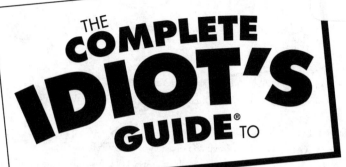

Tarot Spreads

Illustrated

by *Arlene Tognetti* and *Carolyn Flynn*

ALPHA

A member of Penguin Group (USA) Inc.

ALPHA BOOKS

Published by the Penguin Group

Penguin Group (USA) Inc., 375 Hudson Street, New York, New York 10014, U.S.A.

Penguin Group (Canada), 10 Alcorn Avenue, Toronto, Ontario, Canada M4V 3B2 (a division of Pearson Penguin Canada Inc.)

Penguin Books Ltd., 80 Strand, London WC2R 0RL, England

Penguin Ireland, 25 St Stephen's Green, Dublin 2, Ireland (a division of Penguin Books Ltd.)

Penguin Group (Australia), 250 Camberwell Road, Camberwell, Victoria 3124, Australia (a division of Pearson Australia Group Pty. Ltd.)

Penguin Books India Pvt. Ltd., 11 Community Centre, Panchsheel Park, New Delhi—110 017, India

Penguin Group (NZ), cnr Airborne and Rosedale Roads, Albany, Auckland 1310, New Zealand (a division of Pearson New Zealand Ltd.)

Penguin Books (South Africa) (Pty.) Ltd., 24 Sturdee Avenue, Rosebank, Johannesburg 2196, South Africa

Penguin Books Ltd., Registered Offices: 80 Strand, London WC2R 0RL, England

International Standard Book Number: 978-159257-550-3
Library of Congress Catalog Card Number: 2006927523

10 09   8 7 6 5

Interpretation of the printing code: The rightmost number of the first series of numbers is the year of the book's printing; the rightmost number of the second series of numbers is the number of the book's printing. For example, a printing code of 06-1 shows that the first printing occurred in 2006.

Printed in the United States of America

Note: This publication contains the opinions and ideas of its authors. It is intended to provide helpful and informative material on the subject matter covered. It is sold with the understanding that the authors, book producer, and publisher are not engaged in rendering professional services in the book. If the reader requires personal assistance or advice, a competent professional should be consulted.

The authors, book producer, and publisher specifically disclaim any responsibility for any liability, loss, or risk, personal or otherwise, which is incurred as a consequence, directly or indirectly, of the use and application of any of the contents of this book.

Most Alpha books are available at special quantity discounts for bulk purchases for sales promotions, premiums, fund-raising, or educational use. Special books, or book excerpts, can also be created to fit specific needs.

For details, write: Special Markets, Alpha Books, 375 Hudson Street, New York, NY 10014.

Publisher: *Marie Butler-Knight*
Editorial Director: *Mike Sanders*
Managing Editor: *Billy Fields*
Acquisitions Editor: *Randy Ladenheim-Gil*
Book Producer: *Lee Ann Chearney/Amaranth Illuminare*
Development Editor: *Lynn Northrup*
Production Editor: *Megan Douglass*
Copy Editor: *Keith Cline*

Cartoonists: *Shannon Wheeler/Becky Harmon*
Illustrator: *Kathleen Edwards*
Book Designers: *Kurt Owens/Bill Thomas*
Cover Designer: *Bill Thomas*
Indexer: *Brad Herriman*
Layout: *TnT Design, Inc./Chad Dressler*
Proofreading: *John Etchison*

To all intuitive readers who desire more.
—Arlene Tognetti

To the two most intuitive people I know, Emerald and Lucas.
Always trust what you know deep in your heart.
—Carolyn Flynn

Contents at a Glance

Contents

Introduction

Got questions? Tarot's got answers.

The journey of life is uncertain. Will you find your fortune? Will you find your true love? Will you make your mark on the world?

Life is full of challenges and triumphs. It is full of choices—good ones and bad ones. We choose, then we stumble, then we choose again. We grow wiser and kinder and, hopefully, we know ourselves better.

Tarot holds up the mirror to your life, revealing the shape of you. A Tarot spread is like great personal theater, presenting the different actors in your personal story. Unlike a play that you just watch from the audience, however, you are the player in the middle of it. You can improvise. If you know the challenge ahead, you can prepare for it—or accept it.

That's what the Tarot can do—equip you to be an active participant in your life. It's a magnificent journey of self-discovery. As you enter upon the Tarot's journey of insight, may you always be amazed and enlightened. May you grow wise, beautiful, and strong.

How to Use This Book

This book is divided into a five-part exploration of how to use Tarot spreads to gain insight and answers to all your questions:

Part 1, "So You Want to Read the Tarot?" introduces you to the basics of Tarot reading, including a guided tour of the Major and Minor Arcana.

Part 2, "Tarot Spreads to Answer Your Questions," gets right to how to use some of Tarot's most classic spreads, using the suits of the Minor Arcana: Wands, Cups, Swords, and Pentacles.

Part 3, "Looking at the Pictures on the Cards," takes a deeper look at the Royal Court cards, the imagery and numerology, and the upright and reversed meanings of cards.

Part 4, "Looking at the Bigger Picture," takes you a step back, where you can look at cards for patterns, placements, and timing.

Part 5, "Doing Readings," puts your knowledge to practical applications, where you can improve your readings. You'll find a checklist for readings, a visual glossary to all of the Tarot cards, as well as tips about how to prepare your deck.

Following these parts you'll find three useful appendixes: a glossary, a resources guide, and a collection of all the Tarot spreads we teach you in this book.

Extras

Throughout each chapter of this book, we've added five types of extra information in boxes to help you learn even more about how to read Tarot spreads:

Lantern of Truth

These quotes give insight, humor, and encouragement on reading the Tarot.

Tarot Reader

These definitions provide more illumination to a specific aspect of Tarot.

Ask the Cards

These boxes contain short, practical tips that help develop your Tarot reading techniques.

Temperance

These cautionary tidbits help steer you clear of doubts and fears about reading the Tarot.

Foolproof

These practical tips will get you started on working with Tarot spreads so that you begin to feel confident about your readings.

Acknowledgments

From Arlene:

As Carolyn and I wrote this study of Tarot spreads, it was my hope and goal that sharing information to help others grow was the most important part. I thank Carolyn for being patient with the process and holding positive affirmation on the completion. I thank our book producer, Lee Ann Chearney of Amaranth Illuminare, for being there all the time with the utmost enthusiasm for our team.

I thank my friends, family, and students, who would say to me, "You do so much for the public, when do you have time for *you*, Arlene?" To that I say, "Sharing the Tarot with many *is* Arlene, and empowering others to the insight and magic of Tarot is time well spent."

We could say there is a symbiotic relationship between Arlene and her work. They are one and the same, and we are all connected. We all grow together!

Blessings to all who read and work the variety of spreads in this book. May all your goals manifest.

From Carolyn:

I would like to acknowledge the infectious enthusiasm of my co-author, Arlene Tognetti, who is so very in the moment that she might be a Tarot card herself. Many thanks go to book producer Lee Ann Chearney for sending me work that makes me a hit at parties—but seriously, I thank you for sending me a lifeline. You have helped me in many more ways than you know. Thanks to Alpha Books for its commitment to publishing books such as this that encourage people to learn new skills and gain insight about themselves. Mostly, though, I would like to thank you, the reader, and encourage you to believe that you can trust the great wellspring of intuition deep within.

Finally, I want to thank my twins, who bring me joy every day as they turn their wise eyes on the world. And I want to thank my Creator and Source, who continues to bless me with wisdom, strength, and grace amid the chaos, shedding light on my path so that I may see the way.

Thanks to the Illustrator

Warm thanks to graphic designer and computer whiz Kathleen Edwards for her inspired illustration of the Tarot spreads we offer to readers in this book. Always professional, cheerful, pragmatic, and adventuresome, we count Kathy as a friend and invaluable talent. Thanks as well to Bobbie Bensaid for her encouragement and support for the Tarot and U.S. Games Systems, Inc. for permission to reproduce the wonderful Universal Waite Tarot deck.

Trademarks

All terms mentioned in this book that are known to be or are suspected of being trademarks or service marks have been appropriately capitalized. Alpha Books and Penguin Group (USA) Inc. cannot attest to the accuracy of this information. Use of a term in this book should not be regarded as affecting the validity of any trademark or service mark.

In This Part

Part 1

So You Want to Read the Tarot?

If you're ready for the full story, then let's get down to basics. We introduce you to the Tarot and then give you a guided tour of the Major and Minor Arcana. As you'll see, both Destiny and Free Will play a large part in shaping your story. We show you how having Major Arcana cards in a Tarot reading reveals what you have to work with, whereas having the Minor Arcana cards in a reading reveals the choices that are yours to make.

In This Chapter

- Getting the lay of the land—Tarot-land!
- The Three-Card and Seven-Card spreads
- Telling a story: Celtic Cross spread
- Intuition: life in the fast lane

Chapter 1

Surrounding the Question

Does he love me? Is she Ms. Right? What kind of work will bring me bliss? And could you just show me, please, where the money is?

Every day is a winding road, so the song goes. Every day is full of choices: new opportunities, new friends, new loves. But how can we make the most of them? And how can we deal with life's little roadblocks? These are the kinds of problems people bring to Tarot. When they do readings to interpret Tarot spreads, they are looking for practical solutions.

More and more people turn to Tarot for answers in the here and now. A little insight here, a little insight there—and suddenly the road of life isn't so challenging. Tarot provides that nudge to your intuition so you can make choices. And besides all that, it's a fun way to gain insight about yourself, your loves, and your friends.

A Guide Map

We like to think of a Tarot spread as a guide map that helps you navigate life's uncertainties: the rocky waters, the calm times, and the changes ahead. Together, you and the Tarot have some awesome navigating ability.

Tarot doesn't just show you the future: it reflects your state of mind and reveals empowering information through its symbols, colors, and design. Tarot presents choices and encouragement. It's a wonderful tool for personal empowerment.

This book assumes that you already know a little bit about the Tarot, or at least you are somewhat familiar with the cards. But even if you don't know much about Tarot cards or doing Tarot readings—not to worry! As we go along, interpreting spreads, we explain the meanings of cards in the examples. And we offer a full summary of each Tarot card in Chapter 17. There, we have summaries for each card in the 78-card Tarot deck, and you may use that as a handy reference as you practice interpreting the spreads in each chapter.

In this book, we use the Universal Waite deck, available from U.S. Games Systems, Inc. (usgames.com) and from many bookstores and metaphysical stores. Although there are many decks from which to choose, we recommend starting out with this one. If you are just getting started with Tarot, you also may want to use one of Arlene's other books, such as *The Complete Idiot's Guide to Tarot, Second Edition,* or any of the books in *The Intuitive Arts* series (see Appendix B).

When it comes to reading your guide map, remember these three factors inform the interpretation of all Tarot readings:

- The meaning of the card
- The meaning of the position in the spread
- The question of the *Querent* (the person you're reading for: either yourself, or someone else)

Tarot Reader

A **Querent** is the person who is asking the question of the Tarot. It's the person for whom you are doing the reading. If you're doing a reading for yourself, then you are the reader and the Querent, too.

Tarot Basics

The Tarot is made up of 78 cards, 22 Major Arcana and 56 Minor Arcana.

You'll notice that the 22 Major Arcana are mostly people, such as the Emperor or the Hermit; the embodiment of attributes, such as

Justice or Temperance; or universal forces, such as the Moon or the Sun. These cards represent archetypes, or personalities, that are universal through all times and cultures. These archetypes often show up in myths, the stories that transcend cultural boundaries to tell the story of humankind. In other words, these are role models, the people or forces that guide you through the Journey of Life. We delve into them further in Chapter 2.

The Minor Arcana, on the other hand, are about the choices you make in everyday life. They give you practical insight into what's going on. The Minor Arcana are divided into four suits—Wands, Cups, Swords, and Pentacles—which correspond to four areas of life—creativity, love, thoughts, and material things. We discuss them in Chapter 3, then go in more depth with each suit in Chapters 4 through 7.

Take a Position

In a Tarot spread, you lay out the cards in a configuration. Each card has a meaning based on where it falls. You can know what area of life a card is speaking about by its position. The position also indicates whether the card is speaking to you about the past, present, or future. The position tells you a lot: whether the lesson is one you have mastered or one you need to learn, whether your wish will be granted, or whether something stands in the way.

You can learn more about what a Tarot card means by the cards next to it. When reading a spread, you may initially have two possible interpretations of a card. The cards around it can tell you which interpretation fits. Make notes about both interpretations and consider the nuances of each. Pay attention to the one that feels true or has the most energy. We call that the card interpretation that resonates—like the sound of a bell hanging in the air. This is your *intuition* talking to you. (We tell you much more about intuition later in the chapter.)

Tarot Reader

Intuition is the ability to know or perceive without conscious reasoning. You just know. You don't know how you know, but you know. When you listen to your intuition, you are collecting information from more sources than just logic and facts. You know immediately, and you know with deep certainty.

If you hit a snag when interpreting a card, you can throw down another card, asking for further elaboration. Make your next question more specific: *Is this about me, or is this about my mother/father/sister/brother? Is this about the past, present, or future? Is this about my money or my relationship?*

Or you might want to use a new question and another spread.

That's the wonderful thing about Tarot. You can always ask a follow-up question.

What's the Spread?

Three classic spreads in Tarot are the Three-Card spread, the Seven-Card spread, and the Celtic Cross. Notice that Tarot honors numeric symbolism: many spreads stick to the numbers 3, 7, or 10. That's because Tarot and numerology are linked—just as Tarot and astrology are. Tarot is full of references to mythology and religion, too. We explore them all in this book.

In Tarot spreads, the Three-Card spread mirrors the essential spiritual energy of trinities in the universe:

- Father, Son, and Holy Ghost
- Body, mind, and spirit
- Yesterday, today, and tomorrow
- Morning, noon, and night
- Girl, mother, and grandmother
- The heavens, the earth, and you

Past   Present   Future

Three-Card spread.

pg. 7

Draw three cards right now from your Tarot deck. First, consider the possible meanings of each, according to the trinities we've just listed. Don't worry too much about whether you *know* what the cards mean; *feel* the cards in relation to each concept. How does the feeling of card 1 change depending on whether it describes the concept of "Father, body, yesterday, morning, girl, or the heavens"? Or card 2 as it describes "Son, mind, today, noon, mother, or the earth"? Or finally, card 3: "Holy Ghost, spirit, tomorrow, night, grandmother, or you"? Next consider the underlying message or energy of the three cards together as they move to a point of clarity or completion—the infinite eye at the top of the pyramid.

The Three-Card spread is ideal for a daily reading, just to check in with the situation around you. Think of it as a quick fix, a head start, or a cosmic overview. This spread draws on the numerological power of the number 3, the strength of the triangle or pyramid that lifts from a sturdy foundation toward a vantage point of ultimate joy—it's the view from your Third Eye!

Arlene recommends that you take a Three-Card reading every morning, with your tea or coffee—just ask the deck, "What will my day be like?" If you do it seven days in a row, you'll start to notice that certain cards come up again and again … and then the following week, they don't. This is an excellent way to get to know *your* cards. Day by day, you'll start to gain an understanding of how certain cards depict influences that wax and wane in importance as you master the lessons of life.

Ask the Cards

Just before doing a reading for someone else, you may want to do your own quick Three-Card reading, especially if you are having a day of upheaval. This can be a good way to check in with yourself, clearly defining your own energy and issues so they won't get in the way of the reading you're about to do. Doing so may point out troubling feelings or may help put some events in perspective.

The Seven-Card reading is based on the number 7 as the spiritual number. This reading adds more spiritual insight into a situation, or more inspiration. The cards are divided 2-3-2, with the first pair about past issues; the middle three about present conditions and developing events; the final two about the outcome. You can use both the Three-Card spread and the Seven-Card spread to delve into issues that involve a timeline. The Seven-Card spread gives more context and nuance, whereas the Three-Card spread quickly gives context in time, over time, or through time (your choice!).

Past

Future

Present

Seven-Card spread.

A Celtic Cross Story

And the Celtic Cross? It's a time-honored spread; so, let's take a look at its shape and its history.

The Celtic Cross spread originates from the Druid storytelling tradition, in which people told stories around a campfire. Think of each of its ten positions as a speaker who has a little piece of the story to tell—similar to a chapter. Each card, or chapter, adds up to a whole picture storybook.

The Celtic Cross is a terrific spread to use to go deeper into a situation. Here's a look at what the positions mean:

1. **Self.** This is who you are (or your Querent). This is your essence, your core self.

2. **Opposing Forces.** Readers often lay this card sideways, sometimes overlapping the Self card, because it signifies a force that is working against the Querent's true nature or presenting a challenge in the Querent's ability to express his or her true nature.

3. **Background/Foundation.** This card indicates the origin of your question. It could be about your background—your family of origin, your childhood—something that's shaped you. It reveals why you asked the question.

4. **Recent Past.** This card points to events that have led up to this day. The influences of these events are fading from view, but they have created the present.

5. **Near Future.** This card reveals events that are taking shape. This is what's just on the horizon. This card reveals an event that has the potential to occur. It shows you that the event is attainable. If it's a negative card—something you don't want—you have the choice to avoid it, if you act on the advice shown in the spread.

6. **Higher Power.** This card may represent your higher power by whatever name you wish to use: God, Allah, Buddha, Creator, Source, Goddess, the Divine. Or it may represent your highest and wisest self. It can represent aspects of both.

7. **Issues/Fears.** This card points to your fears about the challenge ahead. It reveals your tendencies, which you can counteract if you turn to your allies and follow the advice of the Advice card.

8. **Allies and Supporters.** These are your loved ones, your friends, the helpful people in your life. Or it could be others who have influence, negative or positive, on the situation. This card shows how your question affects those near you, and it shows who among your circle of family and friends will be your best ally. It doesn't have to be a person. It can be a talent, a resource, or an organization.

9. **Advice.** Here is your assignment. If you take the advice of this card, you can favorably influence the outcome. You can take the information in this card and use it to thwart your own worst tendencies, to face fears and worries presented by the Issues/Fears card (position 7). If you take the advice of this card, you can remove the obstacles revealed in the Opposing Forces card (position 2).

10. **Outcome.** Here is how it all turns out. This card represents the long-term solution. This card and the Near Future card (position 5) indicate the timing of events. If you don't want this outcome, look to the other cards for the choices presented to you. If you do want this outcome, look to the Advice card (position 9), Issues/Fears card (position 7), and Higher Power card (position 6) for ways to maximize your effort.

The Celtic Cross can be used to delve into just about any area of life. And if the spread brings up another question, you may use the Outcome card (position 10) as the Self card (position 1) in a subsequent reading, to get further illumination.

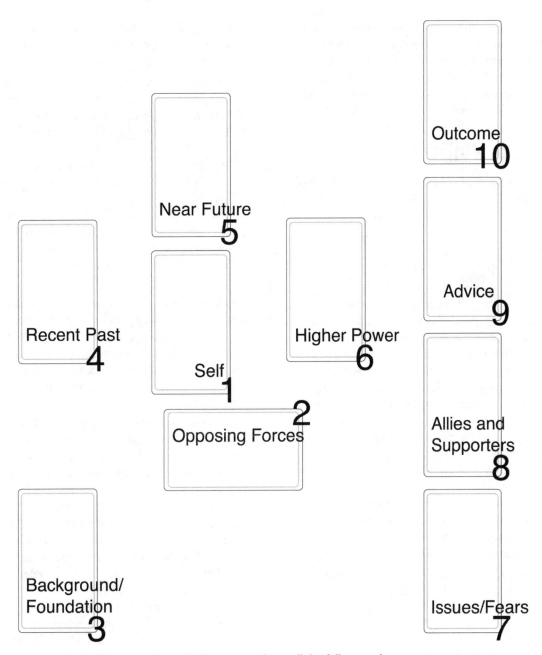

Near Future
5

Outcome
10

Advice
9

Recent Past
4

Self
1

Higher Power
6

Opposing Forces
2

Allies and
Supporters
8

Background/
Foundation
3

Issues/Fears
7

Tarot's Celtic Cross spread uses 10 cards to tell the full story about your question.

Arlene likes the Celtic Cross spread because of its natural flow. Perhaps one of the most beloved Tarot spreads, we use the Celtic Cross in examples throughout this book, deepening your understanding of how to use and interpret this versatile spread.

Tarot Is a Mirror

No Tarot reading occurs in a vacuum. The cards are snapshots—recording in small images the energy that surrounds you and your reading. Think of them as a webcam, scanning to pick up activity—in all nooks, crannies, and corners. The cards pick up on energy that you are not necessarily aware of in your conscious mind.

Because all of this energy is influencing us all the time, it's a good idea to tune in to your surroundings before you start a reading. Your mental and physical states influence what you see and understand in the Tarot. If you are worried about meeting a due date for an assignment, about how a loved one is feeling, or if you are angry with a boyfriend, it will affect which cards you notice and why. If you're asking a question about school or career but still replaying the silly fight you had with your boyfriend, don't be surprised if the Page of Cups comes up. There's nothing like a whimsical fish jumping out of a cup to remind you it's time to lighten up! The Tarot is always aware of the thoughts you have on simmer in the background.

That happens. The Tarot is like a mind scanner, seeking out all the thoughts we are sending out. So sometimes it picks up on scattered or distracted energy. The Tarot is always trying to bring your energy to consciousness, then clarity. A clear mind arrives at clear answers.

Arlene reminds people as they are beginning to learn how to interpret a Tarot spread that, if the energy doesn't feel right on the first three cards, it's okay to start again. If you are reading for someone else, check in with him or her as you deal the first cards. If your Querent nods upon seeing a card and elaborates, saying something like, "Oh yeah, that's my brother. I've

been worried about him," then the reading is right on. But if it just doesn't gel—listen to your intuition and start again.

When Arlene sets up for a reading, whether for herself or for a Querent, she makes sure the surroundings are quiet and comfortable so she can focus on the energy of the moment. It's important that there are no distractions—no cell phones ringing, no outside noises. No other people should be in the room—you want to keep the energy field to yourself and the person you're reading for. That's important for Arlene because when she reduces the stimuli, she can summon her powerful sense of intuition and hone her focus on the energy of her Querent.

When Arlene gives a reading for a Querent, another reason she requests that no other person be in the room is because it's important to her that the lines of communication be clear and open. Another person can influence the reading so that the messages and interpretations are murky.

The most important connection is that between the reader and the Querent. There should be a mutual exchange of energy—a connection. You want the Querent to feel comfortable with being open—to trust that any facts or feelings revealed will be held in confidence. You want the Querent to feel safe that you will not judge him or her. This is true when the Querent is yourself (sometimes we can judge ourselves more harshly than anyone else ever could), when it is someone we know and are close to, such as a friend or family member, when it is someone who is just more of an acquaintance, or when it is someone we don't know at all. The Tarot should *always* be a source of comfort and encouragement, not good or bad, right or wrong.

So when you're ready to start a Tarot reading, relax. There's no need to rush, be too eager, or worried about what the cards will reveal. Because that's sometimes easier said than done, Arlene often uses meditative music to set the mood for a session.

Lantern of Truth _____

Last night I stayed up late playing poker with Tarot cards. I got a full house and four people died.

—Steven Wright, comedian

The Role of Intuition

Intuition's where it's at, baby. It makes a Tarot spread more than the sum of its parts. Look at the wand in the hand of the Magician card of the Major Arcana. Intuition is like that—the force that brings it all together. Intuition is the mystical fourth factor of interpretation, the guiding force of Tarot.

We define intuition as knowing something is true without knowing how we know it. It's a gut feeling. It just feels right. When you shuffle the cards and meditate on your Querent and the question, open to your intuition. Remember that intuition links what's hidden within our hearts with the answers that lie in the universe.

Intuition helps us make connections faster—faster than our rational minds, which require proof. Intuition may eventually yield the proof that verifies the decision you made, but people who develop their intuition will often tell you that they "just know" that something is right for them. That knowing is so solid that they make the decision without requiring the proof. They move ahead with unity of mind, heart, and action.

Temperance _____

Tarot loves an open mind. Don't worry if you feel hesitant about interpreting the cards because you haven't done it enough to feel confident. It's actually a big asset to be fresh and new. Sometimes our emotions or our experiences can cloud a reading. So remember that Tarot doesn't ask that you know all the answers—all you have to know is the questions. And let yourself be open to what the cards show you.

Do I Have to Be Psychic?

You don't have to be a psychic to read Tarot cards. However, Arlene believes everyone is psychic—just that this trait is more developed in some than others. Some of us are more trusting of logic and reason, but we all have intuition. Cultivating your intuition is a matter of training yourself to listen to gut feelings and hunches. Listen. Notice. Pay attention when your head says yes but your heart says no, when the butterflies gather in your stomach. Follow the path. If what you see in the cards through your intuition doesn't feel right, it doesn't. Listening to your intuition is letting yourself know what you already know.

Tarot abounds with examples of both brands of wisdom—logical wisdom and psychic wisdom. The King of Swords, the Queen of Swords, the Emperor, the Hierophant—all are about reason. But the High Priestess, the Hermit, and the Moon are symbols of wise counsel. They are about noticing the undercurrents of life, what might be felt but not immediately understood.

Foolproof _____

To get the most out of this book, you may want to start a Tarot Journal to collect notes about your spreads. At the top of each page, write the date and the question. You may want to refer back to your readings later to find patterns—cards or symbols that appear often. We have found a good way to do that is to make notes in the margin tallying the cards in a reading. You also may want to use colored tabs to identify topics (relationships, money, health) so you can easily refer back to readings on a similar topic.

Full of Meaning

So as you can see, Tarot spreads are guide maps full of meaning. The deeper you go, the more you know. Symbols abound on Tarot cards, derived from Christianity, the Hebrew Kabbalah, and Egyptian and Greek mythology. As we teach you different spreads, we also teach you to start noticing the connections and patterns in the cards. Through interpreting the Tarot, you'll find lots of meaning on this winding road of life.

Let's start by doing two exercises suggested earlier in this chapter.

A Week of Three-Card Spreads

Every day for a week, record your Three-Card spreads in the following worksheet. If you are an artist—and even if you aren't!—you may also want to try your hand at sketching in the basic card imagery, too. That way, individual cards may spring back to mind more easily later on if you're not quite able to recall card images just by reading "4 of Pentacles" or "3 of Cups."

Notice any connections or patterns between and among the cards that occur to you: the name numbers, images, cards … anything you see or feel. Next to each spread, write your thoughts about how accurately the cards seemed to describe that day's energy. How does your week of Three-Card spreads stack up?

Three into Seven

From your week of Three-Card spreads, pick one spread where some or all of the meaning remains elusive to you, something you can't quite figure out. To look more deeply …

◆ Place a new card next to card 1. What more do you see?

◆ Place a new card to the left and to the right of card 2. What more do you see?

◆ Place a new card next to card 3. What more do you see?

Your Week in the Cards

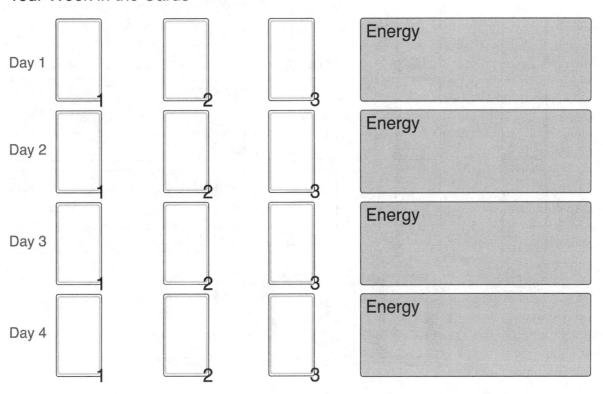

Day 1

Day 2

Day 3

Day 4

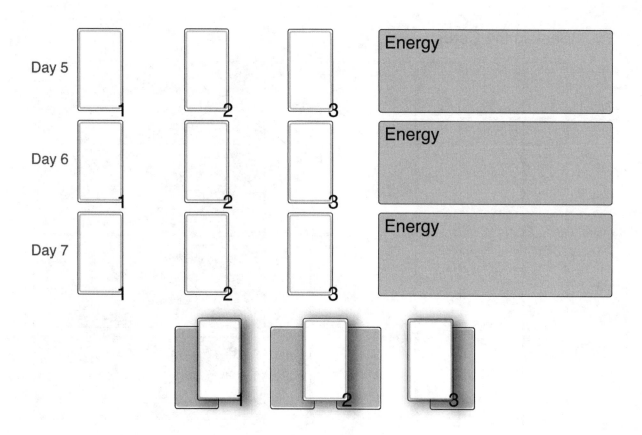

The Least You Need to Know

◆ Four factors are key in interpreting a reading: the meaning of the card; the meaning of the position in the spread; the question of the Querent; and intuition.

◆ The 22 Major Arcana cards are personality archetypes that guide you on the Journey of Life.

◆ The 56 Minor Arcana cards show you your day-to-day choices.

◆ Many of Tarot's classic spreads are 3, 7, or 10 cards—numbers that have spiritual significance.

◆ Tarot's Celtic Cross spread tells a story about your question.

In This Chapter

- ◆ Major Arcana cards tell the story of a lifetime
- ◆ The big, bad, and ugly cards
- ◆ Mentors and masters
- ◆ Your Life Path card

Chapter 2

Destiny

Want to know the story of your life? Meet the Major Arcana. In these 22 cards of the Tarot, you encounter your destiny. These cards shape the people, places, and things that mark the path of your journey in life.

And what's so cool about the Major Arcana is that while your destiny is uniquely yours, we all get to learn the lessons these cards hold, just in different ways. At different times, every person gets a chance to learn the state of no fear in the Fool, or the balance and sure hand of the Chariot, or the deep water and luminescent emotions of the Moon. In this chapter, we show you how all the Major Arcana players figure into a Tarot reading.

Your Personal Sound Track

Chances are you have a favorite song or two. This is the song that always reminds you of the time you met someone special who changed your life or the time you were moving across the country to take on a new adventure. Perhaps it reminds you of a bittersweet time of your life and you always get a lump in your throat when you hear it. Each time you hear this song, you measure how far you've come. When you hear it, you know every word. You already have it downloaded on your iPod at the start of your favorite playlist.

The Major Arcana cards of the Tarot write the sound track of your life. They accompany you through your ups and downs, guiding you as you meet life's challenges and grow along the way.

> **Lantern of Truth** _____
>
> Your vision will become clear only when you look into your heart ... Who looks outside, dreams. Who looks inside, awakens.
> —Carl Jung, Swiss psychiatrist

A Student of Life's Lessons

The Major Arcana, often referred to as the Destiny cards, show you what you were given to work with in life. They identify your personality type and reveal the key personalities who have influenced and shaped you (a teacher, parent, or friend, for example). These cards point the way to your unique purpose in life.

Maybe you've already noticed the Major Arcana are numbered, starting with 0 for the Fool and ending with 21 for the World. The Fool sets out on the journey, knapsack in hand, so innocent and so fearless that he doesn't even know he is about to step off a cliff. But all great journeys begin with this state of no fear. Wise people say love is blind and when we are blind again we fall in love. That is to say when we are so fearless that we don't see all the risks, that's when we set out.

The World card is the end of the journey, when you attain the highest level of spiritual wisdom and self-knowledge. This is when you find your place. You understand why you are here. You have found your unique purpose and carried it out. The World card is the fulfillment of all lessons.

Does this mean the journey is at an end—that if you cycle through all the way to the World, all is done and, like, you die? Not at all. (And the Death card doesn't mean you die either!) The World represents completing one cycle of development. (Just as the Death card often represents the passing of the old influence and the start of something new.) Now you get to start all over again—on new lessons, young and innocent and fearless like the Fool. And so the journey begins again.

Cycle of Self

The first 10 cards of the Major Arcana, beginning with the Fool and ending with the Hermit, are the basic lessons of life. These lay the groundwork for the journey ahead. They form the first cycle of our experience. Indeed, examine the cards and notice they represent teachers, each possessing a unique brand of wisdom. Remember the significance of the number 10, the same number of cards as in the Celtic Cross spread. The number 10 reduced to 1 (1 + 0 = 1), is the number of initiation, the seeker, the self. Whenever you see a card from the Cycle of Self in a Tarot reading, examine how that card's wisdom reflects a part of yourself, or whether it might represent a particular person or energy.

- ◆ **The Fool:** Energetic adventures
- ◆ **The Magician:** Empowered creativity
- ◆ **The High Priestess:** Intuitive insight
- ◆ **The Empress:** Birthing abundance
- ◆ **The Emperor:** Architect builder
- ◆ **The Hierophant:** Conventional wisdom
- ◆ **The Lovers:** Peaceful duality
- ◆ **The Chariot:** Spiritual idealism
- ◆ **Strength:** Healing fortitude
- ◆ **The Hermit:** Spiritual illumination

Cycle of Self: The Fool is the beginning of the first cycle of life.
The Hermit represents the completion of the first cycle.

Cycle of Tests

The next cycle begins with the Wheel of Fortune. You are up to speed on the person you are supposed to be an expert about—*you*. Now you are ready to make waves in the world. The Wheel of Fortune card says the path is wide open. Your life is what you make of it. But there are challenges ahead: you must be fair and honorable, the Justice card tells you. You must be balanced and patience, says the Temperance card. You need to rein in your indulgences and addictions, taunts the Devil card. And there are cards to really shake you up: the sacrifice of the Hanged Man and the upheaval of the Tower. Not to mention Death. There are seven cards in this cycle; the number 7

signifies spiritual growth. Whenever you get a card from the Cycle of Tests in a reading, consider its energy and how that energy matches past, present, or future influences (something that's happened, is happening, or may happen in the future).

- **Wheel of Fortune:** Karmic gambler
- **Justice:** Truth mediator
- **The Hanged Man:** Redeeming sacrifice
- **Death:** Transforming rebirth
- **Temperance:** Calm peacemaker
- **The Devil:** Obsessive addiction
- **The Tower:** Sudden breakthrough

Cycle of Tests: The Wheel of Fortune starts the second cycle, when you take your chances and head out into the big wide world. This cycle culminates in the cathartic change of the Tower.

Cycle of Attainment

Finally, the last cycle, which begins with the Star, shows you how it's all coming together. In this cycle, hope and faith and perseverance begin to pay off. You reap the rewards. Much of this cycle comes through internal transformation, which is now possible because of all the lessons you learned in the previous cycles. There are five cards in this cycle; the number 5 resonates to the energy of change. When you see a card in a reading from the Cycle of Attainment, consider what kind of culmination its energy might signal.

- ◆ **The Star:** Faithful inspiration
- ◆ **The Moon:** Imaginative emotion
- ◆ **The Sun:** Happy contentment
- ◆ **Judgement:** Cosmic awakening
- ◆ **The World:** Highest self

Foolproof

Let's compare the cards that start each cycle: the Fool, the Wheel of Fortune, and the Star. Notice how their energy is different. The Star seems so quiet compared to the other two, doesn't it? That's because it is. For the Fool the energy is kinetic. For the Star the energies are internal and subtle. Anytime you notice a subtle contrast as in the energy of these cards, let it guide you in your interpretation. That's right—trust your instincts!

Cycle of Attainment: The Star launches the final cycle, starting
you off with great clarity, hope, and faith.

The Big Aha

The word *arcane* comes from a Latin word for secrets. Each of the Major Arcana cards represents an aha—okay, now I get it. What once was a secret is now just a done deal. You know it. You've got it down. You have learned to embrace the warmth of the Empress, to wield the sword of Justice, to raise the Hermit's lantern and illuminate your soul.

But Major Arcana cards do more than shed enlightenment; they shine the light on life's turning points, too. Turn the corner successfully … and you get to move on. If you guessed the Devil is one of these cards, you're right. Are you strong enough to break the chains that bind you? Judgement is one, too, and represents an awakening. In Judgement, you know the truth of your life now and you're not going to live any other way. Judgement is assessment time. You look at everything you have accomplished and you look at it all. This is internal review. You take stock of the physical, emotional, mental, and spiritual. You hit a level of universal awareness, where you see what's right for you and how that fits in with the whole pattern of the World. You've left the Devil's addictions behind. *Oh, I see what this is for,* you say. Now it all makes sense. And just when you think you know it all … (Yes, you *are* the Hermit, owning your own wisdom, deep in the place where you form your basic beliefs about life.) … the Tower comes along the way to shake up those beliefs, to send you in another direction, one you probably hadn't planned on.

In every sound track a melody recurs. That's kind of how the Major Arcana cards work when they show up in readings. You repeat some melodies in your life. But if you are learning and growing, each time you come around to that life lesson—no matter what that lesson is about—you're smarter, surer.

In any Tarot reading, look first for the melody of the Major Arcana cards and meditate deeply upon their positions, their order, and possible meanings in the context of the question you're asking. What karmic energy is embodied, tested, or fulfilled? Where is your big aha?

The Ugly Cards

And now a word about the "ugly" cards. You already know which ones we're talking about—the ones you think you don't want to get. Okay, we can say them: the Devil, the Tower, and Death.

The Tarot reflects all that is in our lives, including sorrows, grief, or major changes. These three cards are graphic for a reason—they want to get your attention. Their purpose is kind—they want to help you gear up. The better you know a challenge, the more you can neutralize it. Knowledge is power.

Arlene has seen this happen time and time again—people get one of these cards in a reading, and they are prepared for the upheaval or adversity of the card. They recognize it and face it with courage. These cards don't indicate a permanent condition. They show you what's brewing on the horizon and they welcome the possibility or need for change.

> **Temperance**
>
> These destiny cards—do you have any say in the outcome or is it a done deal? Remember the destiny cards shape the situation. They present your life lessons and your mentors. But you still have choices. You may not get to choose your life lessons, but you do get to decide whether you will accept them. It's like this: Harry Potter didn't choose to be the hero of the wizarding world who fights evil in the form of Lord Voldemort. But in *Harry Potter and the Half-Blood Prince*, the sixth installment, he accepts his role with courage and vision.

And remember, anytime a card causes you to gasp or shrink away, just ask another question. Let's say you get the Tower and it troubles you.

Leave that card out, reshuffle the deck, and ask, "What is the Tower telling me?" Deal out a Celtic Cross with the Tower in the first position. This can help you clear up what seemed upsetting or confusing.

Any time you want clarity on the karmic message of a Major Arcana card, use this exercise to gain more insight. Put the card in the Self position of the Celtic Cross spread and learn more about that card's energy for you, or the situation you're asking about.

Give Me a Mentor

Life is full of uncertainty. You don't want to have to go it alone. And you don't have to. With the Major Arcana, you have a companion for the journey. These personalities will be familiar to you. You probably know someone who is just like the Hierophant (a natural teacher) or the Empress (the ultimate domestic goddess). These kinds of personalities are called *archetypes* because we know these personalities well. They are universal to the stories of humankind, from ancient times to the present day.

When the Major Arcana show up in a reading, these cards are your role models, pointing the way for you. If you have mastered the qualities they represent, they show you that you are well equipped for the question presented to the cards. If you have not, they are there to guide you. In other words, the Major Arcana are your mentors.

> **Tarot Reader**
>
> An **archetype** is a personality that is universal in human experience. These personalities figure in myths and stories, and guide us in our psychological development. Swiss psychiatrist Carl Jung identified archetypes as part of our psyches—the universal father, the universal mother, the universal masculine, the universal feminine. Other archetypes are the teacher, the liberator, the athlete, the alchemist, the earth mother.

Your Life Path Card

Each of us has a Life Path card, a card in the Major Arcana that represents unique lessons we must master in our lifetimes. You figure up your Life Path card based on the numerology of your birth date. For instance, Arlene's birth date is February 4, 1952. February is the second month, so it's a 2. Reduce Arlene's birth year by adding the digits:

2 = **Month**
4 = **Day**
1952 = (1 + 9 + 5 + 2) = 17 (1 + 7) = 8.
So, 2 + 4 + 8 = 14.

The number 14 is the Temperance card. Reduce the result further, and it goes down to 5 (1 + 4 = 5). So Arlene is Temperance and the Hierophant, and those cards represent her Life Path, blueprints for her life lessons.

When Arlene first realized those were her Life Path cards, she was in her early 20s. She said, "You mean I don't get the Empress? I don't get the Sun?" The Hierophant—that was kind of like getting the pope. And Temperance—well, that told her she would have a lifetime of developing patience. She told her reader, "I don't want to be patient. I want things to happen fast." Her reader said, "You see, that's why you got it."

Temperance and the Hierophant are Arlene's Life Path cards.

But Arlene has developed more patience—more than she ever thought she could. As time goes on, she is more and more certain those cards are for her. She has learned mastery. The last thing she ever thought of doing with her life was teaching in the public school system, which is what the Hierophant first suggested to her. Now she teaches Tarot at Pierce College in Tacoma, Washington. And when she was younger, she had an anti-establishment mentality—after all, she's a baby boomer. But now that she's older, she appreciates our society's institutions such as banking and education. Temperance has taught her to adapt in order to support the higher good of family, community, and society.

So when you do your Life Path spread, you may meet cards that feel a little weird to you at first. That's because you have yet to become those cards. But you'll get there.

Carolyn has two Tarot cards that are her personal Life Path symbols: the Fool and the Emperor. (Although it would be much better slumber party talk to be the High Priestess, Carolyn accepts these roles!) Notice how Carolyn also had trouble accepting her archetype? Arlene has noticed that many people, when they find out their Life Path card, shrink away. "I wanted the Magician and the Empress—what happened?" is often their reaction. But these archetypes represent what you need to learn as opposed to what you have already mastered—which would seem familiar to you. As a creative, free-spirited type, Carolyn would not have thought to embrace the Emperor, but that's just what the cards are telling her to do.

The Fool and the Emperor are Carolyn's Life Path cards.

The Fool and the Emperor seem like two opposites—the Fool the picture of unlimited self-expression, the Emperor the very paragon of discipline. How could those two coexist in one person's Life Path? This dichotomy shows up a lot in the 5 of Wands, a card Carolyn gets often. As discussed in Chapter 3, when we explore the Minor Arcana, this is how her Life Path theme is presented in her day-to-day choices. It's your job to master the qualities of your Life Path card and integrate it into your personality—into your very soul.

Figure Your Life Path Numbers and Cards

◆ Your birth month: _____.

◆ Your birth date: _____ (reduce to one digit, if needed).

◆ Your birth year (reduced to one digit): __+__+__+__=____.

◆ Add it all together: birth month ___ + birth day ___ + birth year ___ = ____. Reduce result to one digit, if needed: ___ + ___ = ___.

◆ My Life Path numbers are ___ and ___. My Life Path cards are _____ and _____.

Your Personal Year

Each year, you get a Personal Year card that defines your lessons for that year. Your year starts with your birthday. Figure your Personal Year card the same way you figure your Life Path card, except you use the current year instead of your birth year. For instance, both Carolyn and Arlene were on a 4 year during the writing of this book. Here's how we calculated Arlene's:

2 (Arlene's birth month)

4 (Arlene's birth day)

+ 2005 (2 + 0 + 0 + 5) = 7;

(2 + 4 + 7) = 13 (1 + 3) = 4.

A 4 and a 13 correspond to the Emperor and Death—a very interesting combination. Death means out with the old, but Emperor is about building something.

Here's Carolyn's Personal Year:

12 (1 + 2) = 3.

21 (2 + 1) = 3.

2005 (2 + 5) = 7.

(3 + 3 + 7) = 13 (1 + 3) = 4.

It's a good idea to calculate your Querent's Life Path and Personal Year cards before you do a reading. It will help you get to know that person's mission in life right from the start.

Ask the Cards

Whether or not she's your Life Path card, the High Priestess figures prominently in guiding your ability to read the Tarot. She's the archetype of intuition. Spend a few moments meditating, focusing on this card. Let yourself remember times when you have sensed something was coming or something wasn't right—and you were right. Allow yourself to start to open up to noticing patterns and themes around you.

Life Path Spread

The Life Path spread gives you a quick road map of your life lessons. By using only the 22 Major Arcana cards for this reading, you are calling on the higher power of understanding how those lessons fit into your life's purpose.

Separate all the Major Arcana from your deck. Take out your two Life Path cards (if you only have one, that's okay). As you shuffle the remaining Major Arcana, focus on this question: *How am I learning my Life Path now?* Now spread five cards around your two Life Path cards, moving clockwise.

As you deal the cards, meditate on what you believe to be the biggest issues surrounding your life experience in the past, at the present moment, and also meditate on where you'd like to take your life in the future.

◆ **Record your thoughts and your cards.**

My Life Path cards are _____ and _____.

My five Life Journey cards are:

1._____

2._____

3._____

4._____

5._____

◆ **The Past**

My biggest thing shaping my life so far has been:

_____

_____

My hope for transforming the challenges of the past and building on the foundation of what's good from the past:

_____

_____

The cards in my reading that deal most with the past:

_____

_____

◆ **The Present**

The thing I really want or need to do right now:

_____

_____

My hope for manifesting what I want right now:

_____

_____

The cards in my reading that deal most with action in the present:

_____

_____

◆ **The Future**

My biggest thing hope for the future is this:

_____

_____

When I see myself in the future, I most want:

_____

_____

The cards in my reading that point most strongly toward creating my best Life Path:

_____

_____

◆ **Commencement**

Here's what I've learned from this Life Path spread:

_____

_____

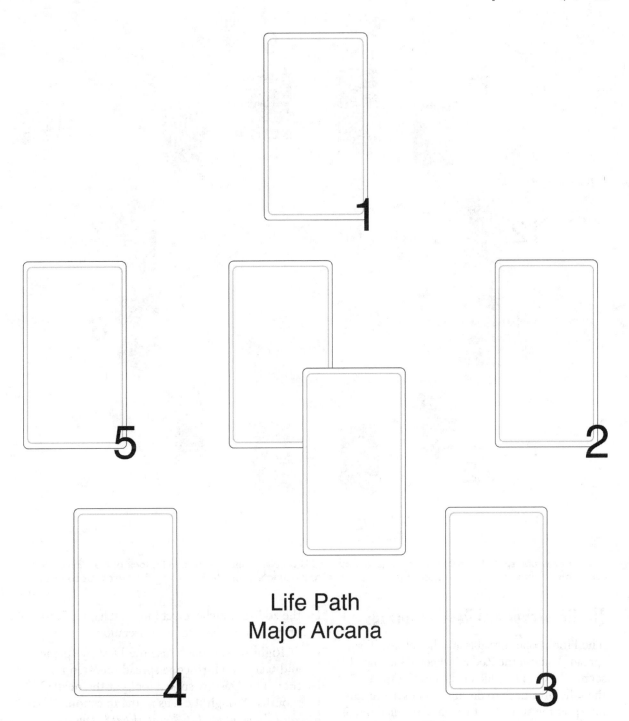

Life Path
Major Arcana

The Life Path spread is a good way to map out your life lessons.

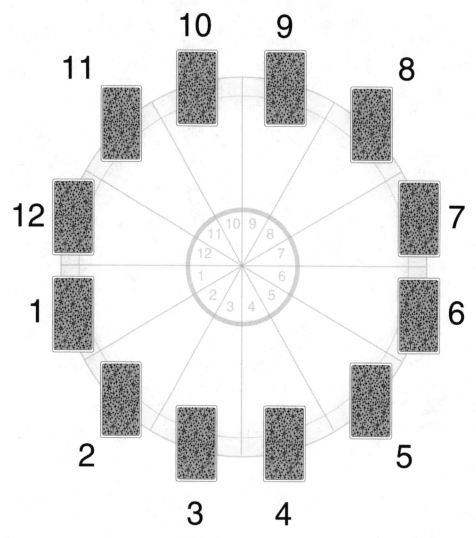

The Horoscope spread uses the complete Tarot deck and is a quick, simple way to get a look at the 12-month period ahead. The Destiny spread uses the Zodiac wheel to illuminate your Life Path using the Major Arcana cards.

The Horoscope and Destiny Spreads

The Horoscope spread is another classic Tarot spread. You use the Zodiac wheel, which has 12 segments, each of which gets a card. (You use the full Tarot deck to do this reading.) You can interpret the spread in two ways. A quick way is to interpret each of the 12 cards as a month in the upcoming year, with the first card being the first month, the second card being the second, and so on. For a more in-depth reading, you look at the spread in relation to the houses of the zodiac, which we get into in Chapter 7, to bring another layer of interpretation.

Right now, though, use the Destiny spread and take the Horoscope spread one step further. The Destiny spread looks at the next 12 months through the lens of the question, *"How am I doing on my Life Path? What lessons are ahead?"* For this one, you use only the Major Arcana cards, spreading 12 cards around the wheel of the zodiac.

Record the cards from your spreads in the worksheet.

Horoscope Cards	Destiny Cards
Month 1	
Month 2	
Month 3	
Month 4	
Month 5	
Month 6	
Month 7	
Month 8	
Month 9	
Month 10	
Month 11	
Month 12	

A Bright Destiny

The Journey of Life is just a start. Now you know more about your Personal Year ahead and the 12 months that will unfold within it, as well as your Life Path card and your Destiny reading. The future, as it *always* does, looks bright! But how do you meet the tests and challenges along the Journey of Life? That's where the Minor Arcana come into play.

The Least You Need to Know

- The 22 Major Arcana cards tell the story of your life.
- The Major Arcana are archetypes— universal personalities that shape human experience.
- Knowing the forces that shape your destiny can equip you to meet uncertainties along the road of life.
- Your Life Path card is a card that is unique to you and defines the lessons you are learning in life.
- Your Personal Year card shows you the assignments you have pulled for the year.
- The Life Path, Horoscope, and Destiny spreads provide more insight into the big picture of your life.

In This Chapter

- ◆ The Minor Arcana: your choices
- ◆ Wands, Cups, Swords, Pentacles, the suits of Tarot: your life stage
- ◆ The numbers of Tarot
- ◆ Your Free Will

Chapter 3

Free Will

So some things are decided for you when you come into this life and are readily apparent, such as where you are born and who your parents are and whether you are a boy or a girl. Other karmic influences are less obvious but can be illumined through the Major Arcana cards. But the Minor Arcana cards show you that life, ultimately, is what you make of it; it is the sum of your actions, mind, body, and soul. You have Free Will. Your life is about the choices you make and the Minor Arcana present those choices. Minor Arcana are the cards of Free Will.

In a Tarot reading, the Minor Arcana reveal the nuances of your everyday life. They reveal the energy of the moment. They can provide an uncanny take on what's going on for you right now. The Minor Arcana also illumine what choices you may have about the outcome of the question your Tarot reading is shedding insight upon.

All the World's a Stage

The Minor Arcana are the stage where you play out the story of your life. The Minor Arcana cards come in four suits—each representing an area in which you function:

◆ **Wands** are about your personal power—how you create and manifest your passionate ambition.

◆ **Cups** are about how you love, live in joy, and connect to your emotional nature.

◆ **Swords** represent the realm of the mind—thinking and decision making. Thoughts have wings!

◆ **Pentacles** are about your resources—not just your money, but your talents, skills, time, and energy as well as how you use them.

Notice that within each suit of the Free Will cards, there are royal cards, called the Royal Court. Unlike the 22 Major Arcana, these cards are not representative of your karma or your personality, but rather a role you may assume. So you may become the Queen of Swords or the Knight of Pentacles for a short time to accomplish a goal or face a challenge. Or you may meet someone who plays that role for you and who influences events in your life in a significant way. We talk more about the Royal Court cards in Chapters 8 and 9.

Tarot Reader

Free Will means you still have a choice in the matter. You may not get to pick the topic but you do get to decide what you make of it. For instance, it was Harry Potter's destiny to be an orphan when the evil Lord Voldemort killed his parents. But it's his choice to become a wise, brave wizard who fights evil.

When Minor Arcana cards come up in a reading, they show that choices can be made to swing events in one direction or another. They often reveal to you a situation that you have not been conscious of—one that you must now deal with to reach the desired outcome. For example, look at the 3 of Swords, the card with a large red heart pierced through with three swords. Many Querents are surprised to find this card in their Tarot readings, and are often puzzled at first by its meaning, and what to do about it.

The 3 of Swords card tells you that you have suffered an emotional loss that cuts deep and it urges you to reconcile your feelings so you can move forward. When this card, or any Minor Arcana card that surprises you, appears in a Tarot reading consider the unconscious emotional depth and power its meaning *empowers* you to explore, and how the card challenges you to think or act or feel something new or different from what seems readily apparent on the surface.

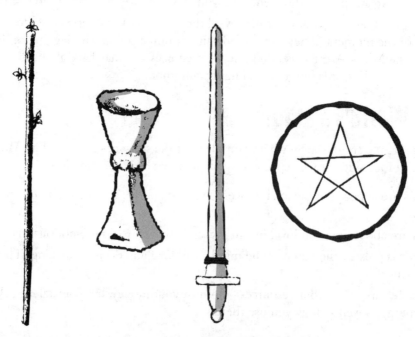

Wands, Cups, Swords, and Pentacles are the symbols of Tarot's suits and the visual metaphors of enterprise/effort, joy/love, action/thought, and abundance/talent.

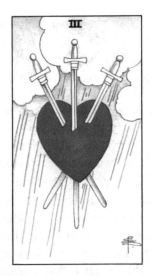

Tarot's Minor Arcana cards often reveal hidden emotions or situations or give clues to future action when they appear in readings. The 3 of Swords indicates grief, a piercing emotional hurt.

Starting Something New, Finishing Something Old

Each of the Tarot suits matches up with a season, both literally and metaphorically:

◆ **Wands are spring.** It makes sense that Wands, the suit of enterprise and growth, would be associated with spring. Everything in this suit is about getting something started. Numerous Wands in a Tarot reading indicate movement toward something new and the need for a creative view or solution.

◆ **Cups are summer.** Cups are about hitting that smooth glide, when all that you have set into motion just goes right along. They are associated with summer, when everything is in full bloom, when the crops are thriving and the harvest ahead looks good. The love and support of friends achieves that for us—making our endeavors in the world more meaningful because we achieve our work for the ones we love and share the rewards with them.

A lot of Cups in a Tarot reading indicates that the circumstances surrounding your question have great emotional import and the outcome depends on love.

◆ **Swords are fall.** Swords are associated with fall, when we harvest. So the Sword becomes like the scythe. Swords cut to what matters. They present choices and they represent decisions. Here is where you sort it out. Many Swords in a Tarot reading indicate there's quite a lot happening and much action surrounding the question.

◆ **Pentacles are winter.** Pentacles are connected to winter and you'll even notice one very wintry card (the 5 of Pentacles). Pentacles are about security—about establishing a base camp for your life so that you have somewhere to come in from the cold. They are also slow-moving, like winter, which is a season of stillness when plants lie dormant and animals hibernate, collecting and conserving energy. A lot of Pentacles in a reading indicates you are finishing something, but something very important—perhaps something that will serve as a foundation for the next cycle.

Lantern of Truth

Chance is always powerful. Let your hook be always cast; in the pool where you least expect it, there will be a fish.
—Ovid (43 B.C.E.–17 C.E.), Roman poet

Alchemy: Blending the Elements

Each of the Tarot suits matches with an astrological sign of the zodiac and its corresponding Element. In readings, you'll want to look to see who might have that astrological sign, or how the energy or interplay of the Elements might be manifesting.

- **Wands are Fire: Aries ♈, Leo ♌, and Sagittarius ♐.** Wands are a very ambitious suit, and their enthusiasm is infectious; it spreads like Fire. Wands were what was used to carry a torch at night, so they represent not only the creative fire that drives a project, but illumination—bringing what was in the darkness to light.

- **Cups are Water: Cancer ♋, Scorpio ♏, and Pisces ♓.** Cups are Water, which heals, soothes, purifies, and transforms. That's why they are the suit of compassion.

- **Swords are Air: Gemini ♊, Libra ♎, and Aquarius ♒.** Swords represent the world of ideas and thoughts—and so they are Air. Ideas are light and quick-moving, like swords.

- **Pentacles are Earth: Taurus ♉, Virgo ♍, and Capricorn ♑.** Pentacles are the resources of the Earth, the soil that provides nutrients to the plants that grow.

The Elements work together to present choices and represent decisions and actions in your life. Air lets Fire breathe, which is why the Swords of action and the Wands of creativity are often seen together in readings. Like wood, Fire needs Earth to burn, meaning you need resources to make your creative endeavors happen. Water can temper Fire, which is to say you need balance between love, life, and work. All work and no play can be very dull, you know!

Water is made of air molecules—hydrogen and oxygen. Love needs Air to breathe or else it is smothering. Fire heats Water, making steam. Fire is the passion; Water is the love. Earth absorbs Water. It tempers Water when it runs too high, as our emotions sometimes do.

Achieving Balance: The Diamond Spread

The Elements represented in the Tarot suits balance each other. You can get a take on how balanced you are each day by doing a Diamond spread. The Diamond spread amounts to four cards arranged in a North, East, South, and West layout. The classic Diamond spread uses the whole deck; if you want a take on how balanced your Elements are, however, just use the Minor Arcana only. Analyze the spread for Fire, Water, Air, and Earth. Notice which are strong and which are absent. Elements that are absent are ones that you want to emphasize on that day to bring you into balance.

When you have two cards for one Element in your Diamond spread reading, that Element energy is strong—go with it! But if you have three cards in one Element, you need to look for balance. (Especially if that Element is Water! You might turn into a spigot on that day because you're too sensitive.) When you have two cards of one Element and two of another there is a balance to be achieved between them. For example, if you have two Cups and two Pentacles, the message may be not to think too much about business, to balance love and work, or to be kinder in the way you approach business. If you have two Swords and two Pentacles, you are going to be *very* grounded in how you make decisions on that day.

Temperance

Sometimes it's hard to focus on a reading because you have so much going on in your head. If the cards that come up seem scattered and unfocused, it's okay to take a break from the reading, get centered, and reshuffle. If the reading is for a Querent, make sure you are not putting your stuff into a reading for someone else. If you start over a third time and get the same scattered energy, it's probably not you but the situation you or your Querent is asking about. Go ahead and read the energy as you see it, recognizing a lot of unfinished business, uncertainty, and doubt about the situation.

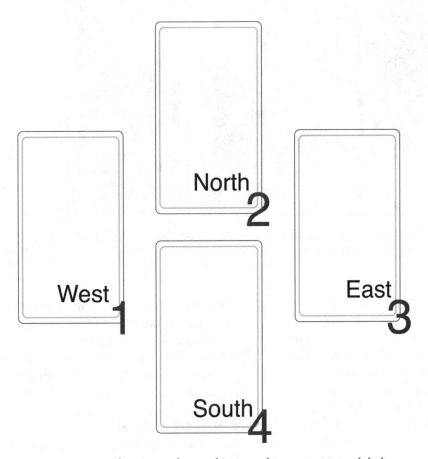

The Diamond spread is a good one to use to seek balance.

These Tarot cards in a reading indicate out-of-balance energy
that needs to be refocused or redirected with right intent.

Out-of-Balance Energy

Three cards from Tarot's Minor Arcana in particular can point to something being out of balance: 2 of Wands in reversed position, 5 of Swords, and 5 of Wands. (We discuss reversed cards in more detail in Chapter 11.) These cards indicate that your Querent is off-center, that his or her energy is dissipated, scattered, fragmented, out of focus. When these cards appear in a Diamond reading, that out-of-balance energy is intensified.

Lessons of Life

Although the Major Arcana show us *what* we have to work with, the Minor Arcana show us *how:* they present our daily lessons. To see how the Minor Arcana play out the energies of the moment, let's take a look at the number 8 card from each Tarot suit. The eighth Major Arcana card is Strength, the karmic energy of power/effort, resolve, and compassion. As you examine the number 8 cards of the Minor Arcana suits, contemplate how each one uses that karmic energy to describe a real-time situation.

The 8 of Wands is pure ambition in motion; you're hitting the mark. The 8 of Cups marks a decision to leave something you've built to look for something different, something more spiritually fulfilling. The 8 of Swords shows how the fear of indecision might bind your strength and prevent you from action. The 8 of Pentacles shows the rewards of strength and talent; look at all those Pentacles stacked to the sky—and you're still creating more!

Continue this exploration into how the Minor Arcana express the in-the-moment energies of the Major Arcana. The Fool (0) represents you in this exercise: your playful openness to investigate and discover new meanings. Lay out the cards of the Major Arcana numbered 1 through 10, along with the corresponding card from each Tarot suit. (Use the Ace for the number 1.) This takes you from the Magician (1) to the Wheel of Fortune (10). Examine each group of cards closely to reveal the relationships that emerge between and among them.

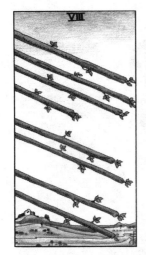

Compare the karmic energy of Major Arcana cards and their Minor Arcana real-time mirrors.

The Major and Minor Arcana cards numbered 1 through 10. How do their energies resonate?

THE LOVERS. THE CHARIOT. STRENGTH. THE HERMIT. WHEEL of FORTUNE.

THE EMPEROR. THE TOWER. THE DEVIL. THE HANGED MAN. DEATH. THE SUN. JUDGEMENT.

The first row of seven Major Arcana cards in a Daily Lesson spread reveal the day's karmic influences. What might this sample reading reveal?

QUEEN of CUPS. KNIGHT of PENTACLES QUEEN of SWORDS.

The second row of cards in the Daily Lessons spread uses the Minor Arcana and reveals real-time choices, opportunities, and challenges. How do the forces of Destiny and Free Will resonate for your Querent's day in this sample reading?

Daily Lessons Spread

To better understand how you are equipped for your life lessons, start out with a Daily Lessons spread. The first part of this spread uses the Major Arcana. This will show the karmic lessons that may come up for you during the day and how they relate to the big picture of your life—what this life is all about *for you today.* Deal seven cards. Here's a sample reading.

Caution! This day holds karmic energies not for the faint of heart. This reading can reveal some of the most important lessons you'll learn in life. It's not uncommon for your Life Path card to show up often here, as it did in this reading (note the Emperor was first). The combination of the Tower, the Devil, the Hanged Man, and Death is extremely potent—some really, really big lessons here. But if our Querent learns them, contentment and awakening are ahead.

Now let's take this back down to the daily level in the second part of the Daily Lessons spread and look at some practical choices for the day using the Minor Arcana. The daily cards show that steady, hard work (three Pentacles cards) and clear, logical thinking (two Swords cards) are the way to navigate the changes ushered in by the Tower, the Hanged Man, and Death. The 6 of Pentacles and 10 of Pentacles indicate that summoning the discipline of the Emperor will pay off. The Knight of Pentacles is the steadfast harvester, and he, too, brings the lesson of discipline closer to the awareness of the Querent. Note there is the challenge of no Wands energy in this day's lessons.

When you read your Daily Lessons spread, look first at the Major Arcana's lessons and think deeply on how they reveal *what you have to work with.* Only after you have done this meditation proceed to deal the Minor Arcana cards to see insights into *how* you can make choices as your day unfolds. Look, too, at the Major/Minor Arcana card pairs to see if patterns or resonances or big ahas come to the surface.

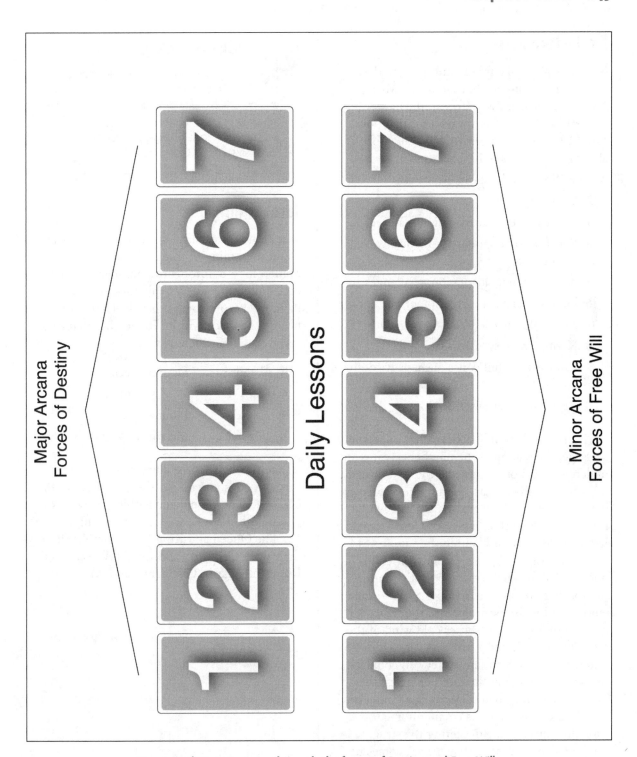

Tarot's Daily Lessons spread reveals the forces of Destiny and Free Will.

By the Numbers

Numbers play a big role in interpreting the Minor Arcana, just as they did in the Major Arcana. An Ace is always fresh—the new energy of the 1, whereas a 5 is always a turning point, and a 10 is a commencement. We talk more about this in Chapter 10, but here's a start:

Ace (1) Spark of the spirit, beginnings

  2 Unity, balance

  3 Creative, celebratory, vision made real

  4 Spirit becoming matter, practicality, foundation

  5 Turning point, adaptation, challenges

  6 Harmony, love, hearth, home, safe harbor

  7 Mystical, inner wisdom

  8 Karma, mastery, prosperity

  9 Completion, full consciousness, wisdom attained

  10 Beginning again with wisdom

Even though each Tarot card has a specific message, the energy of the numbers creates an undercurrent. For example, in the 6 of Swords, the woman and child are leaving their sorrows behind, crossing the placid waters to a new home and safe harbor. The 6 of Cups is the happy childhood card, and it often indicates that a memory or a person from your childhood will show up in your life. Both come after the turning point of the number 5 card—the emotional loss in the 5 of Cups, the treachery in the 5 of Swords, the bitter cold wind of the 5 of Pentacles. In the 5 of Pentacles, the two huddled figures don't know they can come in from the cold, but in the 6 of Pentacles, the man is receiving a bonus that is due him. The man in the 6 of Wands is coming home to victory after successfully mastering the struggle in the 5 of Wands. Notice that "*home*" comes up in all of the number 6 cards.

Ask the Cards

If you get two or more of the same number in a reading, you can bet that the energy of that number is strong in the choices the Querent is making. A reading with a lot of fives says "Adapt," whereas a reading with a lot of sixes says "Come home."

Tarot Timing

The Minor Arcana are generally pretty clear about the timing of things. In addition to numerology, a Tarot card's number *does* indicate something pretty explicit—the number of days, weeks, or months that the choice will need to be made within. Remember that each suit works at a different rate:

◆ Wands   Days to weeks

◆ Cups   Weeks to months

◆ Swords   Hours to days

◆ Pentacles   Months to years

Ace through 10 are quite literally one through 10, so if you get the Ace of Cups, the choice will need be made within one week or one month. Pages are 11, whereas Knights are 12. The Queen and King have a timing all of their own. Call it royal timing! (We explain the Royal calendar in Chapters 8 and 9.)

Past

Future

Present

The Past, Present, Future spread

Past, Present, Future Spread

The Seven-Card spread from Chapter 1 is another way to sort out whether the choice at hand is one you have already made or will need to make. In addition to interpreting the timing by the numbers and suits, look more deeply at the timing revealed by each card's position in the past, present, and future sequence:

◆ **Past.** Card 1 represents background—an event that shaped you to make your choices, whereas card 2 deals with the more recent past, events that are now fading in influence.

◆ **Present.** The middle three cards represent factors in the present situation, revealing things to you that you may need to know in order to decide.

◆ **Future.** Of the final two cards, the first card represents events taking shape in the near future, whereas the last card represents the outcome.

Foolproof

What if you have two interpretations for a card? Maybe it applies to love but it could mean something for work, too. Or maybe it seems like it is happening right now, but you wonder if it's hinting at an event taking shape for your future. Draw upon your intuition. Usually the first thought is the truest, purest thought. And let the idea dwell in you for a while. Remember when you are doing a reading, you can come back to that card. The cards around that card will reveal more to you.

Destiny vs. Free Will

You can analyze every spread for Destiny vs. Free Will. In a Celtic Cross spread, if there are four Major Arcana cards out of ten, that indicates that Destiny may be at work with the lessons being learned but the Querent still has Free Will. If the spread has shown six or more Major Arcana, the lessons would be one of a cosmic level. Note also *where* the Destiny cards come up in the spread; card positions of the Major Arcana reveal deeper nuances and provide clues about how to interpret the right action of the Minor Arcana cards and their positions, too.

For example, if a Major Arcana card comes up in the Recent Past and Near Future positions (cards 4 and 5), it may indicate that the lessons of the moment are vital to the Querent's personal growth. If a Major Arcana card such as the Hierophant shows up in the Ally position (card 8), this could indicate that the Querent will have more than your average kind of help. And if a Major Arcana card such as the Magician falls in the Advice position (card 9), it may indicate that the lesson will resonate—that is, if the Querent takes this advice, it will matter, not only for this desired outcome but for learning a new way of being.

The Choices Ahead

Use the Minor Arcana in a spread to get a sharper, clearer take on the choices that need to be made. Sometimes we already know what we need to choose to embrace and choose to exclude but we're just not ready to do it. An insightful reading of a Tarot spread may be just the thing to help you or your Querent move forward, especially if the indicated outcome is something he or she truly desires.

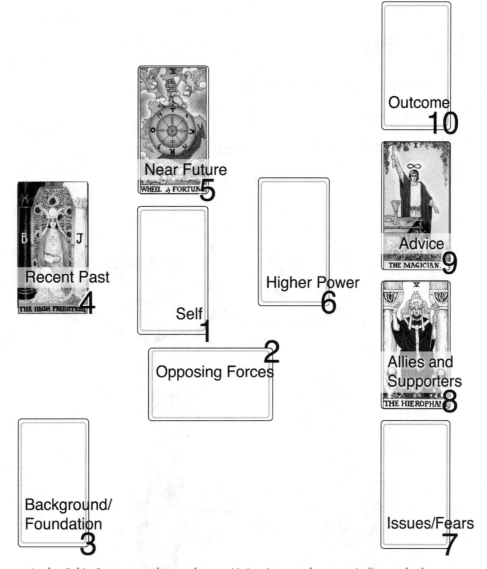

In the Celtic Cross spread, anywhere a Major Arcana shows up indicates the lessons, help, or challenges are very important and lasting ones.

The Least You Need to Know

◆ The suits of the Minor Arcana represent different arenas of life in which you play out your destiny and your choices.

◆ The suits of the Minor Arcana are associated with seasons.

◆ The suits of the Minor Arcana are linked to the astrological Elements of Fire, Water, Air, and Earth.

◆ The numbers of the Minor Arcana indicate the stage of development for the choice being made.

◆ The numbers of the Minor Arcana indicate the timing of the lesson at hand.

In This Part

Part 2

Tarot Spreads to Answer Your Questions

Now the story can unfold. The next four chapters explain Tarot's classic spreads (and a few more!). By examining the suits of the Minor Arcana—Wands, Cups, Swords, and Pentacles—we give you lots of ways to use and interpret Tarot spreads.

Are your questions about feelings? Making something happen? Deciding what to do? Want to know about your love life? About money or health? Armed with knowledge of the archetypes of the Major Arcana and a good understanding of the suits of the Minor Arcana, you'll find Tarot spreads that can help you answer just about any question.

In This Chapter

- ◆ Discover your creative allies
- ◆ Your Life Path and creativity
- ◆ Astrology and your destiny
- ◆ The Celtic Cross story: imagination and initiative
- ◆ The Wish spread: from wish to vision

Chapter 4

About Creating Something

Fire is what gets this party started. Fire is the energy behind the Tarot's Minor Arcana suit of Wands, and that's why this suit is all about creativity. Fire is the energy of creating in its purest form—the beginning. Think: spark of passion, gleam of an idea, flame of initiation, the bonfire that purifies. Fire is an idea moving into action.

In the suit of Wands, we find out all about your creative energy—how you imagine, how you create, how you initiate. If you or your Querent have a knack for enterprise, you'll find it in the Wands.

Make It Happen

Notice that the wands in the suit of Wands are all tree branches, budding with new leaves. That's the growth. In the days before electricity, long branches were used as torches to carry light. That's the fire—the creative passion that drives a project forward.

Creativity brings about growth and expansion, and the suit of Wands depict the qualities that bring that about: the leadership of the King of Wands, the ambition of the Queen of Wands, the courage of the Knight of Wands, the calm assurance of the 3 of Wands, and the ultimate good fortune of the 6 of Wands.

Temperance _____

Why is a wand the metaphor for creativity? A magic wand brings something forth out of thin air. It is an instrument that makes something appear that wasn't there before. The magic behind the magic wand is your focus, your intent, and your vision. It's like those advanced nonverbal spells Harry Potter and friends master in *The Half-Blood Prince*, as six-year wizards at Hogwarts. With a nonverbal spell, Harry can make something happen just by devoting a great deal of concentration to it. That's the power behind the suit of Wands.

Wands and the Magician

From the Major Arcana, though, comes the ultimate symbol of creativity: the Magician. The Magician is the one who manifests, seemingly from the ether. Many of the images and symbols from his card carry over into the rest of the Tarot, and when the Magician shows up with a lot of Wands in a reading, you can be sure there is a strong creative aspect to the question. Once you are familiar with the symbols of creativity, you can look for them in other cards that come up in spreads. It can give you a good gauge of the role creativity and growth are playing in any question, whether the question is about money or love or whatever is being asked about.

THE MAGICIAN.

The Magician holds a magic wand, high and confident, as he looks upon a table containing symbols of all four Tarot suits: Wands, Cups, Swords, and Pentacles (that is, containing all the Elements: Fire, Water, Air, and Earth). The objects on the table represent the Magician's many talents. He recognizes his talents, and he will use his wand to turn them into something tangible. The wand he holds aloft points to heaven and the earth, suggesting unity between higher power and human power. The Magician is the conduit. His energy is the spark of energy that flows from the fingertips of God to Adam in Michelangelo's "Creation of Adam" on the ceiling of the Sistine Chapel. All is in alignment to bring forth what must be born.

Archetypes for Creativity

Are there other members of the Major Arcana that represent creativity? We thought of a few, and here's why:

◆ **The Lovers.** Well, yes, there is that reproduction thing. That's pretty creative, you know, making a new person. But aside from that, there is the wonder that comes when two people in love come together, the weaving together of their hopes and dreams, their sorrows and their joys. (Remember the Lovers card carries the number 6, which is the home.)

The Lovers card can represent the balancing of yin and yang, feminine and masculine energies, the beauty of one flowing into the other. Out of the effort to balance those forces comes great creativity. Looking through the rest of the Major Arcana for examples of the balancing of opposite energies, you'll find it in the black and white pillars of the High Priestess and the black and white sphinx of the Chariot. When you see the Queen of Wands paired with any of these cards, you can be sure that the outcome of the question lies in balancing opposite energies. The black cat at the feet of the Queen of Wands represents the balancing of light and dark.

These cards hold strong creative energies in Tarot readings.

- ◆ **The Chariot.** When this card comes up with the Knight of Wands, you are definitely going somewhere. This card represents action and change, and ultimately, victory over adversity.

- ◆ **Strength.** When this card comes up with the Queen of Wands, watch out. There's a lot of courage and stamina here. Notice the lions on the throne of the Queen of Wands? Lions are associated with the astrological sign of Leo, the sign of creative self-expression. The Strength card also is about unconditional love, which calms our fears of the unknown as we move forward to create something new. Notice also the infinity symbol above her head—just like the Magician.

  And while we are comparing Strength with the Queen of Wands, notice that the Queen of Wands sits on a throne with lions, demonstrating her courage and fierceness. Also notice that a black cat sits at her feet. That cat represents intuition, and it reminds us that intuition plays a strong role in creativity.

- ◆ **The Moon.** This is the card of the imagination, and where would creativity be without a sense of the imagination? This card reminds us to examine the undercurrents of life. The dog and the wolf remind us that creativity has a sense of wildness. To create something original, you must let yourself be untamed for a while.

Foolproof

Add to your list of creative archetypes by brainstorming a few of your own. Think of people who are wildly creative, who are filled with a passion for their work. Think of your favorite writer, movie director, painter, poet, rock star, or songwriter. List your favorite movies, books, songs, or paintings and name the creative forces behind them. Think about which of Tarot's creative archetypes that person resembles.

Creativity in Action, Step by Step

Creativity is a process. Let's use the Tarot to take a deeper look at how a creative project comes together.

The Life Path spread that we introduced in Chapter 2 is the perfect reading to do if you are not sure where to pour your talents. Consider it a career counselor of sorts. It will help you identify not just your strengths, but the work that *you and only you* were *meant* to do.

Here's a look at Carolyn's Life Path reading. At the time, she had accomplished some goals in her career and creativity areas and wanted to know where to go next. Her Personal Year card coincided with one of her personal Life Path cards, the Emperor, which is why so many of her goals had been accomplished in that year. (Paradoxically, she got Arlene's two Life Path cards in her reading: Temperance and the Hierophant—which makes sense because they closed out the year by writing this book together.)

 ◆ **Personal Life Path cards:** the Fool, the Emperor

Carolyn's Life Path reading, using the Major Arcana only, reveals clues to her creative destiny.

♦ **Life Path reading:** the Lovers, Wheel of Fortune, Temperance, the Hierophant, the Star

The Lovers card indicates a desire for balancing opposing forces, and Temperance further supports that desire, depicting a balanced flow. Both cards, as well as the Wheel of Fortune, have angels, and this indicates that Carolyn's next steps will be spiritually guided. The Hierophant suggests she will meet wise ones who will teach her, showing her the ropes. And the Star indicates the outcome will be greater clarity.

And now, Arlene's Life Path reading.

Arlene's Life Path reading is centered on her two teachers, the Hierophant and Temperance. Her lifetime lessons of conventional thinking (the Hierophant) and patience and adaptation (Temperance) provide a nice balance to the intuition seen in the Moon and the Star. The Justice card suggests that although she has an unconventional career, as a Tarot reader, what motivates her is a sense of fairness and honor. The Magician card reminds her that she excels at manifesting ideas into reality, and the Wheel of Fortune indicates that she always has a measure of good luck and serendipity in all she pursues.

Arlene's Life Path reading, using the Major Arcana only.

Take a Life Path reading to the next dimension by doing the Destiny spread we introduced in Chapter 2. You can go deeper into the personal creative energy of the Querent by comparing the Tarot cards that come up around the astrological wheel against the positions of the planets in your Querent's astrological birth chart. In astrology, a birth chart is a map of the heavens at the precise point in space and time that you were born. In the past, calculating a birth chart was a time-consuming and tedious chore. But thanks to computers and the Internet, anyone can create their own charts using software such as Astrolabe's Solar Fire program, get a birth chart easily from one of the many reputable astrology websites, or get a birth chart and reading from a professional astrologer such as Arlene.

Arlene's Destiny reading.

Here is a Destiny reading for Arlene, along with her birth chart. Arlene's Sun sign is Aquarius, while her Moon sign is Gemini. Notice that her Rising sign is Pisces, a very intuitive sign. These three signs are your astrological Power Points. The Rising sign shows you the person you are becoming in this life. The Moon and the Star, paired with the intuitive and dreamy Pisces, say that Arlene will continue to develop her psychic and creative sides with discipline, teaching it to others. The Star card suggests she will do it with clarity and imagination, and the Wheel of Fortune suggests that the destiny she creates of that is only limited by her imagination.

Try a Life Path and Destiny reading for yourself. They will help you get clear on your unique talents and gifts, identifying creative projects and inspiring you to move forward. Next, we will use four subsequent Celtic Cross spreads to analyze the steps to launching a creative project. As you examine these, keep an eye out for the Wands, and other creativity cards.

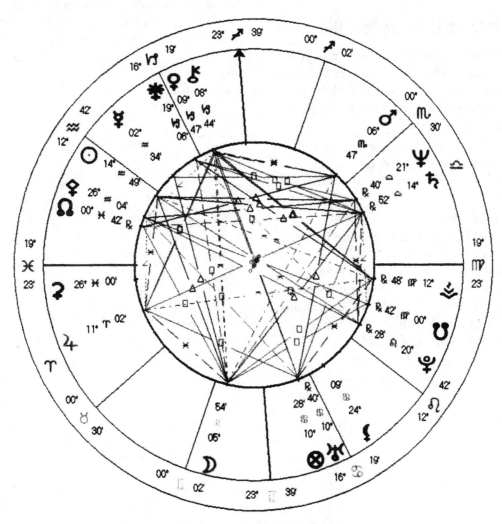

Arlene's astrological birth chart.

Ask the Cards

Notice that in the Magician card, he has the ingredients for his creative project before him, on the table. Use a four-card Diamond spread to advise you (or your Querent) on whether all the conditions are present for a project. Look for a balance of all the Elements: Fire (passion), Water (heart), Air (soundness of mind), and Earth (grounding). This reading will reveal what strengths you have to utilize.

1. Celtic Cross: Defining Your Bliss

The Life Path and Destiny spreads give you the big picture. They show you your individual creative purpose. They reveal the talents you have to work with and the lessons you are learning. They set the stage.

But these spreads don't pinpoint your bliss—the endeavor that brings you joy. So let's use our first Celtic Cross spread to ask "*What is my bliss?*"

Here are the cards:
1. Self. 2 of Pentacles. **2. Opposing Force.** King of Wands. **3. Background.** The Fool. **4. Recent Past.** 7 of Pentacles. **5. Near Future.** Knight of Swords. **6. Higher Power.** 5 of Cups. **7. Issues.** 10 of Pentacles. **8. Allies.** King of Pentacles. **9. Advice.** 5 of Wands. **10. Outcome.** Queen of Swords.

The two Wands cards that turn up here are in Opposing Force and Advice (positions 2 and 9), indicating that the Querent is being presented with choices and lessons about her creativity. The King of Wands could be a mentor she needs to welcome into her life, or he could be a role she needs to assume, becoming her own confident, enthusiastic encourager. The 5 of Wands in the Advice position nudges her to resolve the struggle between the desire for full self-expression and the need for discipline to achieve her goals. The two Swords cards—in Near Future and in Outcome (positions 5 and 10)—indicate that if she does, she will move forward swiftly and wisely.

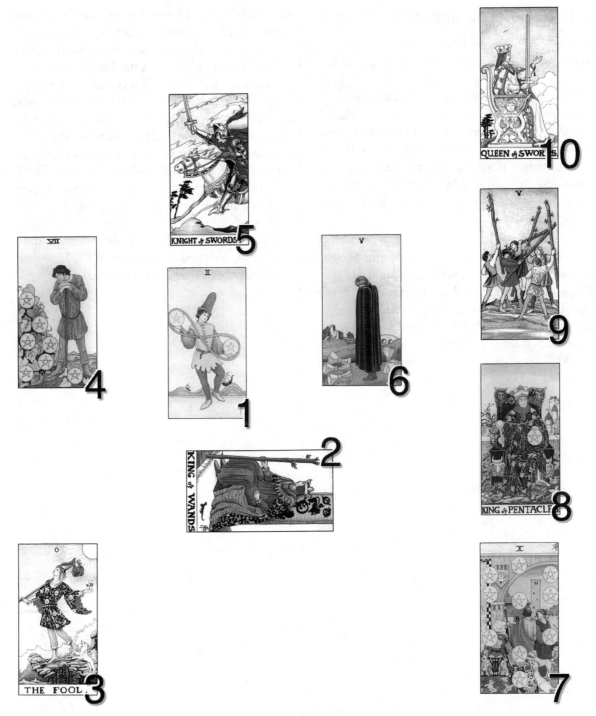

1. Celtic Cross Reading: Define Your Bliss.

2. Celtic Cross: The Initiative

Great beginnings are what creative enterprises are made of. Let's use a Celtic Cross spread to ask how to get started, carrying over the Queen of Swords card, which appeared in the Outcome or tenth position of the previous Celtic Cross, as the Self card, the first card in our new reading. This technique of designing a subsequent reading from the Outcome card is a good way to build step by step toward a full spectrum of answers about a major, big picture, life question.

Here are the cards:
1. Self. Queen of Swords. **2. Opposing Force.** Ace of Wands. **3. Background.** Knight of Cups. **4. Recent Past.** Page of Wands. **5. Near Future.** 7 of Swords. **6. Higher Power.** Queen of Wands. **7. Issues.** 4 of Wands. **8. Allies.** 4 of Cups. **9. Advice.** Death. **10. Outcome.** Ace of Swords.

Wow! What a powerful reading! Wands and Swords are dominant, indicating lots of positive, forward-thinking, action-oriented energy. The Queen of Wands is the Higher Power (position 6), the force that presides over the Querent's new endeavor. The Ace of Wands as Opposing Force (position 2) indicates there are obstacles to getting started, but the Ace of Swords as the Outcome (position 10) indicates that the Querent will resolve that issue. The 7 of Swords in the Near Future (position 5) presents a choice: Sometimes this card indicates a sense of futility that must be overcome. The Death card in Advice (position 9) nudges the Querent to let go of old ways of thinking that hold her back from getting started.

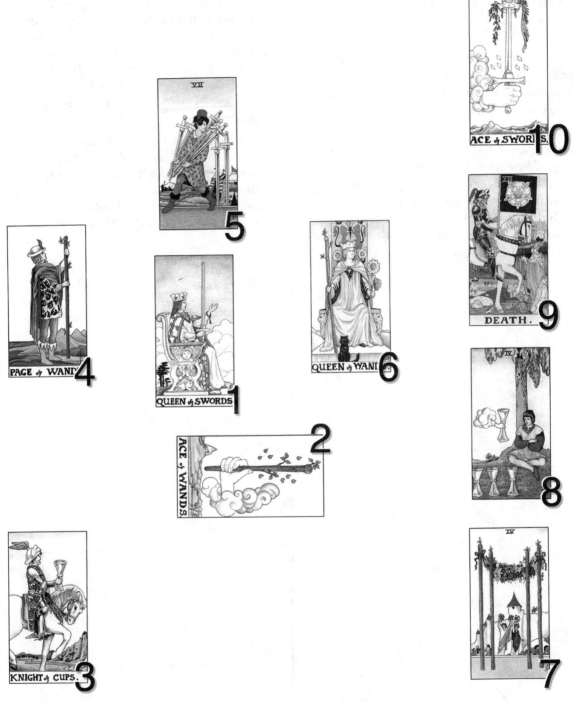

2. Celtic Cross Reading: Initiative.

3. Celtic Cross: Collaboration, Your Creative Allies

Let's say our Querent gets going on her project. She's going to need allies and supporters. Who will collaborate with her on this project? Notice we carried over the Ace of Swords.

Here are the cards:

1. Self. Ace of Swords. **2. Opposing Force.** King of Pentacles. **3. Background.** 10 of Pentacles. **4. Recent Past.** Queen of Pentacles. **5. Near Future.** Wheel of Fortune. **6. Higher Power.** 4 of Swords. **7. Issues.** Emperor. **8. Allies.** King of Swords. **9. Advice.** 9 of Cups. **10. Outcome.** Hanged Man.

The King of Swords shows up in Allies (position 8), indicating her own logical mind— or a logical person—will be her ally, which is supported by the presence of the ever-logical Emperor in the Issues (position 7). The 9 of Cups in Advice (position 9) indicates that if she stays focused on her wish and draws upon her logical mind, she will achieve it.

Let's scan back over the previous spreads for Allies (position 8): King of Pentacles, 4 of Cups. But also notice the King of Pentacles shows up in *this* reading as an Opposing Force (position 2). Also scan for Higher Power cards (position 6): 4 of Swords, Queen of Wands, 5 of Cups.

3. Celtic Cross Reading: Creative Allies.

4. Celtic Cross: Alchemy, Turning Lead to Gold

Let's carry over the Hanged Man for the next step: turning lead into gold. This is *alchemy*, a miraculous transmutation of ordinary things into something extraordinary. Sometime creativity is not about creating something out of the air, but rather about blending things together. It's synthesis. It's the acumen to recognize that two things together can become more than the sum of their parts. Or it's the knowledge that in letting go of the old, something new can emerge.

This kind of creativity has a grace and gentle wisdom about it. It's not the unleashing of creative power that we see in the Magician. It's more the energy of the Queen of Wands, who blends the power of logic with intuition, recognizing that both have their place. Or in the case of the Hanged Man, changing the old patterns.

Here are the cards:
1. Self. Hanged Man. **2. Opposing Force.** 10 of Pentacles. **3. Background.** 6 of Cups. **4. Recent Past.** Queen of Wands. **5. Near Future.** Queen of Swords. **6. Higher Power.** The Magician. **7. Issues.** The Fool. **8. Allies.** The Moon. **9. Advice.** 5 of Cups. **10. Outcome.** 2 of Pentacles.

Tarot Reader

Alchemy was an early form of chemistry, studied in the Middle Ages. In alchemy, the goals were to transmute baser metals such as lead into gold (as in the Magician card) and to discover the elixir of perpetual youth (as depicted in the Fool card). The process has philosophical and magical associations, and it was often guarded with secrecy. In a broader context, alchemy is the miraculous change of one thing into something truly magnificent.

Wow! Did we make that happen—summon the ultimate alchemist, the Magician, as the Higher Power (position 6)? No, it really just came up. And about synthesis: this reading indicates the Querent will synthesize the best energy of the Queen of Wands in the Recent Past (position 4) with the Queen of Swords in the Near Future (position 5) to achieve the Outcome (position 10) indicated in the 2 of Pentacles. The 2 of Pentacles tells her that she will build on her investment in her creative endeavor—her efforts will multiply.

3. Celtic Cross Reading: Alchemy.

Imagination in Action: From Wish to Vision

If you can imagine it, you can do it. Creativity starts with an idea you can imagine. Physicist Albert Einstein said that the imagination was more important than knowledge. The Celts equated the imagination with the soul—it was that vital. In his book *Creativity: Where the Divine and Human Meet* (see Appendix B), Matthew Fox says the imagination "operates at a threshold where light and dark, visible and invisible, possibility and fact come together." (Notice how it echoes back to the dual energies of the Lovers card?) The imagination allows for the invisible and not-quite-possible to exist for a while. It is the entrance into the realm of creativity.

Let your imagination give form to the possibilities. Being able to visualize it can be more essential to your success than hard work and focused intent. That's why *Power of Intention* (see Appendix B) author Wayne W. Dyer says, "Your willpower is so much less effective than

your imagination." Your imagination allows for expansion, for immensity beyond belief. It liberates you, and as the French philosopher Bachelard said, takes you to the "the space of elsewhere."

The Wish Spread

But how to turn it from a mere wish to a vision you put into action? Try the Wish spread. The Wish spread uses 15 cards arranged like a cross. In the center is a card that you (or your Querent) selected to symbolize the wish. Let your Querent shuffle the deck as he or she makes the wish. Fan out the remaining 77 cards, and from that have your Querent pick one card at a time, until he or she has picked up 15 cards, still keeping them face down.

Again, have your Querent shuffle the 15 cards. Lay them out in the following spread. Note that the cards go from the inside out, centered on the wish.

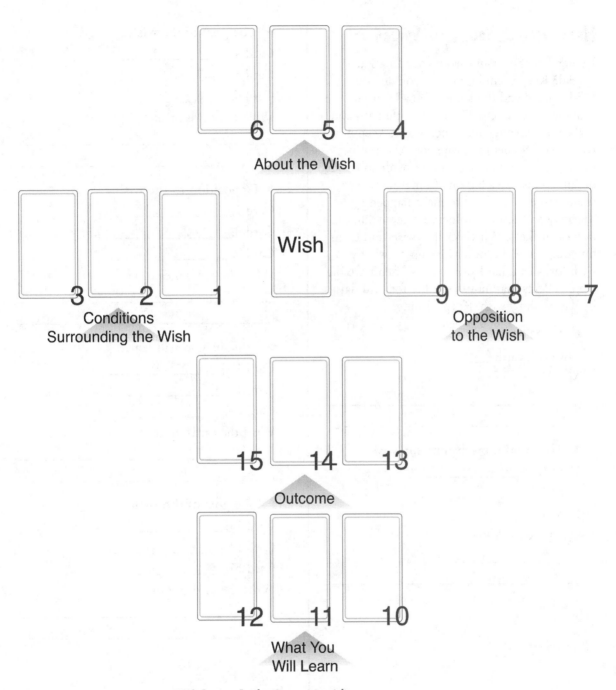

Wish card. The Querent's wish.

Cards 1, 2, 3. The conditions around the wish.

Cards 4, 5, 6. The wish or the goal of the wish.

Cards 7, 8, 9. Opposition to the wish.

Cards 10, 11, 12. Lessons you will learn.

Cards 13, 14, 15. The outcome.

Meditating on Your Wish Spread

Remember the lessons from your Life Path spread? Keep them in mind as you do your Wish spread and think about how what you are wishing for can help direct your Life Path and make your dream come true. Always keep positive intent. Sometimes, we know, this can be hard to do if your situation is difficult and your dream seems like a big one (sometimes, even small wishes seem hard to make happen). Tenacity and resourcefulness are the hallmarks of wish-makers. Whatever the twists and turns on your Life Path, never give up on what you wish for; small, hard-won moves often have big ripple effects that move your life forward day by day, wish by wish. Keep wishing!

◆ **My Wish.**

My Wish card: _____

My Wish:

_____

_____

◆ **The conditions around my wish.**

Card 1:_____

Card 2:_____

Card 3:_____

What the cards mean:

_____

_____

◆ **The goal of the wish.**

Card 4:_____

Card 5:_____

Card 6:_____

What the cards mean:

_____

_____

◆ **Opposition to the wish.**

Card 7:_____

Card 8:_____

Card 9:_____

What the cards mean:

_____

_____

◆ **Lessons you will learn.**

Card 10:_____

Card 11:_____

Card 12:_____

What the cards mean:

_____

_____

◆ **The goal of the wish.**

Card 13:_____

Card 14:_____

Card 15:_____

What the cards mean:

_____

_____

The Creative Life

You can use Tarot spreads to get a better view of your creative endeavors. Through the Life Path, Wish, and Celtic Cross spreads, you can develop a better sense for your talents, your vision, and your direction. Going deeper with your questions and using these spreads, you can develop the imagination and confidence that you need to set the world on fire.

Lantern of Truth _____

Your true passion should feel like breathing; it's that natural.

—Oprah Winfrey, television talk show host and humanitarian

The Least You Need to Know

◆ Wands are the suit of growth, expansion, vision, and creativity.

◆ Creativity symbols show up in the Major Arcana cards of the Magician, the Lovers, Strength, the Chariot, and the Moon.

◆ The Life Path and Destiny spreads can give you insight into the talents you have to work with and the lessons you are learning about creativity.

◆ The Wish spread can give you a full picture of your wish and help you turn it into a solid vision.

◆ Look for Wands cards in your Celtic Cross spreads to find out how to move from imagination to action.

In This Chapter

- ◆ Your heart mentors
- ◆ The Yin/Yang spread
- ◆ Getting to know your soul mate
- ◆ Finding your compatibility quotient
- ◆ Letting go

About Feelings and Emotions

For questions of the heart, there is no better place to turn than the Tarot suit of Cups. That's because the Cups are the vessel for all things emotional.

The suit of Cups can help you map your emotional style. It can show you how you love and how you forgive. It can point you toward your soul mate. It can show you why you came together. Well, we just can't wait—let's find out what the suit of Cups has to say in Tarot readings about all matters of the heart.

The Place of the Heart

Water is the image of Cups, and it's the energy behind emotions. All the words we use to describe water define the energy of emotions: *flowing, purifying, turbulent, choppy, clogged, overflowing, outflowing*.

The images of cups and water are about love, friendship, family, romance, and home. They reveal the realm of the heart—your capacity for compassion and forgiveness, your capacity to give and receive, your capacity for *transformation* through love.

> **Tarot Reader** _____
>
> Why is water the metaphor for emotional transformation? Good question! One answer may be that water cleanses. Water can purify. So water can transform. Water *does* transform, from liquid to ice (solid) to steam (air). Think of baptism. **Transformation** is defined as changing form, condition, or nature. It is the ever-unfolding process of psychological and spiritual growth.

Wise Heart Archetypes

Water is an image that runs throughout the Tarot, not just in the suit of Cups. The suit of Cups may be the ultimate academy for the study of emotional wisdom, but there are wise hearts amid the archetypes that make up the Tarot, especially the Major Arcana.

Whenever you see water imagery in a card that comes up in a Tarot reading, it indicates some emotional aspect is present in the issue at hand. It can indicate a relationship, or it can indicate the emotion that will define your attempt to meet the challenge of a situation.

Some of the more obvious Water Element cards are the Star and Temperance, which both show the flowing of emotions from two cups. They are about clarity and emotional balance.

The Empress and the Queen of Cups go hand in hand, as rulers of emotions. Both suggest the nurturing quality of love. The Moon and the High Priestess suggest the intuition that comes from being emotionally tuned with others. Theirs is the current of knowing that flows beneath logic and wisdom.

The Strength card is sometimes called the unconditional love card because of the tender way the woman is petting the lion (and remember the lion symbolizes creative self-expression). Of course, the Lovers card has to be about love—right?

Supporting Players

Combine the placid waters of the 2 of Swords with the Full Moon high in the sky, and you have the picture of emotional stability and strength. She is just one of many examples of the way emotions show up in suits other than the Cups, playing a supporting role in a Tarot reading in defining the emotions present in the Cups cards.

On the other hand, the surf's up in the 2 of Pentacles. The sea looks invigorating. This card, as well as the Judgement card, suggests emotional movement.

A river runs through other cards, such as the Ace of Wands and the 8 of Wands. In both cases, the river suggests that emotional clarity (like that of the Star) will support the creativity and enterprise of the Wands in a new endeavor. The same river shows up again in the 8 of Wands, the card that says that all is good with your endeavors. If these show up in a reading with the Star, the power of emotional clarity is magnified.

Swords cards depict decisions, and the presence of water in these three—6 of Swords, 8 of Swords, 10 of Swords—indicates that decision is about an emotional issue. The 6 of Swords is about leaving sorrows behind. The decision has been made to cross the river (emotions) to go to the other side. In the 8 of Swords, the water is in puddles at her feet, scattered. This card is about being imprisoned by fear, and in this card her emotions are poured out around her. The 10 of Swords is about fear of emotional ruin. The calm water in the background suggests, though, that this is the end of the cycle. This card presents the opportunity to move ahead.

One other card seems simply to be inescapably about emotions: the 3 of Swords shows three swords piercing a heart, and indeed, it's about grief and loss.

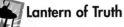

Yin and Yang

The Lovers card is the ultimate yin/yang card, balancing the feminine (yin) and masculine (yang) energies of the Universe. Several cards, including the Lovers, the Chariot, Temperance, and the Star, to name a few, depict dichotomies—the dynamic of two intertwined opposites.

Yin is the quality of receiving, being open, being loyal and faithful, of holding a space for another. In love, yin is the quality of listening, understanding, nurturing—just being there. It is the quality of trusting and allowing yourself to be open to love. Cups are a metaphor for receiving love. The suit of Cups has yin all over it.

But it has yang, too, because without yang there would be no yin, and vice versa. Yang is the quality of just going for it. The Knight of Cups depicts the yang of love—he is riding forth to greet his true love. The Ace of Cups, too, is about an outpouring of love.

This Yin/Yang reading can be done in conjunction with a Compatibility reading (coming up) to give a full picture of the successful aspects of a romantic pairing. It uses 16 cards in total. Each person has a yin column and a yang column. Each card within the column represents an arena of life—thought, emotion, spiritual growth, and physical strength (mirroring the energies of the four Tarot suits). For each person you want to ask about, shuffle the deck as you meditate on that person. Separate the deck into a yin pile and a yang pile. From each pile, draw four cards.

This reading shows how each person is balanced within as well as how two people balance each other out. It can give a good picture of your ability to give and receive love.

Here's a sample reading. Compare Person A's yin/yang balance with Person B's. Person A is female; Person B is male. Note where they are similar. Note where there are conflicts.

Notice when yin images show up in the yin column—the 6 of Cups in Person A's emotional yin column, for instance, indicates a strong emotional current. Notice when a yang card such as the Sun or the King of Wands shows up in the yang column. Both people have strong yang cards in their yang thought column, which indicates they may be strong-willed and creative. Now look deeper: the 9 of Cups appears in Person B's thought yin, which softens the King of Wands, indicating that Person B can slow down and experience contentment. But the Emperor shows up in Person A's yin, which indicates a very disciplined style of thinking, a logic that tempers the creative fire.

Notice where archetypes fall—whether they match up with yin and yang. Where they don't, as with the Empress in yang or the Lovers in yin, you can be sure that's a growth area. That person will find his or her natural tendency tempered by the energy of that card.

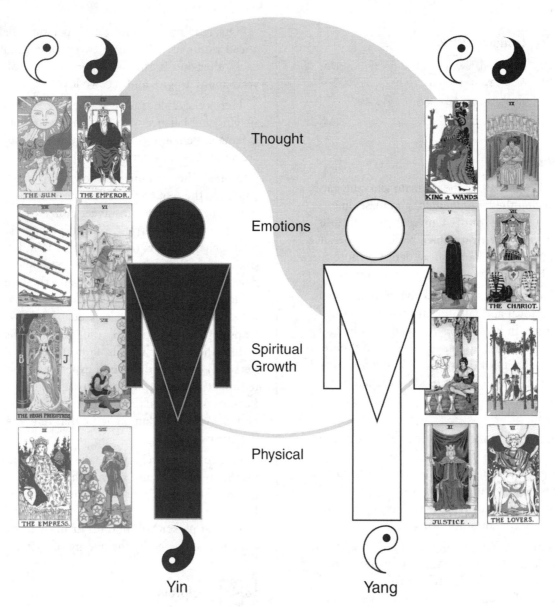

This Yin/Yang spread provides insight in the way two people interact.

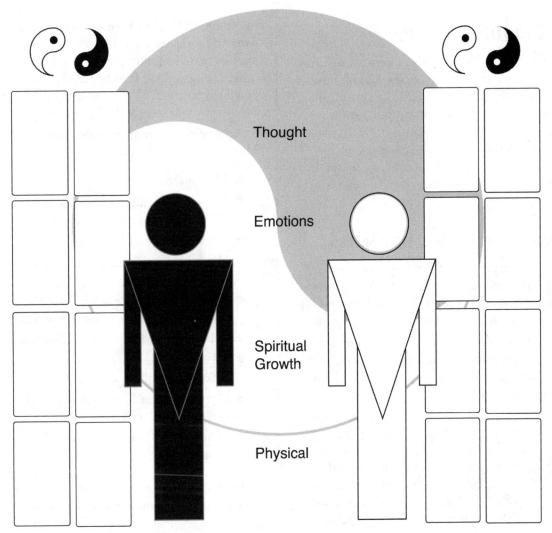

Thought

Emotions

Spiritual
Growth

Physical

This Yin/Yang spread explores the balance of opposite energies in your relationships.

Spreading the Love

The Tarot loves to love you. There are so many ways to look at love through the lens of Tarot. We start you off with a Soul Mate spread, and then we show you the Compatibility spread. Both give insight into the areas in which you and your loved one click. (And ahead, in Chapters 8 and 9, we show you how to use the Celtic Cross to decide if the two of you are a match, using the Royal Court cards.)

Deeper Love: The Soul Mate Spread

What if you are ready for a deeper connection? That's the soul mate connection—not necessarily a lover, but often that's the case, because deep intimacy leads to those true soul connections.

This spread has 22 cards—a lot—but that's what makes it so powerful. In numerology, 22 is a master number, representing some of the highest spiritual workings in our lives.

For this spread, you draw 10 pairs of cards, arranging them in a circle; do this by creating a circle of 10 cards, then adding a second card to each to create your pairs. Adding a second card in this way is often called "covering." Then you draw two final cards and place this pair in the middle of the circle to represent the Querent and the soul mate of the Querent. Each pairing represents the ways in which this couple resonate. In some card pairings, conflicts will appear—but remember, there's no mistake in the friction. This is where you have important work to do that you can only do together. You are like two diamonds, polishing off each other's rough edges. In other card pairings, you'll see harmony. This is where you sing in tune—why you were brought together.

Answer these questions about your Soul Mate.

♦ My soul mate is …?

♦ I'm still searching for my soul mate, but I'd like my soul mate to be …?

♦ What I like best about my soul mate …?

♦ What is most challenging about my soul mate …?

♦ What my soul mate teaches me about myself (that I don't already know) …?

♦ What I am here to teach my soul mate …?

♦ If you are together with your soul mate, what keeps you together …?

♦ If you are apart from your soul mate, how can you become closer …?

♦ What is your hope for your soul mate connection …?

With these questions in your mind, do the Soul Mate spread and explore the answers.

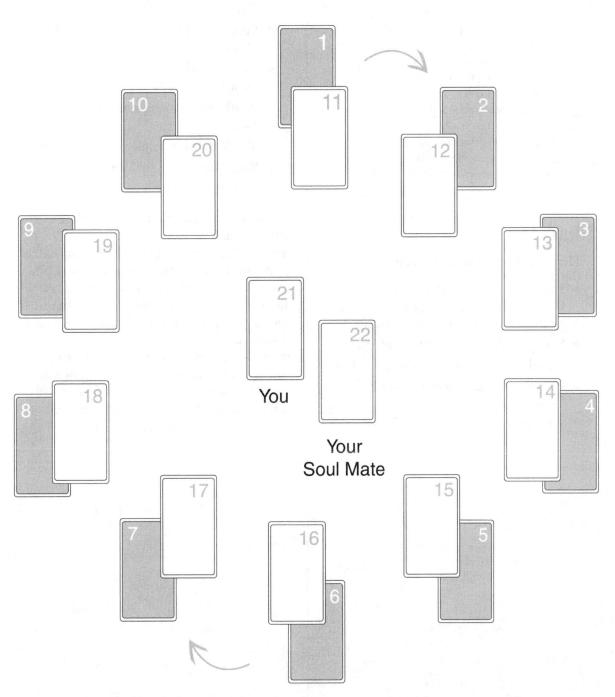

The 22-card Soul Mate spread shows the many ways you and a soul mate come together.

Ask the Cards

Going out? It's a good idea to do a quick Three-Card spread to ask about your ability to give and receive love and friendship before meeting a friend, loved one, or romantic partner for a get-together. The cards may reveal areas where you need to give more in the quality of your attention, or they may reveal areas where you are needing too much, seeking answers from others that you already have within. It will help you recalibrate and get your give-and-take in balance.

Arlene's Soul Mate

Here is Arlene's soul mate reading:

◆ **First pairing:** Hanged Man R, covered by Fool R (more about reversed cards, noted by the letter *R*, coming up in Chapter 11)
◆ **Second pairing:** 2 of Cups, 2 of Wands
◆ **Third pairing:** Queen of Cups, 9 of Cups
◆ **Fourth pairing:** Queen of Swords, 7 of Wands R
◆ **Fifth pairing:** 7 of Swords, Chariot

◆ **Sixth pairing:** Knight of Pentacles, 3 of Cups
◆ **Seventh pairing:** Page of Swords R, Death R
◆ **Eighth pairing:** 5 of Pentacles, 5 of Swords
◆ **Ninth pairing:** Knight of Cups, 4 of Wands
◆ **Tenth pairing:** Emperor, 7 of Pentacles
◆ **Soul Mates:** Page of Wands, King of Swords

The final card pair in the center? Page of Wands with King of Swords! "This just blows me away," Arlene said upon the revealing of the cards. She knows the King of Swords well. She believes he is her ultimate soul mate because he always shows up in her readings, no matter what spread Arlene chooses, in a Future or Outcome position as a future husband or teacher or master—someone who has a lot to share with Arlene. Note that the Royal Court cards may represent different soul mates we'll have throughout our lives (or different expressions of the same person at various stages of life).

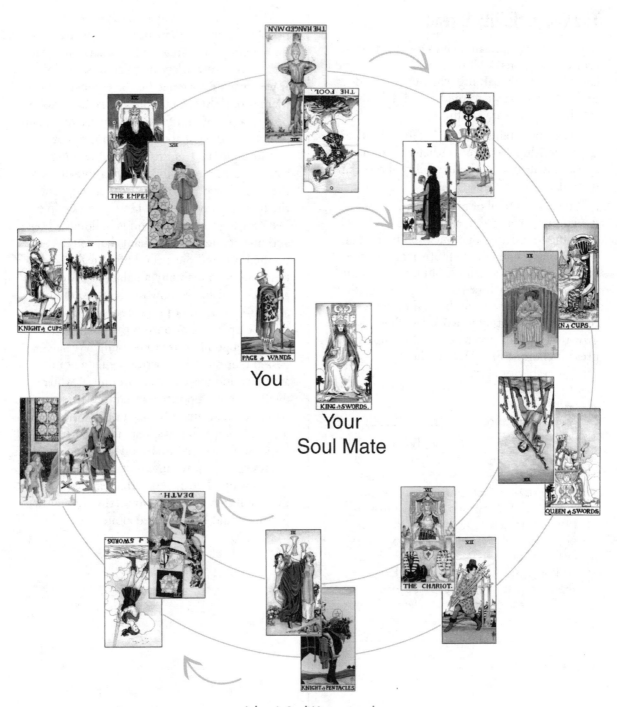

Arlene's Soul Mate spread.

The Compatibility Spread

Try as we might, relationships can be messy. Our expectations don't mesh with others', and it can be positively baffling when the other doesn't understand what we wanted—or didn't want. Inevitably, there are conflicts.

Ah, compatibility. It's the bread and butter of relationships, and guess what—Tarot has a spread for it. It's the Compatibility spread, quite naturally.

There are a total of nine cards. Five are drawn first, arranged in a clockwise circle. They form the foundation of compatibility in your relationship. The final four are arranged in a staff to the right, starting from bottom to top. These cards show how you will grow together. If Major Arcana show up here, they show you that it's your Destiny to work together on growth. If Minor Arcana cards show up, they present choices, Free Will, on how you can grow together or apart.

Temperance

Sometimes our emotions become a flood. Cards that warn you when your emotions are running too high or are too intense are the 5 of Cups, the Tower, 3 of Swords, or 8 of Swords. Other warnings that it's time to slow down show up in the 4 of Swords, which advises retreat or convalescence, or the 10 of Wands, which may be telling you that you are doing too much. The Devil and the 7 of Cups may warn that you are getting too far off center and heading for a fall—just like in the Tower.

We need to be compatible with so many people in our lives: our partners, our parents, our friends, our sisters and brothers, our teachers, people we work with or go to school with. If we have kids, we need to be compatible with them too, right? Sometimes we're like two peas in a pod with the people we relate to, and sometimes the collaboration is not so cozy or comfortable. Here's the remarkable thing: sometimes the most difficult relationships are the ones that produce the most change, and the most positive results. Here's an example. We have a good friend who is building a house and his architect is a brilliant, but tough-minded pro and our friend often feels like he has to fight to maintain a balance between the architect's vision of how the house should be and his own vision of how he wants his house to be. Here's a relationship that needs to succeed for a good house to be built! We suggested that our friend write the name of the architect and place a heart around it, while meditating with positive intent on their compatibility. It seems silly but it does work. Use Tarot's Compatibility spread to explore any important partnership or collaboration, and always keep positive intent at the heart of the relationship. The synergy, that is, the power, of the result may be more wonderful than either partner could have created alone.

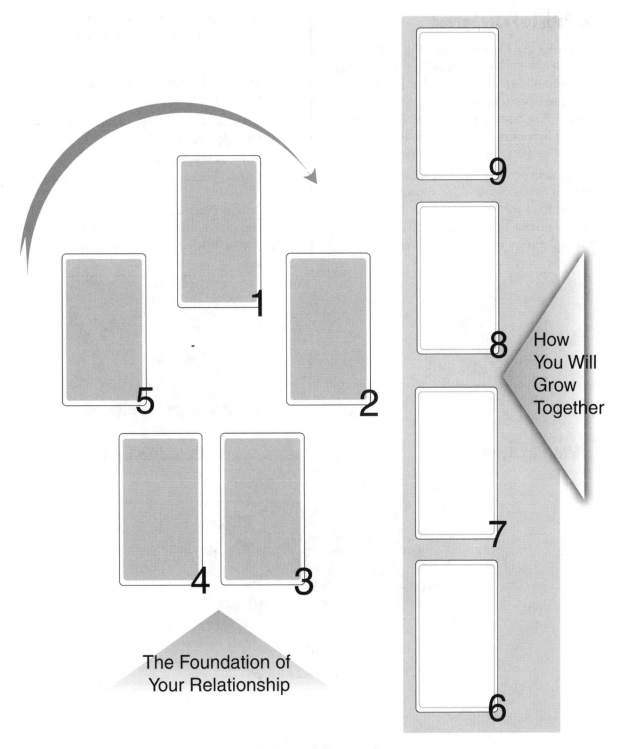

The Compatibility spread.

The Path to Peace Spread

Boundaries can become an issue in a relationship unless we grow comfortable with speaking our truth. Not talking about what we need, want, and desire can be the downfall of a relationship. But boundaries that are too strong can be a barrier to an intimate relationship. You may end up alone in your fortress.

This seven-card Path to Peace spread is a variation on the Seven-Card spread, often referred to as the Magic 7, which draws on higher spiritual knowledge. The Magic 7's spiritual exploration of past, present, and future is taken higher in the Path to Peace spread and reveals what you need to know to walk the line toward bliss.

- ◆ **Path to the Past:** Card 1 Truth, Card 2 Conflict
- ◆ **Present:** Card 3 Anger, Card 4 Sorrow, Card 5 Lessons
- ◆ **Path to the Future:** Card 6 Acceptance, Card 7 Ultimate Peace

A Path to Peace reading, for yourself or for a Querent, is about becoming more authentic—getting your truth in line with another's.

Path to the Past

Path to the Future

Present

The Path to Peace spread.

Forgive Me: The Letting Go Spread

Sometimes you just need tolerance and compassion. These two traits go a long way to creating the space for the forgiveness that transforms. That kind of grace can do miraculous things to a relationship. The Path to Peace spread can show you the choices to make to heal a relationship. When you can't heal it,

however, it's time to forgive and let go. This Letting Go spread will help you (or your Querent) grieve a relationship that has ended.

It's a spread with six cards using the whole deck. Cards are dealt in three and three—two trinities. The first three are what you are hanging on to, the next three show you how to let go.

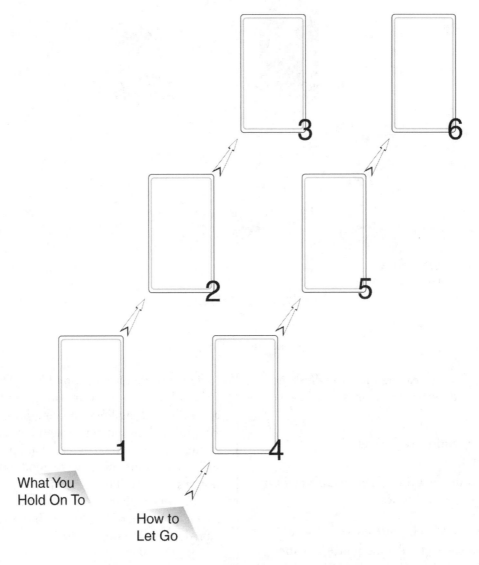

The six-card Letting Go spread is arranged in two trinities.

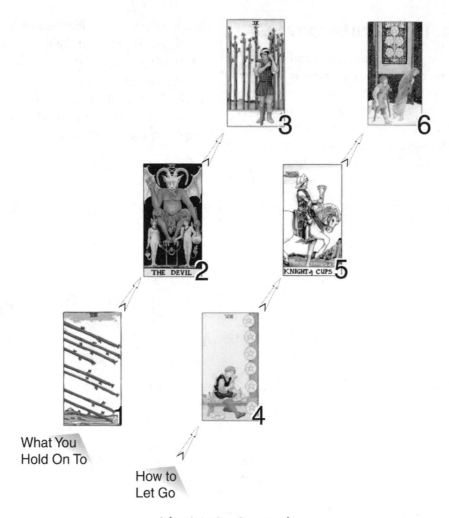

Arlene's Letting Go spread.

Arlene did this reading on her ex-husband, though it had been many years since they were together.

- **First trinity:** 8 of Wands, Devil, 9 of Wands
- **Second trinity:** 8 of Pentacles, Knight of Cups, 5 of Pentacles

As the 8 of Wands came up, she acknowledged that she had had a lot of love and affection for him. When the Devil came up, she said, "You betcha!" To the 9 of Wands, she said, "That's true. It took me a long time to let go."

The 8 of Pentacles showed her, "Work on it, Arlene!" That meant work on financial stability and relinquishing lingering emotions. The Knight of Cups bid her to send love and light to the situation, to recognize that love is what happened. Some things were good; others were not; it's all okay. The 5 of Pentacles reminded her to work on her abandonment issues. The strong presence of 8s, though, indicates she has already achieved some mastery.

Power of the Heart

The Yin/Yang spread, the Soul Mate spread, the Compatibility spread, the Path to Peace spread, and the Letting Go spread are among the most transformative spreads you can use. Look for the wise heart archetypes, study the suit of Cups, and look for other emotional symbolism of the cards in your spread to get to the heart of the matter.

The Least You Need to Know

- The suit of Cups is about more than romance. It's about love, family, friendship—all matters of the heart.
- In the Major Arcana, the Star, Temperance, the Empress, Strength, and the Lovers represent archetypes of the heart. In a reading, they work hand in hand with the choices presented in the suit of Cups.

- The Yin/Yang spread shows your ability and your loved one's ability to give and take when it comes to love.
- The Soul Mate spread shows you the areas where you and your soul mate really click as well as the areas where you are working stuff out together.
- The Compatibility spread can give you a good idea of the solid foundations of your relationship as well as how you will grow together.
- The Path to Peace and Letting Go spreads give you insight into healing a relationship that has ended.

In This Chapter

- ◆ Your life advisory board
- ◆ Making decisions with intuition and logic
- ◆ The Celtic Cross cover
- ◆ The Path to the Heart
- ◆ Keeping karma in mind

Chapter 6

About What Makes You Think and Decide

Are Swords good or bad? The answer: it depends on your state of mind.

When it comes to this double-edged weapon, Tarot's suit of Swords can be about decisive action and intelligent power, or it can be about cutting to the truth or experiencing inner conflict. The energy of Swords is the Element of Air, and it represents all the ways our minds make sense of the world.

The Energy of the Mind

The Swords have energy—there's no doubt about that. The four Royal Court cards and the 10-numbered cards are about the realm of ideas. Here is where we initiate something new— the breath of fresh air. Here is where we test our mental sharpness and the agility of our minds to respond to many challenges.

Which card, we wonder, is the multitasking card that reflects our ability to juggle the mental challenges of our high-tech twenty-first-century world? It would have to be the 2 of Swords, where a blindfolded woman holds two swords in a commanding posture, with her back turned to the now-calm sea. Notice how her swords seem colossal!

The 2 of Swords sees with her mind, and she is
ready for anything!

The suit of Swords not only depicts what we
are capable of when our minds are sharp and
focused, as in the Knight of Swords, it also
gives us a blueprint for the care and feeding of
our minds. The Page of Swords plays the role
the page plays in the other suits, as the messenger and teacher; in this case he shows us how
to conduct our world of thoughts and ideas.
The 4 of Swords, on the other hand, might be
called the single-tasking card. A soldier has put
away three swords as he lies in repose on the
fourth. His focus now is on a single task. This
card is often called the convalescence card
because it's about taking the time out to recuperate and retreat from the demands of battle.

Because the Swords have so much energy,
they are about making decisions, getting to the
truth, moving forward. The Ace of Swords, for
instance, is about cutting through dead wood.
Swords represent the path of courageous
growth.

Ask the Cards

How did Swords come to be a
metaphor for the mind? In medieval
times, the way a soldier held his sword con-
veyed his intention. The way the commander
held his sword could indicate truth, peace,
conflict, or out-and-out war. To lay down
your sword was to agree to a truce.

The 6 of Swords represents a courageous choice
to leave behind your tribulations and start a
new course.

The 6 of Swords, for instance, may seem to
be a negative card, as the hunched-over figure of
a woman and child ride across the water in a
boat of swords. But this card is about a courageous choice to leave your sorrows behind and
start anew. It can also represent the objective
mind, focused and intentional. It is the mind
that has considered the whole picture, one that
has distilled all factors into a crystal-clear truth.
The woman and child proceed across the water
with the full knowledge that they have made the
right choice for themselves. It represents the

courage to look at things as they are rather than what you would like them to be.

Although the Swords cards illustrate defeat, which is one of the possible interpretations of the 10 of Swords (another is the death of an old idea to embrace a new one), the energy of the mind is about victory. Ultimately the victory is the ability of the mind to cut to the truth—and accept it and act on it.

Swords cards are very linear—as in one thing leads to another; a cause, then an effect. There is yang, yang, yang all over these cards. They are about action and big, bold choices. Or in the case of some of the more challenging aspects of the Swords, such as the 8 of Swords or 9 of Swords, they are about being presented with a big, bold choice to change. The 8 of Swords presents the opportunity to choose not to dwell in fear; the 9 of Swords presents the opportunity to quell the self-critical mind.

These cards remind us in dramatic ways that our minds are our ally in how we influence the world, and we must always keep the power of our thoughts in balance. So coming back to the 2 of Swords, could this be the card harkening us to mindfulness, that state of being able to stay in the present moment, reminding us to *be here now?*

Your Advisers

The Major Arcana are role models in how to use the power of the intellect and keep it in balance. Let's take a tour of the ways they use ideas, stimulate change, and make decisions. Go through the Major Arcana and identify images of the mind. Remember that the symbol of the mind is the Element of Air. Often the messengers of the mind are represented by clouds or angels. Remember that our thoughts are light. They travel like angels. Notice, too, the instruments of the mind, the staffs and scepters that symbolize wise counsel. And if a sword turns up … bingo!

Here, we have made some notes about some of our favorite Major Arcana cards. We left some blank lines so you can fill in some of your own.

Card	Image of Thought	Style of Thought
Chariot	Air, movement	Swift
The World	Clouds	White swirl of cloud near eagle head indicates purity of thought
Justice	Raised sword	Truth, judgment
The Lovers	Cloud, angel	Angel bestows balanced thoughts
Judgement	Trumpet sound, clouds	Awakening
The Sun	Passionate thought	Swirling red cape
The Tower	Thunderclouds	Truth revealed
_____	_____	_____
_____	_____	_____
_____	_____	_____
_____	_____	_____
_____	_____	_____
_____	_____	_____

Who did you find? Which cards represented ideas, and why? Which cards bring about change by revealing the truth? Which cards make logical decisions?

The High Priestess can be a meditation focus for intuition; the Emperor can be the focus for logic.

Lantern of Truth

A discovery is said to be an accident meeting a prepared mind.

—Albert von Szent-Gyorgyi (1893–1986), U.S. biochemist

Your Decision-Making Style

Some people make decisions by weighing the pros and cons of a situation, collecting a wealth of information and reasoning it out, like the woman in Justice. Others make decisions by listening to their gut. Most of us are a blend. Here's a Tarot reading you can use to assess your decision-making style or that of a Querent who is grappling with making some key decisions.

We'll use the High Priestess as the meditation focus for intuition and the Emperor for logic and reason. Shuffle your Tarot cards as you meditate on decisions you have made in the past

and the way you have made them. When the meditation feels complete, divide your stack into two piles, one for intuition and one for logic.

For each pile, deal a column of four cards, representing Head, Heart, Power, Action.

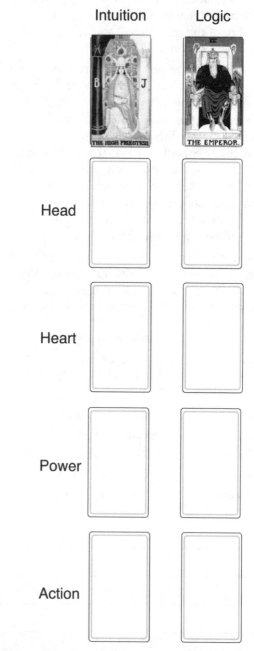

The Intuition/Logic spread can give you insight into the ways intuition and logic play into your decision-making style.

Intuition   Logic

Head

Heart

Power

Action

THE HIGH PRIESTESS

THE EMPEROR.

QUEEN of PENTACLES.

QUEEN of WANDS.

PAGE of SWORDS.

PAGE of PENTACLES.

STRENGTH.

THE HANGED MAN.

ACE of SWORDS.

Carolyn's Intuition/Logic spread.

Carolyn's Intuition/Logic Reading

This reading indicates that Carolyn is clear thinking and balanced of mind, with two Royal Court cards in the Head. The Queen of Pentacles and the Queen of Wands represent grounded intuition and logic with creativity.

The two Royal Court Pages in the Heart area indicate that Carolyn is still learning and growing when it comes to decision making. She is best when she listens to her heart but often must analyze her resources before proceeding. But the Page is always the messenger, and sometimes it can represent children. Arlene's take on it is that Carolyn lets her children guide her in many of her choices and decisions.

The Strength card in Intuition and Power indicates this is the wellspring of her mind power. Her strength derives from courage and creativity. The Hanged Man in Logic and Power shows that she must break her pattern of seeking the approval of others and must listen to her intuition and trust her own logic. The 9 of Cups in Action indicates that if she does, her every wish will be fulfilled. The Ace of Swords shows that actions that derive from this deep sense of trust will be effective.

The pairing of the Hanged Man (the pattern breaker) and the Ace of Swords (which cuts through the dead wood) indicates that Carolyn is often willing to let things go if they are no longer right for her.

	Intuition	Logic

Head		
Heart		
Power	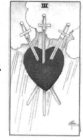	
Action		

Arlene's Intuition/Logic spread.

Arlene's Intuition/Logic Reading

The Star in Arlene's Heart area indicates she always has hope. Her 3 of Swords in Power shows that she is a fighter—she will fight her way through it. Sometimes the way to get her to her intuition, to trusting her inner voice, is to get her mad about it. The 4 of Cups in Action shows that she taps into her Intuition through action, but sometimes she has to retreat first—to go sit under the apple tree.

When it comes to Logic, Justice and Arlene's 8 of Pentacles show she has to process reasoning through her emotions as the 9 of Wands stands guard. The Queen of Swords and the Fool show that when she has, she is mighty!

Try an Intuition/Logic reading for yourself. Record your cards in the following spaces.

	Intuition High Priestess	Logic Emperor
Head	_____	_____
Heart	_____	_____
Power	_____	_____
Action	_____	_____

Temperance

Notice that there is a lot of heart in the Swords suit, and we're not just talking about the pierced heart in the 3 of Swords. Notice the passion with which the Knight of Swords rides out to battle. Notice the despair in the posture of the figure in the 9 of Swords, the defeat in the posture of the woman and child in the 6 of Swords. The interweaving of these images of emotion in these cards reminds us that good decisions are a blend of logic and emotion, listening to both head and heart.

Tarot's Decision Spread: Collecting All the Data

Tarot's Decision spread is a good way to make sure you have done your research and have a full picture before you make a decision. With nine cards in the spread, it allows you to look in-depth at the issues that have led you to this decision point.

Cards are laid out in three columns of three overlapping cards. The first column analyzes events that have shaped you. It shows you how past decisions have created the situation. The second column reveals the conditions of the moment and shows you choices you have before you. The third column reveals the outcome of those choices. And remember, the choice is always yours. So if you see an outcome you don't want, the cards are telling you how to head it off.

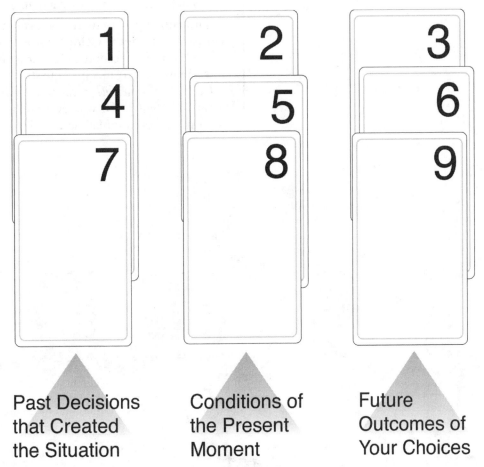

Past Decisions that Created the Situation

Conditions of the Present Moment

Future Outcomes of Your Choices

The Decision spread can help you look in depth at the factors in making a decision.

When You Can't Decide

What if you just can't decide? With any Tarot spread, if you need more information, you can ask a follow-up question by just turning up one more card. Or if you need more information about a particular aspect—the future, for instance, in the Decision spread—you can ask and turn up one more card, placing it next to the cards to which it relates.

I've Got You Covered: A Celtic Cross Variation

An excellent spread to go a little deeper is the Celtic Cover, which takes the Celtic Cross spread one step further.

As you might guess, the Celtic Cover is double your money—20 cards—only when you ask the second question, you lay down the cards in reverse order, moving from Outcome back to Self. Each second-round card amplifies the first.

Or another way to do it is to take the Outcome card of the Celtic Cross and make it the Self card in a second Celtic Cross reading. In this instance, form a new question, as in *So if I did take that new job, what would that mean for my relationship?* Or whatever you might want to find out more about.

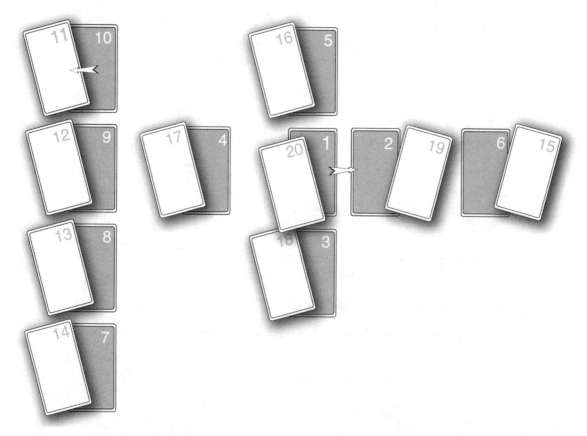

Adding a second round of cards to the Celtic Cross spread is a good way to go deeper into a tough decision.

Foolproof

Although the 2 of Swords can represent the peace that comes when a decision has been made, some people interpret it differently. Instead, they see the two crossed swords as a stalemate and the blindfold as inaction and indecision. Let the other cards in a reading inform you as to which interpretation applies to your Querent.

Path to the Heart Spread: A Heart-Centered Decision

If the decision is really difficult, especially if it's emotional, you might turn to the Path to Peace spread we did in Chapter 5, only do it one better. It can be quite difficult to make a gut-wrenching decision. Sometimes the way to get a clear head is to go through the heart.

The Path to Peace spread guides you to the truth, working through a conflict. To that spread, add three cards that you strip above the seven (making that magical number 10 again). The three cards represent Needs, Wants, and Desires. These cards help you sort out what you have to have, what you want to have, and what you really, really want in your heart of hearts but dare not even hope for.

This spread can be very powerful, sometimes cathartic. Often you'll find it leads not just to a decision, but great peace about the resolution of your situation, as well. You will feel centered and at peace inside. It's often amazing how a reading can help the seeker become calm in the midst of a storm.

Path to the Heart — 8 Needs, 9 Wants, 10 Desires

 Path to the Past — 1 Truth, 2 Conflict

 Path to the Future — 6 Acceptance, 7 Ultimate Peace

Present — 3 Anger, 4 Sorrow, 5 Lessons

For emotionally wrenching decisions, use the Path to Peace spread—only one better, with three extra cards for Needs, Wants, and Desires.

Good Thoughts, Good Karma

The Swords are about personal growth. How could they not be, with all that new energy? Certainly, with all that new energy, they give us the encouragement that if we learn and grow, it will lead to bigger and better things.

Karma is the belief, which derives from the Hindu tradition, that every thought and action we experience has energy. That energy circulates through the world, and eventually all energy we send out into the world comes back to us. In truth, there is no such thing as good karma or bad karma. But people often speak about it that way because when karma comes back to you in the form of a painful lesson, we want to label it. But karma is neutral; and believe us, it's egalitarian. Karma doesn't care how much money you make or what your ethnicity is. Karma just is.

The Karma spread reveals to you your karmic lessons. A *karmic lesson* is defined as a lesson that you were meant to learn in your unique expression. Until you learn it, you repeat it again and again. That's why the energy comes back. When you do master your karmic lesson, you earn the right to move to a higher plane of enlightenment. That means you have realized your full potential and unique purpose in the world, and your contribution to the world is toward the end of the good for all. Sounds great, doesn't it?

> **Tarot Reader**
>
> **Karma** is the concept that all thoughts and actions that we send out into the world are experienced by others and come back to our own experience. That is, if you send kindness out into the world, kindness comes back. **Karmic lessons** are life lessons that you are destined to learn. Behind the concept of karmic lessons is the belief that you must learn from past errors to rise to a new level of awareness.

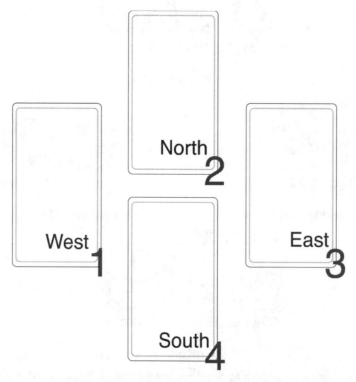

The Karmic spread gives you a picture of your life purpose.

The Karma spread is specific interpretation of the Diamond spread, using four cards to start at the left (like 9 o'clock if you were looking at a clock) and moving in a sequence clockwise. Each card is a part of the story—the lessons you are meant to learn to progress to a higher level of awareness about your life and your purpose.

A Clear Mind, a Strong Heart

In any reading, the suit of Swords is an energizing force, bringing you to clarity of mind and a strong heart, moving you to action. The suit of Swords can be a catalyst for bringing what you want into your life. When these cards show up in a reading, they are bidding you to make clear, quick decisions. They present good choices you can make for yourself in the areas of work, growth, love, and money.

The Least You Need to Know

◆ Tarot's suit of Swords is about the sharp, focused mind.

◆ When you make decisions, you use a little bit of intuition and a little bit of logic. The Intuition/Logic spread can give you insight into your style.

◆ The Decision spread gives an in-depth look at all the factors shaping a decision you need to make.

◆ Using the Celtic Cross Cover can be helpful when you have a difficult decision to make.

◆ The Path to the Heart spread helps answer questions that are deeply emotional.

◆ The Karmic spread can show you the spiritual impact of your decisions.

In This Chapter

- ◆ Abundance in the Tarot
- ◆ Magic 7: taking stock of spiritual resources
- ◆ Zodiac Horoscope spread: mapping out your houses
- ◆ Chakra spread: getting your resources in balance

Chapter **7**

About Your World and Having Stuff

We like to call the Pentacles the "Show Me the Money" suit. But they aren't just about money—they are about having the material to work with, "the right stuff," so that you get what you want out of life.

So after you examine a spread for ideas, decisions, actions, creativity, and love, you know the goals and directions of the Querent. Turn to the Pentacles to see how your Querent is equipped to make those goals happen.

Pentacles: More Than a Bright Shiny Coin

Pentacles can represent money, but in the larger sense, they represent resources and how you use them. So they are often about health, career, home, emotional fortitude, generosity, skills and knowledge, confidence, and good old-fashioned stick-to-it-iveness.

The Pentacles reveal to you how resourceful you are. They show whether you have the ability to bring your needs, wants, and desires to reality. If you are working toward a goal and you need resources, Pentacles in a Tarot reading show you what's available to you.

Pentacles are associated with Earth energy, which is the slowest-moving energy. That means that if you are having a run of Pentacles in your spreads, you are working on something that is going to take some time. Swords, on the other hand, are the fastest suit. Ideas materialize, light as Air, and they become thoughts, plans, and actions—all very quickly. When you see a lot of Pentacles in a reading, you know that the events indicated in the cards are unfolding slowly. It's a message to be patient and stay grounded.

Abundance Archetypes

Many of the Major Arcana serve as signposts to the bounty of Pentacles. So when you see these in a reading that focuses on the issues of Pentacles—anything about money, health, or resources—pay attention to how these destiny makers are shaping the events.

The Empress, for instance, signifies abundance, especially in the realm of home. The Strength card symbolizes abundant good health, as does the Sun. Others that are abundant with flowers include the Fool, the Magician, and the High Priestess. Note that the first four cards of the Journey of Life are strong in imagery of *abundance*, suggesting that we are given much to work with as we set out on our path.

When you see a lot of Pentacles paired with a lot of Major Arcana in a Tarot spread, this is some really major stuff. Remember that a heavy presence of archetypes in a reading indicates some larger life lesson that you have inherited.

> **Tarot Reader**
>
> **Abundance** is the quality of being very plentiful, more than sufficient. Abundance is having a great supply—whether of money, health, wisdom, or rewarding work.

Supporting Players: Resources in Other Suits

Let's take a look, too, at where you'll find resources in other suits. For instance, in the 2 of Wands, the man is holding the world in his hands as he waits patiently for his ship to return. The 3 of Cups is a celebration of abundance. The 10 of Cups is the happy family card—and a good family foundation is the basis of well-being. The 7 of Cups might be called the overabundance card—an embarrassment of riches. When this card comes up, look for Pentacles in the spread to indicate how your Querent might knuckle down and do the hard work to bring grand illusions to reality.

Taking Stock

Like the man in the 7 of Pentacles, who is taking stock of his harvest, you can use Tarot spreads to analyze your resources. Our resources ground us. We may have great ideas (Air, Swords), and we may have a creative, make-it-happen style (Fire, Wands); when it comes right down to it, however, our resources are essential to whether they become reality. What do you have to work with? Like the 2 of Pentacles, where one has multiplied to two, can you make one little something grow into something more? The suit of Pentacles is about multiplying your effort. After the ideas, the passion, and the emotion, you need the real thing. You need tools, and you need hard work.

Notice how many images of tools show up in the Pentacles cards: the hoe in the 7 of Pentacles, the hammer and chisel in the 8 of Pentacles, the scales in the 6 of Pentacles (after all, measuring something and getting hard numbers on it is a great way to make hay).

Use the 7 of Pentacles to focus on taking stock of your resources.

The Magic 7 Spread

The Magic 7 spread uses the Seven-Card spread, only with a spiritual twist. The Path to Peace spread introduced in Chapter 5 is an example of a Magic 7 spread modified for a specific query. The Magic 7 is set up like the Seven-Card spread, with the first two cards about the past, the middle three about the present, and the final two about the future. Only the Magic 7 is about seeking higher knowledge. This is about attaining a higher wisdom about

a subject, so it's good to use on an issue that comes up again and again in your cards. Or if you have a reading that indicates some major life lesson work is at hand, going deeper with the Magic 7 will help you clarify it.

The first two cards reveal the events that have shaped you and prepared you to learn this life lesson now. The middle three cards show you where you are now in your spiritual evolution. The sixth card reveals the steps to take in the future, and the final card—the seventh—represents the spiritual outcome of the question.

What Prepares You for Your Life Lesson

How You Learn

Where You Are Now Spiritually

The Magic 7 spread.

The Zodiac Horoscope Spread

The Horoscope spread is a great way to assess the situation. In the Horoscope spread, introduced in Chapter 2, you spread 12 cards out around the astrological wheel and use each position to represent a month of the upcoming year. In the Zodiac Horoscope spread, we go deeper and associate each card in the reading with an astrological house. What's a house? Think of each house as a stage on which you play out an area of your life. Here's a guide to the houses:

- **First house.** Your physical self, your personality, your early childhood
- **Second house.** Your possessions, your earning ability, your self-esteem (definitely a Pentacles sort of house!)
- **Third house.** Your knowledge, your siblings, your environment
- **Fourth house.** Your home, your family, the foundation of your life

- **Fifth house.** Your creativity, your ability to have fun (especially in romance), your children, your ability to take risks
- **Sixth house.** Your personal responsibilities, your health, your desire and style in helping others
- **Seventh house.** Your primary relationships, your marriage, your business partnerships
- **Eighth house.** Your joint resources, your sexuality, your death, your rebirth
- **Ninth house.** Your ideas about the world: education, philosophy, religion, law; your travel adventures
- **Tenth house.** Your reputation, your career, your social responsibilities
- **Eleventh house.** Your aspirations, your social life
- **Twelfth house.** Your subconscious mind, your privacy, your secrets, your karmic lessons, your hidden knowledge

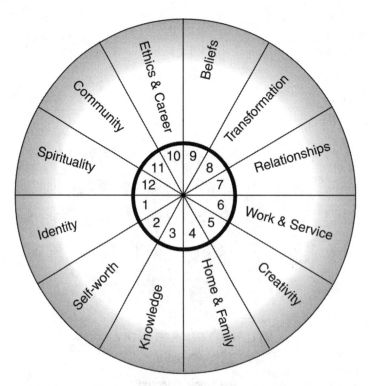

Each of your birth chart's 12 houses represents an area of your life.

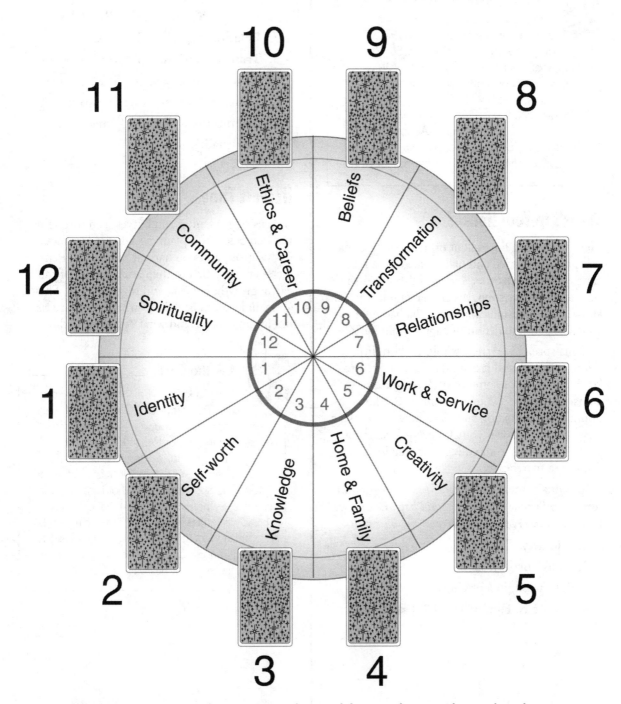

The Zodiac Horoscope spread. Lay out 12 cards on each house and examine how each card carries the energy of that house and gives insight on that house's area of life.

Foolproof

Did you know the astrological signs show up in the Tarot? Of course, you probably already figured out the Sun and the Moon. But every player in the Major Arcana is associated with a sign, such as the High Priestess with Virgo and the Hanged Man with Pisces. Four signs show up in the Wheel of Fortune: Aquarius, Taurus, Leo, and Scorpio. Look in Chapter 17 for a complete guide to the associations.

What's in Your House?

Here is a spread for a client of Arlene's. Deanna was getting married and had worked for a long time to find her partner and establish success in her career. Many strengths and favorable aspects showed up here, indicating Deanna had established a solid foundation of happiness in her life.

This spread is a great whole-person, in-depth reading, and it can take a good hour to read. It's ideal for some of life's bigger questions, especially if your Querent is thinking about a big transition such as a new business or new marriage—or if your Querent is starting out (graduating from college) or starting over (ending a marriage).

Deanna's question: *How will the energy of the astrological houses help me to build happiness in my career and in my relationship with my husband?*

1. **Identity.** The Lover.
2. **Self-worth.** Justice.
3. **Knowledge.** 6 of Cups.
4. **Home & Family.** Wheel of Fortune.

5. **Creativity.** The High Priestess.
6. **Work & Service.** Ace of Pentacles.
7. **Relationships.** The Empress.
8. **Transformation.** 8 of Swords R.
9. **Beliefs.** Judgement.
10. **Ethics & Career.** King of Swords.
11. **Community.** Three of Pentacles R.
12. **Spirituality.** The Star.

Harvest Time

Images of gardening and harvest run through the Pentacles. You plant a seed, and it grows. Crops grow, and you harvest them. The Pentacles are very tied to the natural cycles of the earth: growth, harvest, and regeneration. They are wonderful indicators of what events are rising in importance and what events are fading.

Ask the Cards

Want to know what's new and what's old? This three-card Cycle of Earth reading can show you what's coming and what's leaving, what to nurture and what to let go of. The first card indicates what is new, fresh, exciting—seeds planted that have yet to sprout. The second shows what is ripening in your life—what is flourishing. The last card shows influences that are fading—things to let go of. Let them fall away, the way leaves fall to the ground in autumn, decaying and regenerating the soil with nutrients.

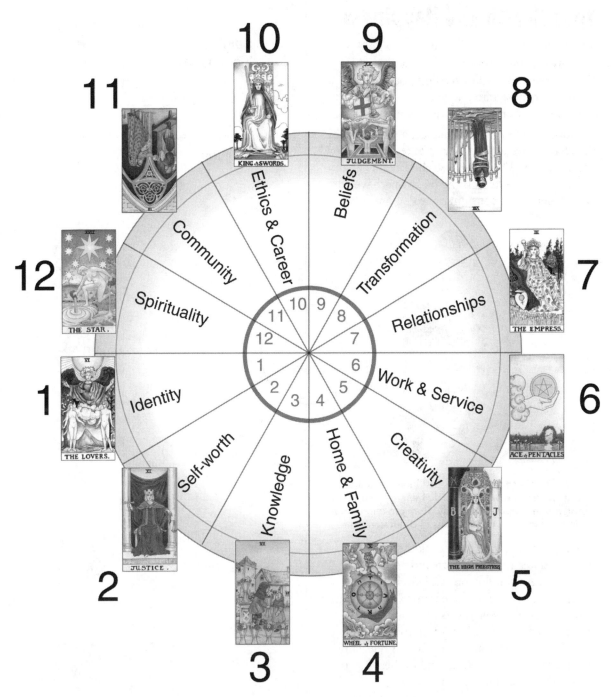

This Zodiac Horoscope spread helped Arlene's client Deanna solidify her goals
as she started a new marriage and enjoyed an established career.
Where is the Pentacle energy expressed?

Your Health and Happiness

The Chakra reading can give you a whole picture of your health—kind of like a physical! Except that the Chakra reading doesn't just check your pulse rate and your blood pressure. It examines your sense of well-being, too.

Good health is about balance, and that's why the chakras are a good way to take stock of how you're doing. That's because the chakras are seven energy centers in the body that have to be in balance for your energy to be optimum.

The chakras come from the East Indian tradition. Each chakra is a whirling pool of energy and light, centered in a part of the body. They are aligned on your spine. Each chakra spins at a different rate.

Let's explore what each chakra governs and how it relates to your health and your power resources. As you do your Chakra reading, compare each card to the energies of its chakra and see how it resonates to your bodymindspirit. After your reading, sit in Yoga's Easy pose or Lotus pose and meditate on releasing the energy of your chakras and on healing to restore balance and harmony.

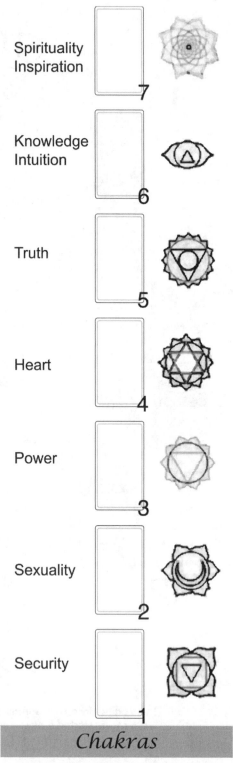

Spirituality
Inspiration

7

Knowledge
Intuition

6

Truth

5

Heart

4

Power

3

Sexuality

2

Security

1

Chakras

The Chakra spread can give you a full bodymindspirit scan.

Security Chakra

Often called the root chakra, this energy center is located at the base of the spine, at the anus or perineum. Root chakra health issues might involve the colon. Emotionally, this chakra is about our need for survival and security. As you were growing up, you formed beliefs about life, love, and money. This chakra is very much about your link to your family. Ultimately, it's about feeling safe.

The energy of the security chakra spins slowly, just like that of the suit of Pentacles. This is definitely an Earth energy sort of chakra. It's about being grounded.

Keywords: Safety, security, survival, retention, groundedness

Color: Red

Sexuality Chakra

Sometimes people call this the allegiance chakra or the creativity and children chakra. It's located just above the pubic bone, and it's associated with the genitals. Sexuality chakra health issues might involve cancer in the genitals, sexual dysfunction, sexually transmitted diseases, infertility—or pregnancy!

So it's obvious why we might call this the creativity and children chakra, but what do we mean by allegiance? Allegiance is the act of deciding to whom and to what you will be loyal. In other words, it's choosing wisely who your romantic and sexual partner will be. But this chakra is about creativity, too—the energy of Fire we find in the suit of Wands—so it's about staying true to your talent and your creativity.

Keywords: Allegiance, creation, sexuality

Color: Orange

Power Chakra

This chakra defines your personal power. It's located at the solar plexus, in the abdomen about where your belly button lies. Power chakra health issues might be in the stomach, intestines, liver, or gallbladder.

This chakra defines your sense of self and your power. If it's in balance, you are assertive in just the right way—not too aggressive or domineering, not passive-aggressive in a "who, me?" kind of way. This chakra also is the home of good boundaries, knowing how much to give and how much to take. Some people refer to it as the chakra of choice because here is where you make your choices by listening to your gut. It's associated with the suit of Swords.

Keywords: Power, assertiveness, good choices

Color: Yellow

Heart Chakra

The fourth chakra is sometimes called the transformation chakra because it's the seat of compassion—the heart. This one links the lower-body chakras to the upper-body chakras, and it's the one that can change all the others.

Some people simply refer to it as the love chakra. From here, all love flows. It's the home of generosity.

Heart chakra health issues might involve heart disease or even respiratory ailments such as asthma. This chakra is associated with the Water energy of the suit of Cups. The heart itself is a like a vase—physically it holds blood, emotionally it holds love. Just as the heart nourishes the body by pumping blood through it, so does our feeling center nourish our emotions by pumping love through us.

Keywords: Love, compassion, transformation

Color: Green

Truth Chakra

This chakra is centered on your voicebox, the place from which you speak your truth. Physical issues associated with the truth chakra might be thyroid problems, neck injuries, laryngitis, or just a sore throat.

Sometimes people call it the expression chakra because it's the outlet for creative expression. Think about great artists or writers who "found their voice," producing their most definitive work. When this chakra is in proper balance, you are able to express yourself well—making it clear what you need, want, and desire in life. This chakra is associated with Swords and Wands.

Keywords: Truth, expression
Color: Blue

Knowledge and Intuition Chakra

This chakra is located in the middle of your forehead, just above your brow, about an inch beneath your skin. Physical issues associated with this chakra might include headaches, eye-strain, or strokes.

Many people call this the Third Eye because of its location and because it's the place in the body where intuition resides. The Third Eye refers to a way of seeing the world in a different way, seeing beyond what is right before your eyes. Someone with a strong Third Eye chakra pays attention to the undercurrents, noticing patterns and synchronicities.

The suit most closely associated with the Third Eye is Cups because intuition has a lot of Water energy. So when a Cups card shows up here, it's doubly powerful. Also associated with the Third Eye is Swords because this is your knowledge base—where ideas come from.

Keywords: Knowledge, skills, intuition
Color: Indigo

Spiritual Chakra

Located at the crown of the head, this chakra is the one most closely associated with heaven. If the first chakra, or root chakra, is the earth, then this one represents the ascendance to heaven. It is also often called the Thousand-Petaled Lotus.

Physical issues associated with this chakra are dizziness, strokes, or neurological issues.

This chakra is sometimes called the chakra of inspiration because it's the meeting point of the knowledge from heaven. This is where we get our most inspired ideas, the kind that seem to just descend out of the clouds. If you get one of the Ace cards in this chakra, where the Wand or Sword or Pentacles is being handed out of the clouds, then you can be sure you will receive an idea straight from your Higher Power. This is definitely an idea that has your own best interest at heart.

Quite naturally, this chakra has the lightest energy—that of Air—and so it's associated most closely with the suit of Swords. Know that when a Swords card shows up here, the power of that card is intensified.

Keywords: Spirituality, inspiration
Color: Violet

Temperance

But what about that 5 of Pentacles card? All the others look good, all that multiplying and harvesting. But in this one, two figures as passing through a blizzard, seemingly unaware of the warm glow of a church where they might seek refuge. Remember the suits cards are about choices, though, so this card is a reminder that everything you need is right here. Balance the impoverished energy of the 5 of Pentacles with a grounding, nurturing Chakra reading.

The World Is Your Oyster

So you see, the Pentacles are an important part of what makes for your happiness and success in the world, and they aren't just about money. Pentacles in a reading show you the areas where you are getting down to the business of making it happen—or where you need to. With a wise investment of your resources, you can find love, creativity, health, and wealth.

The Least You Need to Know

◆ Pentacles show how resourceful you are—how hard you work and how much you stick to it. They show you the areas where your hard work will pay off.

◆ Your resources are more than your bank account. They are your health and emotional fortitude.

◆ The Magic 7 spread reveals information about your spiritual evolution.

◆ The Zodiac Horoscope spread is a good in-depth full-life report on your health, wealth, and talents.

◆ The Chakra spread is a health and well-being spread that shows you how balanced you are.

In This Part

Looking at the Pictures on the Cards

If you want to know more, take a deeper look at the images on the Tarot cards. Noticing the color, imagery, numbers, and symbols on the cards can help you get to the subtler aspects of a reading. Getting better acquainted with the Royal Court cards can help you know who the big players are in the question. Also we get you up to speed on what it means when a Tarot card comes up reversed.

In This Chapter

- Meet the masters of creativity (Wands) and emotions (Cups)

- Look to the leaders in Kings and Queens

- Take on assignments with Knights and Pages

- High-powered pairings

- Royal Court card placements

Chapter 8

Royal Court Cards: Wands, Cups

Meeting the Royal Court cards in a Tarot reading is like meeting the master. Whether it's the King or the Queen, the Knight or the Page, the Royal Court cards represent the full attainment of skills and knowledge in their particular areas.

In this chapter, we examine what the wisest minds in creativity (Wands) and love (Cups) have to teach us.

Who Are They?

The members of the Royal Court may be you or a role you play temporarily. You may find that one particular Royal Court card follows you around for a lifetime, as the Queen of Swords does with Carolyn, showing up quite often when she needs strength, courage, or clarity. Or if you are working on a particular aspect of your life, the Royal Court card who signifies mastery may show up to conduct or complete your training, as with the Queen of Pentacles, who showed up regularly for Carolyn the year she got her writing business off and running. That same year, the King of Pentacles showed up a lot, too, representing two important men who helped her make that happen.

That's just one example of how Royal Court cards also can be important people in your inner circle. They can be family members, soul mates, or trusted friends. Sometimes they are teachers or mentors who will come into your life for a while. They shed light on a particular aspect of your life. Sometimes they are authority figures who bring a specialized expertise that you need, such as a doctor or a lawyer.

Foolproof

If a Royal Court card shows up in your reading, it means your question just tapped into the brain trust. Sweet! All the best and brightest minds have assembled to educate and equip you to meet the challenge of the question at hand and bring to you your most heartfelt desire.

The King and Queen of each suit are the oldest form of mastery, whereas the Knight and Page represent newly obtained mastery. Notice that all the Knights ride horses. Horses always mean that some new level of skill and knowledge is moving closer to you.

Pages are messengers. They bring you helpful information that will educate you. With Pages, it's all about phone calls and e-mails.

Kings and Knights are consciousness that is in motion and expanding. They are consciousness in action. Queens and Pages are centered consciousness. They draw knowledge to them, and the way they teach you is to deepen your understanding. Their wisdom goes within to be examined, whereas Kings and Knights put their new wisdom out into the world to be tested.

If that sounds a little yin/yang to you, there's a reason for that: it is! The energy of Kings and Knights is yang; the energy of Queens and Pages is yin.

Court Card	Meaning
King	Expanding, sharing wisdom
Queen	Deepening, inner wisdom
Knight	Coming closer, developing wisdom; the Knight presents new opportunities to expand wisdom through action
Page	Studying, cultivating wisdom; receiving messages of wisdom

Leaders: Kings and Queens

The energy of Kings and Queens is older energy; so when you look around in your life for whom they might represent, consider your elders. The energy of Knights and Pages is younger. This is someone in your life who is your age or younger but who nevertheless has something to teach you. Sometimes they can be your own children.

Kings and Queens have mastered the knowledge of their domain, and the numbered cards of that suit point the way to the choices they have made. For instance, the 5 of Cups represents an emotional loss, the kind that often happens when you give too much. Trust that the Queen of Cups already knows all about that. Beneath her serene demeanor, there is a story: she, too, knows emotional loss. The 5 of Wands, on the other hand, shows conflict and competition—which can cloud your vision. The King of Wands has been there, done that. He has slogged through it and come out with a list of achievements.

So when you see the Ace through 10 of the same suit in a reading paired with a King or Queen, you are receiving an extra measure of guidance to resolve the conflict at hand and make a better choice.

Assignments: Knights

With the Knights, you are being presented the opportunity to put your knowledge to the test out in the world. Knights ride in on their horses to bring you ways you can achieve a whole other level of mastery. The Knight of Cups recognizes that you have gotten smarter at love, and he brings you an opportunity to try that idea on for size. (Can we ever *really* be smarter about love? We'd like to think so!)

Likewise, the Knight of Wands represents inspired creativity. Feel how fresh that energy is! He believes in you. You can do it!

Spend some time getting to know Tarot's Royals.

Temperance

Knight cards often warn you of something that you need to heed, so listen up! They bring a message up in your consciousness to full awareness. So hear them out. They present challenges and opportunities.

Messages: Pages

The Pages urge you to listen and learn. No matter how much life experience you have, if a Page shows up, you're being told to be more open to learning new ways of thinking and doing. Because their energy is young, the learning here may feel original, fresh—and invigorating. There is a playfulness to the Pages. The fish jumping out of the cup in the Page of Cups—doesn't it just remind you of the fish in *The Cat in the Hat?* Or maybe the clownfish dad voiced by actor Albert Brooks in *Finding Nemo?* Both pretty uptight fish, we'd say! It is through play that we get to that innocent state of mind that facilitates learning. So don't just listen up—lighten up!

The Truly Magic Wands

The Royal Court cards of Wands are true magicians. They have vision and focused intent. Arlene and Carolyn added some celebrities and fictional characters who exemplify the qualities of the Royal Court cards. Here's a handy guide.

- **The King of Wands** is an inspiration for spiritual growth. He is committed to a purposeful life, and he has mobilized all of his energy to pursue it. Like the Hanged Man from the Major Arcana, he is willing to break old patterns and remove all obstacles that might stand in the way of his vision. He is perceptive and insightful.

- **The Queen of Wands** has achieved self-mastery. She is self-assured and has a lot of personal magnetism. You want to get to know her. The black panther at her feet serves as a reminder of the dark places she has traversed and the growth she has experienced.

- **The Knight of Wands** is every artist's best friend because he's all about inspiration. When he shows up in a reading, it means the creative process will flow. Everything is in place: vision, intent, focus. He is committed to growing through the creative process.

- **The Page of Wands** is the liberated spirit of creativity. He represents a new direction.

Wands and Royal Wands

When Royal Court cards show up with other cards of their suit, they indicate that the choice presented in the other cards will likely be successful. For example, the 5 of Wands card is about the struggle between the desire for limitless self-expression and the need for discipline to see a project through completion. But if the Page of Wands shows up in a reading with the 5 of Wands, there is cause for hope. The Page of Wands indicates that the lesson will be learned.

The same holds true if any of the Royal Court cards show up in a reading with the "work-in-progress" cards, such as the 7 of Wands (in which the man is fending off an enemy).

Lantern of Truth

It is better to have enough ideas for some of them to be wrong, than to be always right by having no ideas at all.
—Edward de Bono, British psychologist, physician, and creativity expert

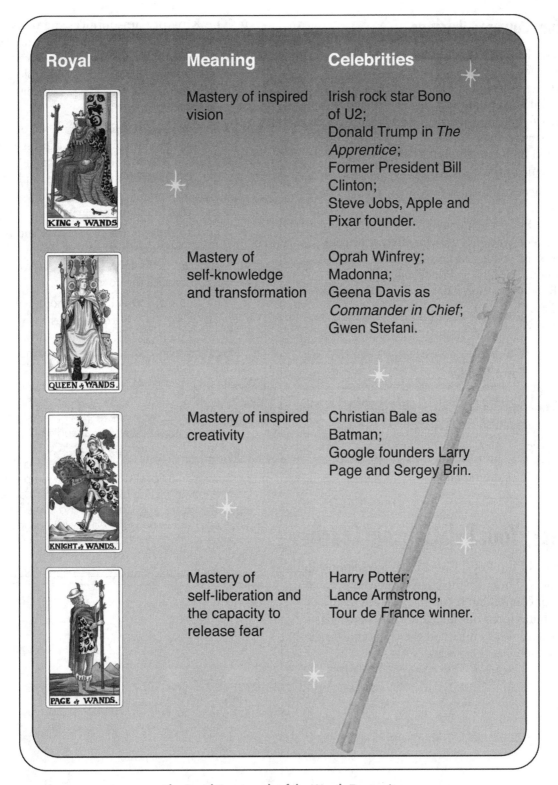

Royal	Meaning	Celebrities
KING of WANDS	Mastery of inspired vision	Irish rock star Bono of U2; Donald Trump in *The Apprentice*; Former President Bill Clinton; Steve Jobs, Apple and Pixar founder.
QUEEN of WANDS.	Mastery of self-knowledge and transformation	Oprah Winfrey; Madonna; Geena Davis as *Commander in Chief*; Gwen Stefani.
KNIGHT of WANDS.	Mastery of inspired creativity	Christian Bale as Batman; Google founders Larry Page and Sergey Brin.
PAGE of WANDS.	Mastery of self-liberation and the capacity to release fear	Harry Potter; Lance Armstrong, Tour de France winner.

The Royal Court cards of the Wands Tarot suit.

High-Powered Pairings

When Royal Court cards of Wands show up with each other or with power-and-vision archetypes from the Major Arcana, you can be assured you are on your way to *mastery* in this area of your life—the rise to a certain level of status, where your skills and knowledge are held in high esteem. Refer back to Chapter 4 for some of the creativity archetypes.

When Royal Court cards show up together, you just got a unified front of wisdom. You may think of yourself as one of them—as the King or Queen of Wands. If the other in that pairing shows up, you have a powerful ally. When you get both the King and the Knight, expect there to be a lot of action. When you get the Queen and the Page, expect to do a lot of listening before you act.

> **Tarot Reader**
>
> **Mastery** is what the Royal Court cards are all about. Mastery is defined as rule or control; the ascendance to victory after a struggle; expert skills and knowledge. Other cards in the Tarot that define mastery include the 7 of Wands and the 8 of Pentacles.

Cups: Your Relationship Coaches

Think of the Royal Court cards as relationship helpers. These are the counselors who keep you out of counseling. If you incorporate their attributes into your life, you will achieve mastery. Here's a summary of the Cups court members and what they mean.

- ◆ **The King of Cups** forgives and transforms. He is the embodiment of kindness and exemplifies trust. He has achieved such a level of mastery that he is able to reach out, unguarded. His presence is spiritually uplifting.

- ◆ **The Queen of Cups** is the model of owning her feelings. She can express her feelings clearly, without blame or judgment. She's compassionate, kind, and nurturing, but she's also honest and congruent. She's got integrity.

- ◆ **The Knight of Cups** wants love and is willing to be vulnerable to receive it. He is a great encourager. He bids you to open your heart to love.

- ◆ **The Page of Cups** loves without jealousy, without a controlling, possessive heart. The Page of Cups knows how to create a relationship that can breathe.

> **Ask the Cards**
>
> When Arlene has more than one interpretation about which way a reading is going to go, she defers to the Royal Court cards. That means she really, really listens to those cards. If a Royal Court card shows up in a Celtic Cross as an Ally (card 8) or Higher Power (card 6), you are in good hands. If a Royal Court card shows up in the Advice (9) position, its advice you'd better take. And if it shows up in Outcome (card 10)? You're on your way!

Royal	Meaning	Celebrities
KING of CUPS.	Mastery of emotional loyalty, commitment; epitome of kindness and compassion	Steven Spielberg; George Lucas; Tom Hanks; Former President Jimmy Carter.
QUEEN of CUPS.	Mastery of emotional integrity, emotional balance, emotional self-management	Gwyneth Paltrow; Scarlet Johansson.
KNIGHT of CUPS.	Mastery of desire; he wants love, and he's willing to be vulnerable to receive it	Matthew McConaughey; Jude Law; Antonio Banderas; The young knight Percival.
PAGE of CUPS.	Mastery of authentic communication; mastery of emotional security; mastery of emotional freedom and objectivity. The Page of Cups loves without jealousy, without a controlling, possessive heart.	Natalie Portman; Reese Witherspoon; Rainer Maria Rilke; Romeo & Juliet.

The Royal Court cards of the Cups Tarot suit.

Two Celtic Crosses: Connecting, Reaching Out

Here's a way to use the Royal Court cards to set up a reading about your love life. Choose a Self card that represents your Querent. Then choose a Self card (card 1) that represents your Querent's love. In this case, to show you how it works, we used the same Royal Court card as Self, pairing with two different Royal Court cards. They are a hypothetical couple, but this does give you an idea of which partner is better

suited for the Queen of Cups—the King of Cups or the King of Wands. Based on these readings, which love interest is more ready for the Queen of Cups?

As you shuffle, meditate on the two people. When shuffling feels complete, divide the deck into two stacks. Then shuffle the individual stacks, one for the Queen of Cups, the other for the King of Cups. Lay out their cards in a Celtic Cross spread. Here's our spreads.

Should the Queen of Cups be with the King of Cups? Will their paths converge? What are their obstacles?

Should the Queen of Cups . . .

1. **Self.** Queen of Cups.
2. **Opposing Force.**
   Ace of Pentacles.
3. **Background/Foundation.**
   King of Swords.
4. **Recent Past.**
   7 of Cups.
5. **Near Future.**
   The Hierophant.
6. **Higher Power.**
   9 of Pentacles.
7. **Issues/Fears.**
   Knight of Swords.
8. **Allies.**
   Temperance.
9. **Advice.**
   Queen of Pentacles.
10. **Outcome.**
    The Moon.

1. **Self.** King of Cups.
2. **Opposing Force.**
   4 of Cups.
3. **Background/Foundation.**
   10 of Swords.
4. **Recent Past.**
   The Fool.
5. **Near Future.**
   10 of Wands.
6. **Higher Power.**
   Wheel of Fortune.
7. **Issues/Fears.**
   10 of Pentacles.
8. **Allies.**
   3 of Wands.
9. **Advice.**
   7 of Wands.
10. **Outcome.**
    Queen of Swords.

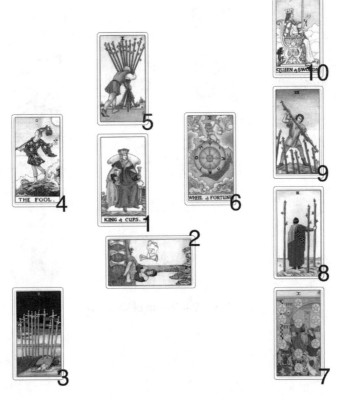

. . . be with the King of Cups?

Or should the Queen of Cups be with the King of Wands? Will their paths converge? What are their obstacles?

What's your take on it? Well, the King of Cups shows up in the Queen of Cups' Recent Past (card 4) when she meets the King of Wands, so it looks to us like the King of Cups is about to become history. Plus we wonder whether the Queen of Swords in the Outcome position (card 10) of the King of Cups means he has his eye on someone else.

Notice, too, which cards came up twice. The Queen of Cups got the Ace of Pentacles both times, the card of new beginnings. Only the Ace of Pentacles came up as an Opposing Force (card 2) to the King of Cups and as an Outcome (card 10) with the King of Wands.

Lots of Knights are coming up here, too. The Queen of Cups got the Knight of Swords in Issues (card 7) on the first round, and the King of Wands got the Knight of Pentacles and the Knight of Wands. That indicates that in both pairings there are some very important assignments ahead.

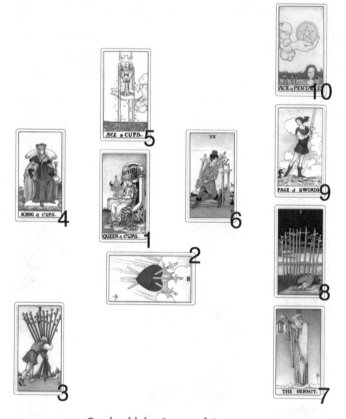

Or, should the Queen of Cups . . .

1. **Self.** Queen of Cups.
2. **Opposing Force.**
   3 of Swords.
3. **Background/Foundation.**
   10 of Wands.
4. **Recent Past.**
   King of Cups
5. **Near Future.**
   Ace of Cups.
6. **Higher Power.**
   7 of Swords.
7. **Issues/Fears.**
   The Hermit.
8. **Allies.**
   10 of Swords.
9. **Advice.**
   Page of Swords.
10. **Outcome.**
    Ace of Pentacles.

1. **Self.** King of Wands.
2. **Opposing Force.**
   The Sun.
3. **Background/Foundation.**
   Temperance.
4. **Recent Past.**
   3 of Pentacles.
5. **Near Future.**
   The Star.
6. **Higher Power.**
   6 of Cups.
7. **Issues/Fears.**
   Knight of Wands.
8. **Allies.**
   Knight of Pentacles.
9. **Advice.**
   8 of Swords.
10. **Outcome.**
    The Fool.

. . . be with the King of Wands?

Friends of the Court: Places, Please!

Those two readings probably gave you a little bit of an idea of how to read Royal Court cards based on their position in a reading. Here's a closer look at how to interpret Royal Court cards in a Celtic Cross spread:

- ◆ **Card 1: Self.** Of course, this means you! It means that you are taking on the attributes of the Royal Court card.
- ◆ **Card 2: Opposing Force.** This usually means that someone is playing a role in your life to challenge you to more wisdom. This person is prepared to teach you something, and you must decide whether you are ready to learn.
- ◆ **Card 3: Foundation.** This can mean that someone who was influential in your background—a family member or a mentor—is an important part of why you're asking the question. It may be someone who helped you, or it may be someone who was instrumental in shaping a belief that you no longer need. Look to the other cards to see if there is something holding you back. If so, the clue might be in the Foundation (card 3).

For example, notice in the previous reading that the King of Swords showed up in the Queen of Cups' first reading with the King of Cups. His appearance in the third position of Foundation, along with the Queen of Swords' appearance in the tenth position of Outcome, indicates that logic, reason, and clear thinking will come into play in this pairing of two heart-centered masters. Might logic get in the way?

- ◆ **Card 4: Recent Past.** The influence of this Royal Court card is diminishing. You are beginning to master the lesson of this card for this cycle.
- ◆ **Card 5: Near Future.** This Royal Court card has arrived to reveal more lessons to you, or it's a role you will assume.
- ◆ **Card 6: Higher Power.** If you have a Royal Court card that likes to follow you around, it often shows up here. When a Royal Court, whether familiar or new, shows up here, it means that the mastery of this card has big picture implications for your life. It's a lesson that will point you to your higher self.
- ◆ **Card 7: Issues.** This card has something to teach you. You have tendencies that undermine your ability to learn the lessons this card represents. To find out how to balance that, look to Allies (card 8) and Advice (card 9).
- ◆ **Card 8: Allies.** This card could be a trusted friend or adviser who will play a key role in the question at hand. Or it could be a person who is influencing the situation, for better or for worse.
- ◆ **Card 9: Advice.** Take this advice if it comes from the Royal Court. Trust us, it's good advice.
- ◆ **Card 10: Outcome.** When a Royal Court card shows up here, you are becoming the master of the abilities this card represents.

The Royal Way

All in all, you're in good hands with the Royals. We are off to a good start in creativity and love. So let's find out in the next chapter about how the Royal Swords and Pentacles bring you clear thinking and material wealth.

The Least You Need to Know

- Royal Court cards represent mastery of a struggle or attainment of higher skills and knowledge in a certain area.

- Royal Court cards may represent you and your strengths, or they may represent mentors and loved ones who are influencing your situation.

- Kings and Queens are leaders, whereas Knights and Pages often deliver opportunities and messages.

- Kings and Knights are about expanding wisdom, whereas Queens and Pages are about deepening wisdom.

- When Royal Court cards show up in readings with the Free Will cards of the Minor Arcana, they bode well for you to learn the lesson and make good choices.

In This Chapter

- ◆ Masters of intention and focus (Swords)
- ◆ Rulers of passionate and practical thinking
- ◆ Assuming the role of prosperity (Pentacles)
- ◆ Learning the lessons of many talents

Chapter 9

Royal Court Cards: Swords, Pentacles

Now it's time to meet the brain trust and the money gods. In the Royal Court cards of Swords, you'll find the best and brightest when it comes to thinking it through to victory. The Royal Pentacles, on the other hand, have the Midas touch when it comes to material worth.

Find out what these cards have to say about who you are, who you might become, and who is there to help you along the way.

Your Task Force

If you need to make a decision, look for the Royal Court cards of Swords in a reading. They point the way to the wisest choices you can make—and the wisest people who can help you.

Here are some of the attributes of the Royal Swords cards:

◆ Focused   ◆ Passionate   ◆ Intentional

◆ Decisive   ◆ Shrewd   ◆ Fair

◆ Logical   ◆ Practical   ◆ Authentic

◆ Objective   ◆ Determined

To some extent, all Royal Swords cards have these attributes, whether it's the wise King, the fierce and magnificent Queen, the courageous Knight, or the studious Page.

Spreading It Out

Let's put what we know now about the Royal Court cards in Tarot suits and Swords into action by looking at the way they figure into spreads.

When you see a Royal card in a spread, always remember that it most often represents a person. Make a few notes about who you think it is:

- ◆ You
- ◆ A role you are playing for now
- ◆ An image you put out to the world
- ◆ A role you are about to assume
- ◆ A person who is influencing you
- ◆ A parent
- ◆ An adviser
- ◆ A lover or soul mate
- ◆ A companion or ally
- ◆ An agent of change for you
- ◆ A teacher

In some cases, it can be someone who recurs often in your readings, as in the case of the King of Pentacles for Carolyn (that's her father!) or the King of Swords for Arlene (that's her soul mate!). Other times, though, it's someone you are going to meet.

King of Swords

The King of Swords is exemplary in his way of thinking things through and making decisions. He's the person to whom you turn for the most difficult decision because he has the ability to examine the most intricate situations for truth and find clarity.

The King of Swords is full of intention. He is very intentional in the way he goes about all parts of his life. He has really thought this all the way through. He can visualize exactly what he needs, wants, and desires. When you get him in a reading, you have reached the pinnacle of knowing, seeing, and acting on your goals.

And he's not just a stubborn dude. He's so clear on what he wants that it's so right, and it all falls into place without great struggle or strife. He doesn't have to do a lot of negotiating to convince others to believe in what he's doing. He's mastered that.

He has achieved a union of heart, mind, and action. All are moving in the same direction. When he shows up in a reading, he is instructing you about how to get your heart, mind, and actions in alignment.

> **Ask the Cards**
>
> Notice that the King of Swords is not all yang—not all doing. He's determined, but he's infinitely aware and in tune. He's still listening, even as he is proceeding forward with his plan of action. That's the symbolism of the butterflies on his throne, the yin side of the King of Swords. Notice also the pair of sea-gulls in the background, suggesting harmony. He is the union of all four levels of consciousness—physical, mental, emotional, and spiritual. That's why it all falls into place for him.

Queen of Swords

When Carolyn was in a high-risk pregnancy with twins, she got the Queen of Swords a lot. That's because there is no better advocate for you than the Queen of Swords. She is a protector. She is fierce, but she's not rash. She acts decisively and thinks clearly and quickly. She can think on her feet. She's sharp.

And her heart is in the right place. This is the outward expression of the Queen of Cups. It is emotional wisdom in action. The Queen of Swords thinks logically, but with a wise heart. She sees all with clarity because she has examined her emotions, and she has mastered them with objectivity and fairness. The Queen of Swords is the counselor, the consultant. In many cases, she is the mask cutter.

Royal	Meaning	Celebrities
KING of SWORDS.	Mastery of intention, focused thinking	Tom Brokaw; Colin Powell; Albert Einstein; Dr. Phil.
QUEEN of SWORDS.	Mastery of logical, focused, objective thinking	Erin Brockovich; Maya Angelou; Christiane Northrup; Gloria Steinem.
KNIGHT of SWORDS.	Mastery of passionate thinking	Tiger Woods; Nicolas Cage; Orlando Bloom.
PAGE of SWORDS.	Mastery of practical thinking, processing logic	Yoda; Harry Potter; Peter, in *The Chronicles of Narnia*.

The Royal Court cards of the Swords Tarot suit.

The Queen of Swords also cuts through all that is unsound—the masks we try to wear, the façade we keep up to protect our most heartfelt desires from being trampled on. There are no pretenses with the Queen of Swords. She is intent on deepening your consciousness. She's not tied to the old ways of doing things. She's a breath of fresh Air. Her insights are filled with wise innocence. She demands authenticity— that's why the masks won't work anymore. Still, it's okay to be vulnerable when the Queen of Swords comes up, because you're safe with her.

Foolproof

Neither the Queen of Swords nor the Knight of Swords likes to be held back. They are ready to get going. So if you see them in a reading, check the other cards to see if you have any cards that are going to slow things down or get in the way, such as reversed cards or cards with the number 4.

Coming Closer: Knight of Swords

The Knight of Swords is passionate thinking in action. He rides forth with no restrictions, no limits. When he comes up in a reading, he's going to get things moving. He doesn't have much patience for lack of imagination. He has already imagined it, and he's going to make it happen. He is the culmination of creativity— when you have successfully completed the curriculum of the suit of Wands, the Knight of Swords shows up to ride forth. He has no question in his mind that his creativity and passion will make their mark on the world. He's the ultimate original, fresh and innovative in his approach. Only problem is, he doesn't like limits. So look throughout the reading for cards that show what might be holding you back.

Learning All About It: Page of Swords

The Page of Swords just gets the job done. He's practical. He finds ways to apply ideas in productive and tangible ways. Forget your doubts. When the Page of Swords comes up, you're getting the signal that it's time to just do it. The Page of Swords swiftly uses his sword to just make it happen, and happen now. The Page of Swords holds back the doubts, the feelings of futility, the concerns about inadequacies. He's not overly idealistic. He has vision, but he's more intent on a step-by-step approach.

Like all pages, the Page of Swords is still a student. He is still learning, and he's enthralled with learning. He's soaking it up like a sponge. He's constantly replenishing his mind and embracing new thinking. He's eager to act rather than just plan. He's got planning down. Now it's time for results.

Lantern of Truth

There's no money in poetry, but then there's no poetry in money, either.
—Robert Graves, English poet

A Wealth of Information

The Royal Pentacles cards are more than just resourceful people. They have the ability to manifest resources and multiply them. They have the ability to sow many seeds and reap the rewards.

That takes not just talent but knowing your talent. It takes knowing how to pull the best out of yourself and others. And it takes good, steady, hard work. The Royal Pentacles are diligent, that's true.

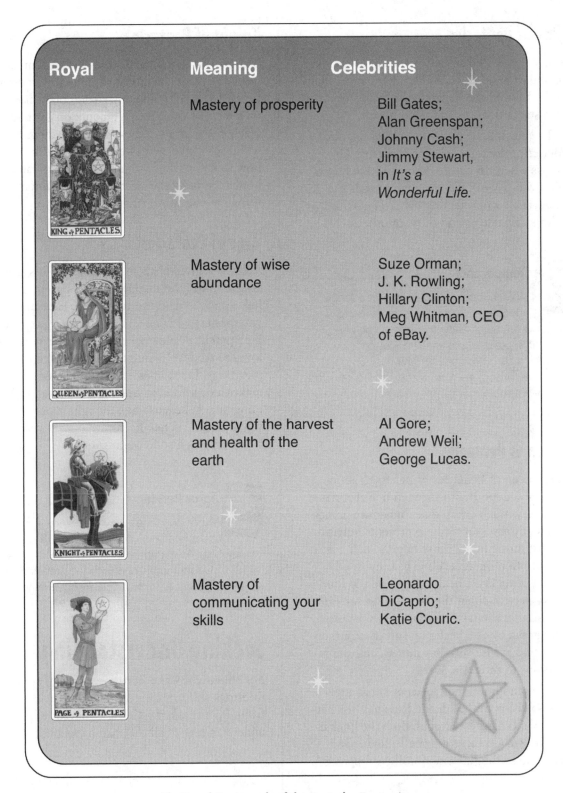

Royal	Meaning	Celebrities
KING of PENTACLES	Mastery of prosperity	Bill Gates; Alan Greenspan; Johnny Cash; Jimmy Stewart, in *It's a Wonderful Life.*
QUEEN of PENTACLES	Mastery of wise abundance	Suze Orman; J. K. Rowling; Hillary Clinton; Meg Whitman, CEO of eBay.
KNIGHT of PENTACLES	Mastery of the harvest and health of the earth	Al Gore; Andrew Weil; George Lucas.
PAGE of PENTACLES	Mastery of communicating your skills	Leonardo DiCaprio; Katie Couric.

The Royal Court cards of the Pentacles Tarot suit.

King of Pentacles

The King of Pentacles is practical. He is successful in material ways. His abundance is tangible. Like all the Pentacles cards, his expertise is in stable finances and good health.

In your life, he plays the role of financial adviser or doctor, healer or harvester. He knows where to put his resources. He knows what will pay off. He also understands the importance of protecting his productivity by valuing his talents and those of others.

> **Temperance**
>
> When it comes to reading about other people's money, it's always wise to read on the conservative side. Everyone wants to ask about winning the Lotto, but remember only the lucky few win. So don't go promising the rose garden or the keys to the kingdom.

Queen of Pentacles

The Queen of Pentacles brings forth abundance and good health through her nurturing. She's very much aware that abundance comes from daily discipline. She represents nutrition, not just in the literal sense of good diet but in consumption on all levels: a healthy mind, a healthy sexuality, a healthy approach to money. She's selective about the people who surround her. All that she takes in must serve the ultimate good. She's a healer and an environmentalist. She is wise with her money, and she is generous to those she loves.

What motivates the Queen of Pentacles is love—a vision for health and happiness for herself and all of her loved ones. Both the Queen and King of Pentacles are gentle, loving and wise. And so they are emotionally prosperous, too.

Knight of Pentacles

The Knight is the harvester—and he works hard. He plants beautiful gardens and bountiful fields. He is solid, like the strong black horse on which he rides. He is an encourager and a teacher. When he shows up in a reading, he will teach you how to become a harvester—how to know where to put your energy and how to complete projects. He helps you manifest what you want. And he's for real.

Page of Pentacles

The Page gives birth to new forms. He's still a *student* under the tutelage of the master, and he's someone who can teach you. He can teach you mastery of your talents and your creativity. He's practical. He's patient. He perseveres. He loves to study. His thirst for knowledge is infectious. He studies everything before he makes a decision. So he's a good person to have on your side because he's thought it out all the way through. When he comes up in a reading, he represents a solid opportunity.

> **Tarot Reader**
>
> All of the Pages play the role of the student, soaking up information like a sponge. As a student of the Tarot, remember that **student** means one who inquires and investigates. A student has an open mind.

Seeking Understanding

For Juliette, it was a hard week, full of strange meetings and lots of movement on the career front. So she asked a Celtic Cross for a better understanding of all that had happened.

Juliette's Hard Week

And guess what … both the King of Swords and King of Pentacles showed up in her reading!

The King of Swords shows up here as an Opposing Force (card 2), indicating that Juliette was not yet willing to look at events with a logical, practical mind. The 7 of Cups in the Foundation position (card 3) shows that she was asking the question because she had been dazzled by all the choices—she had networked with a lot of people that week and been approached by several others. The Devil in Recent Past (card 4) indicates that she might have been tempted to put too much stock in all the attention she was getting, and the 8 of Cups in Near Future (card 5) points her to get quiet and centered to look at the situation more logically.

The King of Pentacles shows up as the Outcome (card 10), indicating that if Juliette takes the more intentional, focused approach of the King of Swords she will realize prosperity.

The King of Swords and King of Pentacles showed up in Juliette's reading to help her approach a whirlwind week of change with a more logical, grounded mind.

Rosanna's Lessons to Come

Rosanna did this reading on her birthday, drawing the Page of Swords in Self (card 1) and the Knight of Pentacles in Recent Past (card 4). She posed a general question about the year ahead, but her specific concerns were about being more focused on making her dreams happen, about having more confidence in her ability and being more effective in the ways she was expending effort.

The Knight of Pentacles in Recent Past (card 4) indicates that Rosanna already has been learning about slow and steady as she goes. The Page of Swords reflects her current state of mind—willing to learn, willing to change in productive and tangible ways. The Page of Swords here is a big confidence booster, showing that she already has learned some of the lessons she is seeking to learn.

And the Queen of Swords in Near Future (card 5) shows that if she takes the Advice of the 7 of Pentacles (card 9), she will master those lessons. The Advice in the 7 of Pentacles is for her to reap what she has sown.

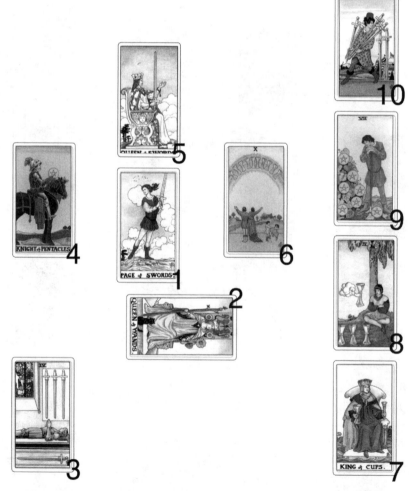

Rosanna wanted to know about having more confidence in her decisions about where to expend her energy.

Great Minds Think Alike

Tune in to the logical minds of the Royal Court Swords and the steady hands of the Royal Court Pentacles to learn about how to use your resources to get all of your best wishes to come true.

The Least You Need to Know

- The Royal Swords are the masters of determined, decisive thinking.
- The King of Swords is exemplary in his logical approach; the Queen of Swords is your best advocate.
- The Knight of Swords is ready to ride forth; the Page of Swords just gets the job done.
- The Royal Pentacles have the ability to multiply their efforts through hard work and wise management.
- The King of Pentacles is the financial adviser, healer, or harvester; the Queen of Pentacles is the nurturer who brings forth abundance.
- The Knight of Pentacles is steadfast; the Page of Pentacles is a diligent student.

In This Chapter

- ◆ Animals, flowers, fruit, and colors
- ◆ Astrology and numerology
- ◆ Myth and religion
- ◆ The Feng Shui spread

Chapter 10

Colors, Numbers, Stars, Symbols

Tarot cards are full of imagery—lots of animals, celestial objects, fruit, flowers, and mythological symbols. The images are often narrative —meaning they tell a story—as in the Tower or the 10 of Cups.

All of this imagery is a strong underpinning to the fundamental meaning of the card. Taking the time to give the cards a closer look and study the images can make your interpretations stronger. In this chapter, we introduce a new spread—the Feng Shui spread—and take you on a tour of Tarot's symbols and metaphors.

Symbols and Their Meanings

Every bit of information on a Tarot card has significance. Becoming an expert reader means taking in all the data. In this section, we discuss some of the most common symbols. Pretty soon, you'll be looking for signs in all the right places—and you'll find it's lots of fun!

Animal Magnetism

Wolves, horses, birds, lions, cats, and fish—the cards are lush with creatures. Here's a guide to what they mean.

Animal	Meaning	Cards
Lion	Courage, stamina, strong heart; fortitude, confidence	Strength Queen of Wands King of Wands 2 of Cups
Horse	Moving closer, moving forward	Knights Death 6 of Wands
Birds	Quail	9 of Pentacles
	Scarlet ibis in tree of the mind, a message from heaven	The Star
	Eagle, sign of Scorpio	Wheel of Fortune
	Dove, Holy Spirit	Ace of Cups
Dog	Happy, carefree	The Fool; 10 of Pentacles
	The tamed	The Moon
Wolf	The untamed	The Moon
Fish	Emotions, imagination, playfulness	Page of Cups

Foolproof

Whenever you're stuck on a card, take a closer look at its imagery. Notice similarities between the imagery on this card and others in the spread. Take notes of mythological or spiritual associations. Notice the colors. All of these handy tricks will help you pull the whole message of the cards together.

Flowers and Fruit

Many Tarot cards are lush with the bounty of the earth, filled with images of roses, pineapples, lilies, and more. Generally, these images suggest abundance and fertility (as in the Queen of Pentacles, the Ace of Pentacles, the 3 of Cups, or the 6 of Cups), but let's take a closer look.

Symbol	Meaning	Cards
White rose	Promise Banner of life	The Fool Death
Red rose	Passion	The Magician
White lilies	Thought	The Magician
Pomegranates	Fertility	The High Priestess
Palms	Intuition	The High Priestess

Notice that white lilies, for instance, symbolize thoughts, so they are closely linked with Swords. When there are a lot of Swords cards in a reading where white lilies show up, you can be sure that a lot of mental activity is occurring around the question.

Color My World

Someone once did a study that proved that sports teams that wear red jerseys seem more formidable than those that wear blue or white jerseys. And everyone knows that red cars get speeding tickets more often than white cars— right?

Color does have the power to evoke certain responses in us. They are called visceral responses, meaning they are intuitive and emotional rather than intellectual.

Because color has such a strong ability to communicate, we can know that it has some pretty clear messages for us in the Tarot. The color palette of the Universal Waite cards is limited, but each color is carefully chosen to have a meaning. The yellow robe, for instance, of the Fool symbolizes the innocent cheerfulness of new life. Red symbolizes the passion for life, whereas white means the attainment of purity of the spirit and clarity.

> ### Ask the Cards
>
> Colors can work together to inform the message of a card—for instance, the passion of red and the clarity of white. Both colors show up in the flag on the archangel Gabriel's trumpet in Judgement and the emblem on the front of the Chariot. A red-and-white emblem also appears on the 2 of Wands, which indicates your endeavor is right on track—blessed by passion and vision. Your head and heart are in the right place.

- **Red** is about passion, desire. In religion, it symbolizes divine love, courage, and self-sacrifice. In astrology, it's associated with Aries.
- **White** is purity of mind and heart. In religion, it's associated with innocence. In astrology, it's associated with Aquarius and Pisces.
- **Yellow** is about joy and vitality. In religion, it's the source of life. In astrology, it's all about Leo.
- **Green** is about life, growth, and harmony. In religion, it's the color of life. It's associated with Virgo.
- **Blue** is about trust, wisdom, truth, and serenity. In religion, it's about faith and contemplation. In astrology, it's associated with Sagittarius.

Red is the color of fire and blood. It's a high-energy color, and it's associated with ambition, power, and determination. Passion is what red is all about, and it's very focused. Red has countless cultural associations—for instance, in Dante's symbolism of color, which established meanings for the colors in stained glass, red was the color of divine love, courage, and self-sacrifice. In astrology, red is associated with Aries, the sign of creativity and manifestation, symbolized in the Magician card.

Notice that the Cups are always yellow, the symbol of joy and vitality. Observe how yellow and cheerful the 6 of Cups is—the happy childhood card.

Notice that the wands sprout green leaves and often are adorned with wreaths. Green is the symbol of growth, love, and transformation, and so it is the engine that drives the expansion of any enterprise.

Notice that the Swords are blue, the color of truth. What might the blue in the quilt of the 9 of Swords mean? What about the canopy of white stars on the Chariot?

Pentacles are golden, suggesting richness, ripeness, maturity, recognition (gold star), true worth (good as gold, solid gold), excellence (gold standard), or good favor (golden child).

Astrology and Numerology

Astrology and numerology add another dimension to interpreting the Tarot cards. Each card is associated with a sign of the Zodiac and is influenced by certain planets.

Astrological associations often provide additional insight—about who is influencing the situation, about the timing, about the area of your life being influenced, or about the advice the cards are giving. A list of astrological associations appears in Chapter 17.

Celestial Objects

The sun, the moon, and the stars are prominent symbols throughout the Tarot—and not just on the Sun and Moon cards.

The moon always symbolizes intuition. The moon suggests the choice to tune in to the emotional undercurrents of life. The connection of psychic and emotions are linked to the suit of Cups. The High Priestess, the ultimate intuition archetype, has a crescent moon at her feet, and her crown is made of the full moon and two crescents. When the moon appears in suits cards, such as the 2 of Swords or 8 of Cups, it's telling you that the choice to be made must be made with intuition. The 2 of Swords suggests that if you are not able to make a decision, you need to get out of your head and into your heart. You need to *feel with your mind.*

Stars adorn the crown of the Empress—12, to be exact, representing the 12 signs of the zodiac. The Hermit is using a star as his lantern of truth, which tells us that he's committed to following the path of enlightenment. Clusters of stars are on the canopy of the Chariot, and in this case, they represent celestial protection. (Now add together the concepts that the stars in the banner represent celestial protection and that the blue in the banner represents the truth. This indicates that higher spiritual truth is a source of safety for your Querent.)

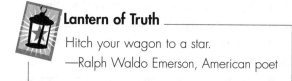

Lantern of Truth

Hitch your wagon to a star.
—Ralph Waldo Emerson, American poet

The Sun represents vitality, as in the Sun card. But it shows up in some interesting places—the Death card, Temperance, the Moon, the Lovers. Wherever it shows up, it means renewal and rejuvenation are on the way.

The energy of the Star—inspiration, enlightenment, and protection—resonates in the imagery of the Empress, Chariot, and Hermit.

WHEEL of FORTUNE.

The Wheel of Fortune card has symbols from four zodiac signs.

Numerology

In addition to the numbers on the cards, there are numeric symbols, such as the infinity symbol (called a *lemniscate*) on the Magician and Strength cards. Infinity is endless, unlimited space or time. On the Magician card, it tells you that the power and passion that the Magician is about to unleash has no limits. A few more steps down the road of life to the Strength card and we see that it means unconditional love—that when we love like that, we open ourselves up to the full range of creative self-expression.

THE MAGICIAN.

STRENGTH.

The infinity symbol reveals potential beyond limits for the Magician and Strength.

But it's more than the numbers—there's numeric symbolism in the imagery. Notice the parts of flowers and stars. The five-petaled rose on the banner that Death carries signifies change and rejuvenation; 5 is the number of change. Notice there are eight points on the big star in the Star; 8 is the number of mastery. This suggests that with clarity, the Star card brings mastery.

Temperance

Symbols on cards can be fascinating—so much so that you can get lost in them for a while as you explore how to use them in Tarot readings. Remember to step back from the details and see how they add up to the big picture. It's a good idea to jot down key directives from each card, such as "initiate" or "trust," as you go so that you don't miss the forest for the trees.

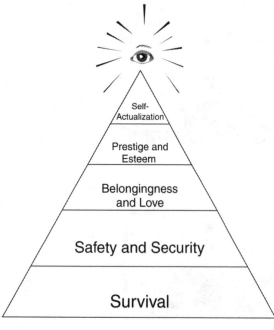

Maslow's Hierarchy of Needs embraces Tarot's divine geometry

Geometry

Beyond numbers are shapes. The square on the angel's breast in Temperance holds a triangle. Once, a friend of Carolyn's pulled the Death card, followed by the Temperance card. The friend started off the reading by saying, "I hope this is good. I need a change." The Death card heard that and showed up. Yep, she was in for change. Carolyn's friend was relieved to know that Temperance was the next step on the Journey of Life—and that's the card she got. The patience and be-in-the-flow of Temperance was just what she needed to understand the turmoil in her life at the moment. She was especially curious about the square and the triangle. Both symbols reinforced the larger message of Temperance: balance. The square represented grounding, in earth, reinforcing the significance of the archangel Michael's left foot being on land. The triangle, which is a trinity, is about spirit manifest on earth. That reinforces the significance of Michael's right foot being in water.

The big changes in the Death card are followed by the patience and adaptation in the Temperance card.

Metaphors and Myths

From archangels to black cats to drops of heavenly light, the Tarot has myth and religion all over it. Many cards are metaphors in and of themselves, as in the Ace of Cups, which is a metaphor for the holy grail. A *metaphor* is an implied comparison that quickly conveys a fully developed understanding. Metaphors can give meaning to us quickly and in ways that are more memorable than direct communication.

> **Temperance**
>
> A **metaphor** is a figure of speech, using symbolism in an implied way. With a metaphor, you don't make a direct comparison, as in "night fell like a curtain." Instead, you say "the curtain of night." Often metaphors are more effective than comparison (called simile) because they are more memorable and more palpable.

It's easy to find some of humanity's most powerful myths, legends, and stories here, from the tree of knowledge on the Lovers card to the divine child on the Sun. These kinds of stories are powerful because they are universal, with variations showing in many cultures.

Jewish

Yods are drops of light from heaven. They represent the life force, and they come from the Jewish tradition. Notice that they show up in many Tarot cards, such as the Ace of Swords, the Tower, and the Moon. The six yods in the Ace of Swords, for instance, protect the sword. The raindrops in the Tower are the hand of God. The raindrops in the Moon are the light of transformation. How did we know that? There are 13 of them, and 13 is the number of transformation—Jesus and the 12 apostles, the number of the Death card.

The divine yod in the Ace of Swords, Tower, and Moon.

Christianity

If you think the Hierophant looks like a pope, you are way ahead of us. He represents the figure who pronounces the conventional wisdom about religion and philosophy in our time.

If the Lovers remind you of the Garden of Eden, you got it! We have talked about how the Lovers card symbolizes the choice for love and harmony, but it also can represent the choice for spiritual knowledge. In this card, the lovers stand beneath the outstretched arms of the angel Raphael, who represents inspiration. Behind the woman is the tree of knowledge, which represents the path of spiritual knowledge.

The pair in the Lovers shows up again in the Devil, this time in chains. This time, though, it's the chains of ignorance—the chains that bind.

Lovers are surrounded by symbols of spiritual evolution in the Lovers card and spiritual bind in the Devil.

If the Hanged Man brought up images of the crucifixion, you're still with us. Notice that even as he hangs, a yellow nimbus encircles his head, and he is meditating peacefully. That indicates that he's at peace with his sacrifice because he knows it leads to a higher good.

Then there's archangel Gabriel, who blows seven blasts on his horn (hmmm … 7, the spiritual number) in the Judgement card.

Ancient Egypt

Two sphinxes are on the Chariot, one white, one black, representing the positive and negative energies of the universe. We see the sphinx again on the Wheel of Fortune. From the myth of the Sphinx, we know that sphinxes represent wisdom, whereas pyramids such as the three in the Page of Wands card are about spiritual enlightenment. Egyptian hieroglyphics adorn the robe of the charioteer, suggesting that the wisdom of that ancient culture goes forward with the charioteer.

Egyptian imagery infuses these cards with ancient wisdom.

Greek and Roman Gods and Goddesses

Venus, the goddess of love and beauty, is just one of the many Greco-Roman goddesses who populate the Tarot. Her emblem is the same as the woman symbol that you often see on public restroom doors. Yep, that's where it comes from! That symbol appears on the High Priestess and the 9 of Pentacles. Any time a symbol repeats on two cards in a reading, you can be sure the energy of those two cards is linked and strengthened.

Repeated symbols of love and beauty reinforce these energies in a Tarot reading.

A Whole-Person Scan

The Feng Shui spread is a good way to get a whole picture of a person. This spread is based on the Chinese art of arranging your space in a way that attracts positive energy to you. The operating belief behind Feng Shui is that the universe is made up of a life force energy, called *chi*. When your chi is good, you bring good things to you. In Feng Shui, your space is divided into nine areas, called *guas*, arranged in an octagon, with one gua in the center, surrounded by eight guas. Each gua represents a different area of your life, and so it is with the Feng Shui spread.

We took this Feng Shui reading and analyzed it for symbols, relating the meanings of the imagery to the areas of life.

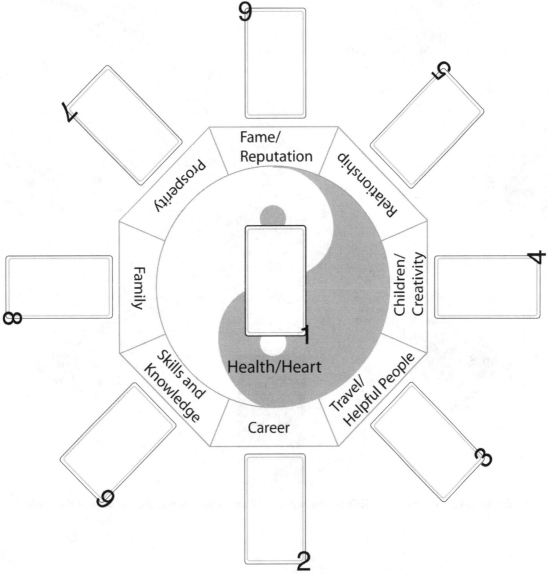

The Feng Shui spread examines nine areas of your life to see what's flowing and what's blocked.

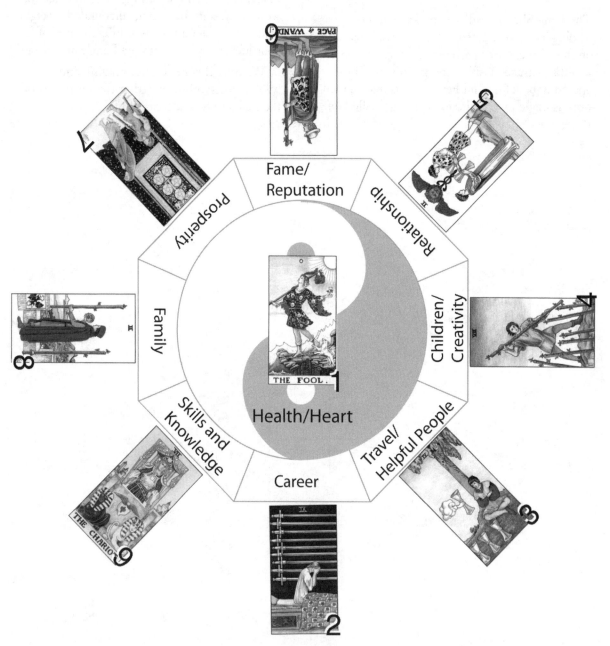

Take notes on the images in this Feng Shui spread. What do they add to the message of the card?

Card 1: Health and Heart

The Fool

Images: Yellow, the color of optimism, vitality; white rose, promise; flowers on flowing tunic

What other symbols indicate this card might mean optimum health?

_____

_____

_____

_____

Card 2: Career

9 of Swords

Images: Flowers on bedspread, the number 9

What do the flowers on the bedspread suggest about the truth of this card? What does the number 9 tell you about whether this is the beginning or the end? What is the choice to be made here?

_____

_____

_____

_____

Card 3: Travel/Helpful People

4 of Cups

Images: Hand emerging from the clouds, verdant tree, green tunic, the number 4

What does the imagery suggest about where help is coming from? What does the number 4 tell you about where the help fits into this person's life (temporary or permanent)?

_____

_____

_____

Card 4: Children/Creativity

7 of Wands

Images: Green tunic, higher position of figure, the number 7

What does the green tunic tell you about the strength and stamina of this person? What does the number 7 suggest about the spiritual dimension of the struggle?

_____

_____

_____

_____

Card 5: Relationships

2 of Cups

Images: Lion, two serpents, garlands in their hair, flowers on the tunic, the number 2

What do the intertwined serpents suggest about balancing male and female energies? Why does the lion have wings, and how does that alter your interpretation of his strength and courage?

_____

_____

_____

_____

Card 6: Fame

Page of Wands

Images: Three pyramids

The Page of Wands tells you that a message is coming. What do the pyramids suggest about the meaning of the message?

_____

_____

_____

_____

Card 7: Prosperity

5 of Pentacles

Images: Stained glass window, pentacles arranged on a verdant tree, the number 5

What does this card tell you about the resources available to these two people?

_____

_____

_____

_____

Card 8: Family

2 of Wands

Images: Red and white shield, the number 2

What does this card suggest about who is coming to help the man? What does its placement in the family gua of this reading tell you?

_____

_____

_____

_____

Card 9: Skills and Knowledge

The Chariot

Images: Black and white sphinxes, stars on the canopy, red-and-white emblem on the chariot

What do the sphinxes suggest about the skills this person brings to challenges? The stars? The red-and-white emblem? The Chariot is the number 7. What does that tell you?

_____

_____

_____

_____

Taking It Beyond

As you can see, this is just a start of what you can learn about the cards through the symbols and images. Wings show up not just on the Lovers and Temperance cards, but also the 2 of Cups and the Knight of Cups (on the helmet of the knight). Pretty soon, you'll start to notice more subtle symbols, such as the rosette in the 3 of Pentacles and the two crossed keys at the feet of the Hierophant. The more you practice with readings, the more comfortable you will become in applying interpretations of these symbols.

The Least You Need to Know

◆ Images of wolves, lions, pomegranates, and roses abound in the Tarot, supporting the larger message of the cards.

◆ Color conveys messages in the Tarot that are often instinctively known because of our many cultural and psychological associations with color.

◆ Each card is associated with an astrological and numerological symbol, which can give added dimension to the interpretation of a card.

◆ The metaphorical images on the cards can convey messages in memorable ways.

◆ Many cards are associated with religion and myth, with messages that speak to our spiritual growth and our role in the big picture of life.

◆ A Feng Shui reading provides a complete look at all areas in a person's life.

In This Chapter

- ◆ Meanings of reversed cards
- ◆ Facing delays and challenges
- ◆ Blocked energy
- ◆ Getting back in balance

Upright and Reversed

But what happens when a card is upside down? Does it matter? Some say yes, and some say no. We say yes. The way a Tarot card lands in a spread shows the way the energy comes to you. And sometimes, it's not direct.

A reversed card, often indicated by the letter *R* after the name of the card, as in "4 of Wands R" asks you to stop and go deeper. Or it may call for a little more perseverance or patience on your part. In this chapter, we explain how reversed cards fit into how to interpret Tarot readings.

The Theory of Upside Down

These days many movies that come on DVD come with bonus material—alternative endings and deleted scenes. Reversed cards are a little bit like that. When they do come up, they add an extra dimension to the story.

Generally, there are several ways *reversed cards* can be interpreted:

◆ The energy of the card is blocked.

◆ The energy of the card is still taking shape in your life, but it's coming the slow way.

◆ The opposite will happen.

If the choices and influences in a card are blocked or slowed down, it's usually because another choice needs to be made. You may not be ready. Or you may need to get more in place before you can be ready. At any rate, when you want to know more about a reversed card, look through a spread to see what other choices are presented.

Tarot Reader _____

Reversed cards in Tarot books are usually noted with a capital *R* after the name of the card, or with the word "reversed" written out. Reversed cards indicate the energy of the card is delayed or blocked; sometimes they mean the opposite of the upright card.

Often a reversed card may indicate an internal struggle. Maybe you are trying to match your expectations against what is really happening. Perhaps it's time for some acceptance in the situation at hand. Or perhaps you need to compromise.

Sometimes a reversed card is telling you that the situation you are facing is really big. It may be an important challenge, and so it may take a while. Look through the spread to learn about the skills and knowledge you need to develop to meet the challenge. Look through the spread for allies, supporters, and role models. A Major Arcana card in the reading may be your companion for the challenge. And if your Life Path card is present (upright!), you can know you are in good hands.

When Major Arcana come up reversed in a reading, no matter the spread, they are important signals that a lesson that needs to be learned is not being learned. A reversed Major Arcana card means that the lessons of the card are not being totally integrated into your life. You have yet to learn its full meaning. For instance, the Hermit upright means that you have the desire to get insight and wisdom, but a reversed Hermit may mean that you are fearful, are not taking in your own wisdom, or are not listening to wise advice from others.

In some cases, a Major Arcana card in reversed position can indicate movement toward a more positive energy. When the Moon is reversed, it portrays good balance,

with mastery, but the Querent still may need to understand the upright side of the Moon—with all of its milky flow and murky currents.

Minor Arcana cards in reversed position almost always indicate delay, difficulty, or a problem that needs particular attention to turn the energy upright again. But there's one important exception to this: all reversed 5 cards in the Minor Arcana suits represent the release of negative energy. Change, change and more change is what number 5 gives us in a reading. You have noticed, no doubt, that the upright 5 cards are often negative, presenting a situation that really needs to change. When the 5 is reversed, the change has happened, and good things are on the way. The question you asked is transforming—you are turning a negative into a positive.

Lantern of Truth _____

Always seek out the seed of triumph in every adversity.

—Og Mandino, author and motivational speaker

A full guide to reversed cards and their meanings appears in Chapter 17. You may refer to it as we take you through examples in this chapter.

Through the rest of this chapter, the sample spreads will help you get a better idea of what reversed cards mean in the context of a reading.

Not Yet, Be Patient

Many times, a spread full of reversed cards is a strong indication that the Querent is stymied about a situation. The person is not yet ready to face challenges and choices that he or she needs to face to get the desired result. That was true for Martha, who wanted to know whether she would ever get married. Five out of 10 cards in her Celtic Cross reading were reversed. When Martha saw that, she exclaimed, "Does this mean I won't? There are so many reversed." Arlene said it meant Martha wasn't quite ready, or her soul mate wasn't. It was important for one or both of them to clear up old issues and heal wounds from former relationships. So Arlene asked, "*What is the appointed time? When will Martha be ready?*" (More about timing coming up in Chapter 14.)

Martha got four reversed cards when she asked when she would be ready to be married.

Martha did get married three years after this reading. Note the prevalence of the number 3 in this spread—the 3 of Swords, the 3 of Wands, the Empress (which was the Outcome card). In Chapter 14, we explain why these three cards point definitively to three years as well as how other cards predicted when she would meet her husband and how long the courtship would be.

Here's a closer look at the reversed cards in the reading:

- **The High Priestess R** in the Near Future position (card 5) indicates Martha is blocking her intuitive side, suggesting that when she can sharpen her intuition about relationships, she will manifest a lasting one.

- **6 of Wands R** indicates that her opportunity to meet someone new is being delayed. The Higher Power position (card 6) is about your conscience or your potential to be your best self. So this delay is about Martha needing to do some inner work before she is ready to meet her mate.

- **The World R** indicates that she doesn't quite have the vision in place, pointing her to getting clearer about the kind of man she would like to share her life with.

- **9 of Swords R** is actually better than upright! Instead of the despair we see in the upright card, the 9 of Swords shows that you will get through a tough time and experience healing. The advice of this card is that patience and prayer will set Martha on the path to finding her new love.

Ask the Cards

What if all cards in a reading are reversed? That can happen in a Three-Card reading. Arlene has seen it often. If that happens, it means that the lessons are being integrated slowly into your life. Your old patterns are changing, and a new attitude about the situation will emerge. Just be patient!

Topsy-Turvy Creativity: Part 1

Remember the series of Celtic Cross spreads we did in Chapter 4? Here's the original spread for "*How do I get started to find my bliss?*"—only the Near Future (card 5) and Outcome (card 10) positions are reversed.

1. Self. Queen of Swords. **2. Opposing Force.** Ace of Wands. **3. Background.** Knight of Cups. **4. Recent Past.** Page of Wands. **5. Near Future.** 7 of Swords R. **6. Higher Power.** Queen of Wands. **7. Issues.** 4 of Wands. **8. Allies.** 4 of Cups. **9. Advice.** Death. **10. Outcome.** Ace of Swords R.

Upright, the 7 of Swords was a negative card, indicating a sense of futility or possibly a deception (maybe by another person, or perhaps a self-deception). Either way, an obstacle was present that was limiting the Querent from getting started. But reversed, the 7 of Swords R tells you that something will be restored. Someone who has been acting against you will come clean. It's time for the truth to come out.

If the Ace of Swords were still upright, this combination would indicate that all barriers to a good start had been removed. But with the Ace of Swords R, it may mean there is too much truth revealed—a truth that harms. The Ace of Swords R attracts opposition. The choice being presented here is to go more gently.

Temperance

Let the reversed cards in a reading help you face your challenges. We tend to hear what we want to hear in a reading, so it's human nature to want to gloss over the negative cards. But reversed cards in a reading may present some of the key aspects to getting the outcome you desire.

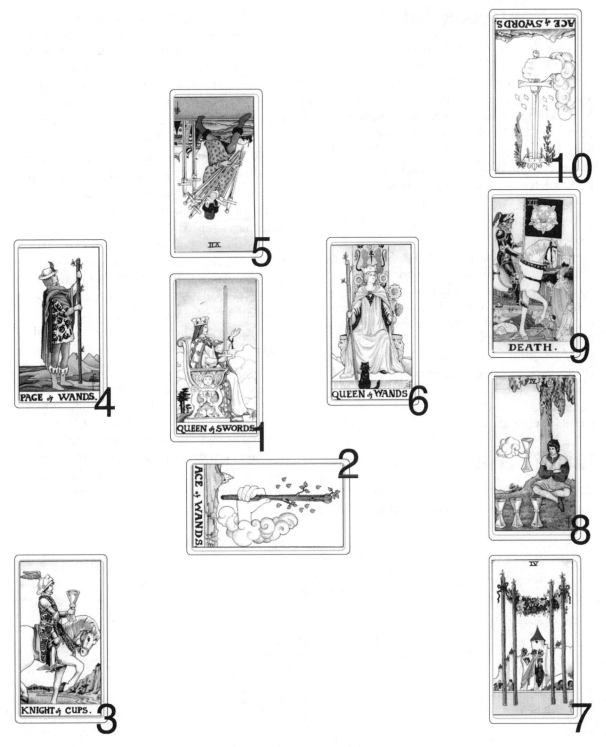

"How do I get started to find my bliss?"

Topsy-Turvy Creativity: Part 2

Let's say the Higher Power (card 6) and Allies/Others (card 8) positions were reversed instead. Here are the cards. **1. Self.** Queen of Swords. **2. Opposing Force.** Ace of Wands. **3. Background.** Knight of Cups. **4. Recent Past.** Page of Wands. **5. Near Future.** 7 of Swords. **6. Higher Power.** Queen of Wands R. **7. Issues.** 4 of Wands. **8. Allies.** Four of Cups R. **9. Advice.** Death. **10. Outcome.** Ace of Swords.

When the Queen of Wands is reversed, she's too aggressive, and she is passionate about everything, even the wrong things. She's a bonfire. Looking at how she combines with other cards here—specifically the Queen of Swords in Self (card 1)—this reading is sending a strong message to back off, be more receptive, and go more gently. The Death card in the Advice (card 9) position suggests that it's time to change all that. On the other hand, the 4 of Cups R suggests it's time for action, to come out of isolation and reach out to others to move ahead on your ambitions.

Stacking the Deck

Okay, so let's take a break here and step back to consider anew this whole concept of reversed cards. If you've spent any amount of time with your Tarot deck, no doubt you've begun to fall in love with a few of your favorite cards, waiting and hoping they'll come up. Other cards you may just feel neutral about, depending, of course, on when and how they appear! And then there are those cards you'd rather avoid, or even just not deal with altogether.

We have one friend who deals with this situation by stacking her deck. When it comes to reversed cards, she orients the deck so that the cards she likes least are reversed for positive outcomes—for her, this means cards such as the Tower, the 4 of Swords (she doesn't have time to lie around!), the 7 of Cups (banish indecision!), and all the 5s. Do we recommend this? Not really! We love our friend, but we know that she knows the Tarot will tell her what it must tell her. You see, the Tarot will find a way to communicate its message, always.

We believe that reversed cards have their own kind of meaning and power, never to be feared. The important thing, though, no matter how you stack your deck, is that you remember that the Tarot is here to help guide you and even with the most difficult of questions, holding a positive intent will help you work through whatever you need to look at.

The Life Path cards of Hierophant and Temperance are grouped with Justice R, the Moon, the Magician, the Star, and the Wheel of Fortune.

Reversal of Fortune: Life Paths

Let's take a look at what happens when a Major Arcana card is reversed. Here is Arlene's Life Path reading from Chapter 4, with Justice R.

It shifts the meaning of her reading, doesn't it? Instead of validating that she is well on her way

to learning the lessons of the Hierophant and Temperance, her Life Path cards, a reversed Justice is nudging her to get back in balance, to seek out the honor in the situation and establish fairness.

But if the Moon had been reversed instead, it might be telling her to let her imagination go for a while—to not be so conventional.

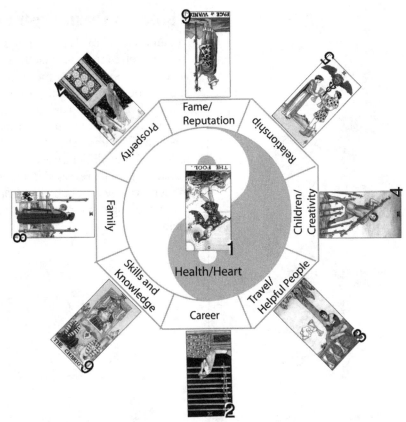

In this Feng Shui spread, several cards appear reversed: Fool R in the heart/health gua, 9 of Swords R in the career gua, 7 of Wands R in the children/creativity gua, 2 of Cups R in relationships, and 5 of Pentacles R in the prosperity gua.

Other Reversals of Fortune

Let's get some experience looking at reversed cards in other spreads, such as the Feng Shui, Chakra, and Karmic spreads. Because the positions in those spreads are specific, the meanings of the reversed cards can have very specific applications.

Blocking the Light: A Feng Shui Reading

Let's return to the Feng Shui reading from Chapter 10. Suddenly, with a reversed Fool in Health, this Querent doesn't look so healthy, wealthy, and wise. It's time to slow down and do some more research about nutrition or exercise to head off or not aggravate a health problem. But the 9 of Swords R in Career and 7 of

Wands R in Children/Creativity both indicate this Querent has triumphed over some challenges. The 9 of Swords R indicates some healing of despair and agony is taking place in the Querent's career. The 7 of Wands R tells us the threat has passed.

Foolproof

Reversed cards can sometimes represent the extreme expression of a card—to the point where the situation is out of balance. In the case of the Moon, it can indicate an imagination out of control, or in the case of the Devil, sexual indulgence. Look to the cards around it to see whether the situation is calling for balance and restraint.

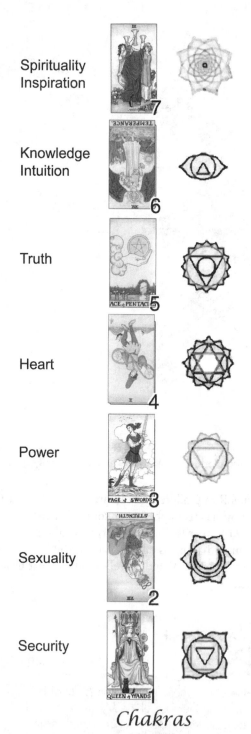

Spirituality
Inspiration

Knowledge
Intuition

Truth

Heart

Power

Sexuality

Security

Chakras

Three reversed cards appeared in this Chakra spread, pointing to areas of the body, mind, and spirit where energy is blocked.

A Different Chakra Experience

When reversed cards turn up in a Chakra reading, they often indicate exactly what's out of balance in the body, mind, and spirit. In this Chakra spread, the Strength card is reversed in the allegiance chakra, known as the Sexuality chakra, directly pointing to some fears about sexual matters. The 2 of Pentacles R in the Heart chakra indicates some difficulty accessing the compassionate side. The reversed Temperance card for the Knowledge chakra may indicate emotions are overruling logic and reason, creating bad judgment.

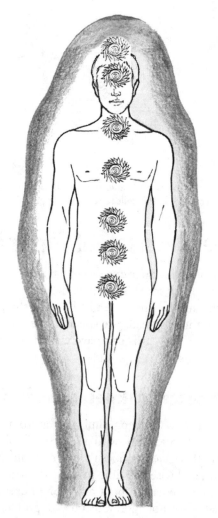

Chakras are energy centers in the body.

Karma Chameleon

Three Major Arcana cards are reversed in this Karmic spread, which indicates that the Querent may not be ready to accept his or her destiny. The Querent will resist the lessons of Death (transformation), Justice (truth and fairness), and the Hanged Man (sacrifice). This reading points to letting go of the old ways of thinking and being, of accepting new truths. What the Querent sees as fair may not be the best way for all concerned. There is a higher truth. The upright Sun promises vitality and renewal should the Querent accept that truth and change courageously. The Hanged Man R indicates that what the Querent must let go of is something he or she holds dear.

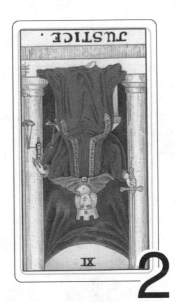

In this Karmic spread, three of four cards are reversed, indicating the karmic lessons will meet resistance.

Gallery of Positive Reversed Cards

Remember our friend who stacks her Tarot deck with cards upright and reversed as she wants them to be? While, again, we don't recommend stacking your deck, we do recommend that you spend some time with your deck, looking for cards that speak to you more positively when reversed. Think about why that might be. Traditionally there are many cards that usually do have a more positive connotation when they are reversed. Our quick gallery of "positive" reversed cards includes the 5s from each suit, 10 of Wands R, 7 of Swords R, 9 of Swords R, the Hierophant R, the Devil R, and the Moon R. Whether positive or challenging, though, all Tarot cards, upright or reversed, point the way toward your highest good and are there to help you find solutions.

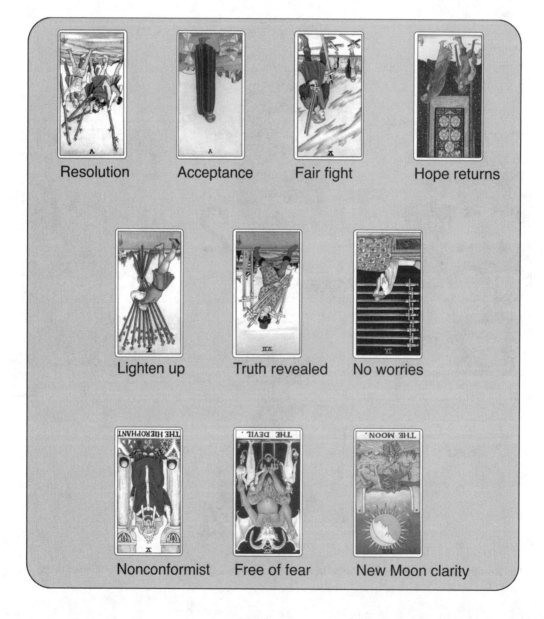

Resolution   Acceptance   Fair fight   Hope returns

Lighten up   Truth revealed   No worries

Nonconformist   Free of fear   New Moon clarity

Taking a Step Back

Reversed cards are just part of life. Sometimes it goes fast; sometimes it goes slow. When you meet the delays and challenges in the reversed cards, just remember you always have choices.

The Least You Need to Know

◆ Reversed cards indicate the energy of the card is being blocked or delayed. Sometimes they mean the opposite of the upright card.

◆ Reversed cards almost always present challenges, lessons to be learned, or advice to be taken. They can sometimes be the key cards to realizing outcome.

◆ When Major Arcana are reversed, the lesson will be learned—it will just take more time.

◆ Reversed cards in Feng Shui readings indicate that the energy of that card is being blocked—just as chi is blocked when the Feng Shui of a space is out of balance.

◆ Reversed cards in a Chakra reading indicate something is out of balance.

◆ Reversed cards in a Karma spread indicate that the person has yet to accept his or her destiny.

In This Part

Part 4

Looking at the Bigger Picture

Now let's take a step back and see how the story is coming together. Where a Tarot card falls in a spread tells you a lot about its role in the story. Patterns appear in the cards, showing how the story is woven together. By taking a step back, you can see the timing of events and choices that are coming into your life as you read and interpret the Tarot.

In This Chapter

- A Love Celtic Cross
- The story of a Wish
- A Chakra spread
- House by house, a Zodiac Horoscope spread

12

Seeing Placements

Sometimes the cards start talking to you: the Justice card advises to be fair-minded; the Knight of Swords says "Heads-up!" But what's that all about? Be fair about what? Stay alert about what?

Placement in a Tarot spread tells you about the answer. Is it talking about the past or the future? Is it talking about someone who will help you or a choice that you have to make? Is it talking about your money or your relationship? This chapter helps you figure out how the placement of the cards gives you context for the story you are reading.

Telling a Story

In the spreads we have shown you, the placement or position of a card has a specific meaning. Each card's placement reveals more and more of the story unfolding. What's fun about this is the spread reveals what you already know about your question, what's going on now, and the potentials for future conditions. Or a placement may tell you that the card is speaking about other people in your life, such as with the Allies/Supporters position (card 8) in the Celtic Cross. In the case of the Feng Shui or Chakra spreads, the placement reveals exactly what area of life or area of your health you need to know about.

With the Celtic Cross and Wish spreads, the Tarot provides a snapshot of each aspect of a story about your question. All of these snapshots add up to a full story, complete with plot, characters, and setting—even a climax and resolution.

Temperance

Remember that what makes Tarot's story-telling style fun is that it still holds the possibility of improvisation. That is, you can still revise the ending. The cards tell a story of today's choices now. But if you make different choices, tomorrow's story could be different. Remember that you always have Free Will.

The Story of Love

Let's take the Love Celtic Cross reading for Stephanie to look at how the placement of the cards add up to a story of love.

Stephanie wanted to keep her question general. Her request was "*Please show me about matters of the heart.*"

◆ **Card 1:** The **Self** position shows where you're at. It's a snapshot of the moment and generally picks up on your energy in the most immediate way. The Self position is the look in the mirror.

In Stephanie's case, the 9 of Swords in Self showed she was letting her worries keep her up at night. Stephanie admitted that she was suffering from insomnia.

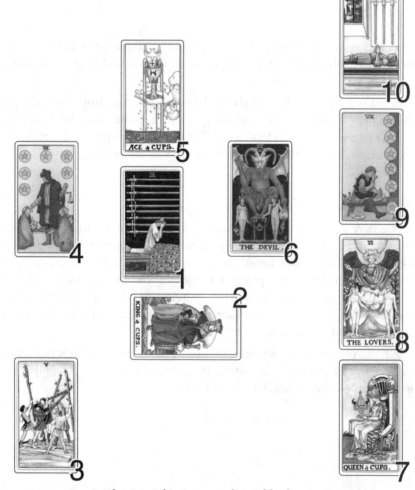

Stephanie's Celtic Cross reading told a love story.

◆ **Card 2:** The **Opposing Force** card shows a factor or a person that is blocking you. It can indicate where you have a choice to make, or it can show you that something you want is being delayed. It can show an external condition—something that needs to be worked through and resolved before you can move forward to the next parts of the story—the Near Future (card 5) and the Outcome (card 10).

In Stephanie's reading, the King of Cups may literally indicate the man about which she has the question, or it may indicate an ideal of love. The man in her life may have fallen short of this ideal, causing her the anguish seen in the 9 of Swords. The block to restoring peace (indicated in the Outcome card, the 4 of Swords) may be resolving the conflict between her expectations and reality.

◆ **Card 3:** The **Foundation** card points to the origin of the question—the reason you are asking. It often depicts a choice or struggle in your family background that is influencing the present situation. In Stephanie's reading, the 5 of Wands in Foundation indicated that in her childhood or in past relationships, she has experienced the struggle between the competing needs, wants, and desires of couples.

◆ **Card 4:** The **Recent Past** (card 4) shows us events that have influenced us but are fading in importance. The 6 of Pentacles tells us Stephanie just got a welcome boost of energy. She confirmed that she had recently had a breakthrough in her insomnia.

◆ **Card 5:** The **Near Future** (card 5) shows us events that lie just ahead. If you want them to transpire, take the advice presented in the spread. If you don't, look through the spread for other choices you can make. For Stephanie, though, the Ace of Cups indicated a chance at a new beginning with love. The Ace of Cups is about loving with a new wisdom, with a balance of giving and taking.

◆ **Card 7:** The **Issues/Fears** card is the Queen of Cups, which is telling Stephanie that her fear is that she's not loving with wisdom and balance. That the King of Cups (as an Opposing Force) and Queen of Cups both showed up here is not just a coincidence. Both are the masters of love, but both show up in challenging positions. This pair are being forced to confront some essential issues about give and take.

That is reinforced in the Lovers and the Devil cards, which are two sides of the same coin. Both of those cards present choices about balancing the best of ourselves and the worst of ourselves. Certainly a relationship that is recalibrating its exchange of giving and receiving brings out those qualities in both people as they negotiate their highs and lows.

◆ **Cards 6 and 8:** The Lovers and the Devil cards show up in the **Allies** (card 8) and **Higher Power** (card 6) positions, respectively, revealing much about the supporters around this couple and their conflict. On the human level, their supporters are loved ones who also have worked through the conflict of giving too much or taking too much. On the cultural level, note that both are archetype cards, which indicates that Stephanie and her love are gaining support from the culture for the work they are doing together.

◆ **Cards 9 and 10: Advice** (card 9) is the turning-point card in a Celtic Cross spread—a climax of sorts. It shows you what you must do to gain or alter the outcome. In Stephanie's case, the 8 of Pentacles was encouraging her that she already had achieved some mastery of the matter at hand and telling her to trust in her skills. The Ace of Cups in **Near Future** (card 5) indicates she may have a fresh start if she does so. But the 4 of Swords in **Outcome** (card 10) underlines just how important it will be for her to retreat, rest, and recuperate.

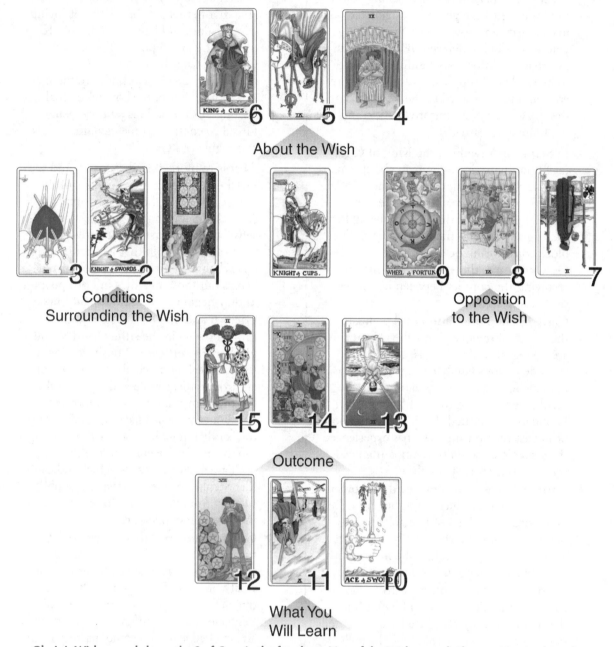

About the Wish

Conditions
Surrounding the Wish

Opposition
to the Wish

Outcome

What You
Will Learn

Gloria's Wish spread shows the 9 of Cups in the fourth position of the Wish spread. That position is about the wish itself, and the 9 of Cups is about the attainment of the wish.

Ask the Cards

Let's cut to the chase. Which cards tell you what's going to happen? In the Celtic Cross, it's the Near Future (card 5) and Outcome (card 10). In the Wish spread, look to cards 4, 5, and 6, as well as 13, 14, and 15. Also keep an eye out for the 9 of Cups. If it appears anywhere in the Wish spread, you'll get your wish. In other spreads, such as the Magic 7, often the last card is read as the Outcome card.

I Wish I May, I Wish I Might

Gloria wanted a full look at a wish she had had for some time—a good romantic relationship in the coming year. This is a look at how all the cards in her Wish spread told the story.

- **Cards 1, 2, and 3: Conditions surrounding the wish.** The three cards in these positions indicate Gloria has struggled with this issue in the past, experiencing some feeling of abandonment and betrayal in the 5 of Pentacles, supported by the swift-riding truth of the Knight of Swords and heartbreak in the 3 of Swords R. The fact that the 3 of Swords is reversed indicates that the heartbreak is healing.

- **Cards 4, 5, and 6: About the wish.** The 9 of Cups says she will get her wish, but the 6 of Wands R indicates there may be a delay. With these two cards hanging out with the ever-lovin' King of Cups, this bodes well for Gloria's wish ultimately.

- **Cards 7, 8, and 9: Opposition to the wish.** Here we look at what has been in the way of Gloria's attaining her wish. The 2 of Wands R is a one-step-up, two-steps-back kind of card, and the 6 of Cups R points to a painful memory from the past. But next to the Wheel of Fortune, these cards suggest that Gloria can still be

in charge of how she decides to respond to these setbacks. She can let them hold her back, or she can learn from them.

- **Cards 10, 11, and 12: What you will learn.** The 5 of Swords R is about getting at the truth behind a conflict, and the Ace of Swords supports that. The 7 of Pentacles tells Gloria that she will learn much from being willing to get to the truth, which will help her avoid the betrayals and heartbreaks of the past.

- **Cards 13, 14, and 15: Outcome.** The 2 of Swords R indicates a decision has been made, and in this case we think the decision is Gloria's choice to examine the sorrow of past relationships. The other two cards here point to a happy outcome—a happy, abundant home in the 10 of Pentacles, and a rewarding partnership in the 2 of Cups.

Foolproof

You have heard the expression "Two heads are better than one," but Tarot likes threes—as in the groupings of three cards within the positions of the Wish spread. That's because three cards add up to a more complete picture, as in the case of the 5 of Pentacles, Knight of Swords, and 3 of Swords R in Gloria's Wish spread. You can use the power of three in any reading to get more insight about a particular position, by adding two more cards around the most puzzling card.

Everything Has a Place

Several Tarot spreads have very specific meanings in their placements, indicating whether the card is about health or money or love. Among them are the Chakra, Horoscope, and Feng Shui spreads. Here's a closer look.

A Chakra Shuffle

Placement meanings can be very specific in a spread such as the Chakra spread. Most often, they indicate what the choice presented in the card is about. The suit of the card gives further meaning to that. For instance, in the Chakra spread, if the placement is telling you that the choice is about love and the suit is Cups, you can be sure this is a matter of the heart and emotions.

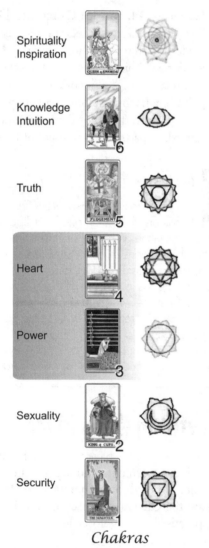

Chakras

The placement of cards in a Chakra reading has very specific meaning.

Also notice how the numbers relate to the placement. For instance, the 4 of Swords fell in the fourth chakra, the Heart chakra in this Chakra spread. In that case, both are indicating that the choice at hand is one that will build a good foundation for matters of the heart.

We already know, for instance, that the Heart chakra is about love, transformation, forgiveness, and compassion. So when the 4 of Swords shows up here, it's telling us that the recuperation presented in this card is about a matter of the heart. The Power chakra is about setting boundaries and making good choices, and the 9 of Swords indicates despair. We know that the Power chakra is associated with Swords—thoughts, action, power. That shows that the way out of despair is through clearer thoughts and better choices.

How would you interpret the other cards in this Chakra spread? Make notes in your Tarot Journal.

> **Lantern of Truth**
>
> It's all about finding the right note at the right place and knowing when to leave well enough alone. And that's a lifelong quest.
> —David Sanborn, American jazz saxophonist

By the Stars

The best way to understand how the card meanings shift in relation to their placement is to look at a few variations. Let's take this basic Zodiac Horoscope spread and see how the meanings shift as one card moves from house to house.

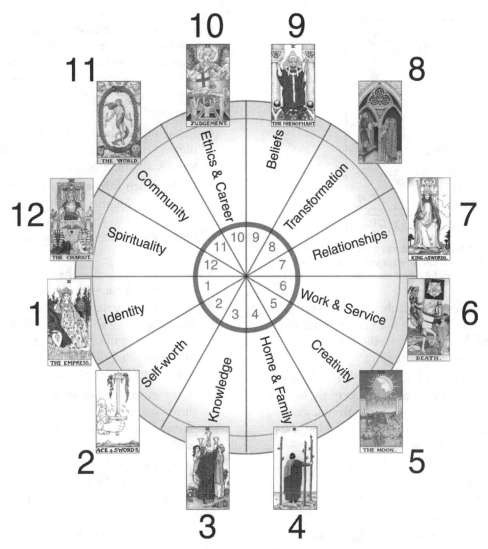

The Horoscope spread matches up Tarot cards with the houses of astrology—the arenas in which you play out your life.

The Ace of Swords came up in the second house, which is about your resources and your self-esteem. Let's take a look, house by house, at how that card's meaning might change as its placement changes.

Here is the card's inherent meaning: the Ace of Swords can be constructive or destructive, depending on its placement. It can cut to the truth, whacking away at dead wood, which presents the opportunity for a new beginning. The sword emerges from the clouds, with the same hand you see in the other ace cards. That represents the Hand of Creation—that this new beginning has as its origin the creator of the universe (however you may define that). The sword holds the crown of peace on its tip and is adorned with the olive branch of peace and the palm of victory. Six yods—which represent the life force of the universe or light from heaven—surround the sword, protecting it.

This card represents new ideas and swift action. It's all coming together, clearly. You have fortitude of mind and a focused vision.

The Ace of Swords' inherent meaning is absolute truth. Each placement in a spread throws a different light on that meaning.

- In the **first house,** the Ace of Swords describes not just your current state of mind, but your most essential way of thinking and functioning.

- In the **second house,** the Ace of Swords indicates new ways of thinking about your resources and possessions. You may no longer think of them as the end but the means to the end.

- In the **third house,** the Ace of Swords indicates you are surrounded by clear thinking. This house specifically refers to your siblings.

- In the **fourth house,** the Ace of Swords tells you about a new direction in your home life. It could mean quite literally the birth of a child, or it can mean a new home. Or it can mean a fresh start for your family.

- In the **fifth house,** the Ace of Swords is showing that it's time to take a risk. This house is about creativity, so it can mean the start of a new project. But this house is also about romance, so it can encourage you to take a chance with a new love.

- In the **sixth house,** the Ace of Swords may be telling you to take more responsibility with your health. Or it can be encouraging you to volunteer in some act of service.

- In the **seventh house,** the Ace of Swords points to a new partnership in business or in marriage. If you are already married, it may mean your relationship is rejuvenated by a renewed sense of partnership and cooperation after getting to a deeper level of truth.

- In the **eighth house,** the Ace of Swords means you are letting go of something old to let something new be born.

- In the **ninth house,** the Ace of Swords indicates a significant shift in your paradigms. That is, you have a new view of philosophy, religion, or the structures of society.

- In the **tenth house,** the Ace of Swords indicates a fresh start in your career or a new focus in your social responsibilities. You are getting to a new truth about your reputation in the world, cutting away at some old thinking, seeing yourself in a new light. You are ready for a new role.

- In the **eleventh house,** the Ace of Swords shows you are now focused on accomplishing some aspirations you may have had for a while.

- In the **twelfth house,** the Ace of Swords is a truth card. What has been hidden will now be seen. It may be something that was in your subconscious, or it may be a clearer understanding of a karmic lesson.

The Soul Has Many Mansions

Teresa of Avila's *Interior Castle* compared the soul to a castle with many rooms through which a postulant would pass on the way to reach perfection with God. Although the Feng Shui spread uses another culture's traditions, the intent is quite similar. Our environment becomes an outer expression of our inner divinity and our soul's progress. Using the principles discussed in this chapter, try a Feng Shui spread, looking deeply into the resonance of card placements in your reading.

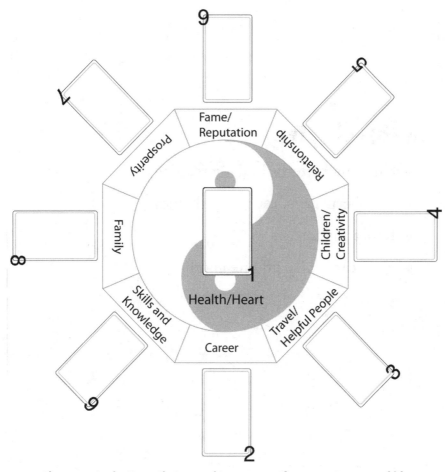

Placement in the Feng Shui spread is very specific to certain areas of life.

Looking Ahead

Now with a full grounding in interpreting symbols, reversed cards, and placements, we can take you to the next step: looking for patterns and weaving it all together. That's what's ahead in the next chapters.

The Least You Need to Know

- Placement in a spread can indicate which part of the story a card is speaking about.
- The Near Future (card 5) and Outcome (card 10) positions in the Celtic Cross spread tell you how your question may end up.

- For an action plan, look to the Opposing (card 2) or Advice (card 9) positions in a Celtic Cross spread. In the Wish spread, look to cards 10, 11, and 12.
- Positions such as the Power position in the Chakra spread or the Prosperity position in the Feng Shui spread are very specific about which area of life the card is addressing.
- The focus of a card's meaning can shift, depending on which position it falls in a spread.
- A card's placement gives you a specific application for the card's meaning.

In This Chapter

- ◆ Charting patterns in daily readings
- ◆ Regular players, recurring themes
- ◆ Repeating images
- ◆ How cards play off one another

Chapter **13**

Recognizing Patterns

In newspaper journalism—Carolyn's profession—there is a saying, "If it happens once, it's a fluke. If it happens twice, it's a coincidence. If it happens a third time, it's a trend."

And so it is with patterns in Tarot readings. Our minds are always looking for similarities, to see how the little details come together to form a big picture. This chapter shows you how to find the common thread in a reading, so that you can take your interpretations to a whole new level.

Looking for Patterns

Whenever you do a spread, you will see that patterns naturally emerge. Notice these little patterns, and they will give you a sense of how the smaller, day-to-day choices fit into the big picture. Soon you will get to the point where you will pick up immediately on patterns (or maybe you are already!). You'll be able to see at a glance that this spread is about love, even if the question at hand might be about health or money.

This happened to Carolyn when she asked a friend to read her cards on her birthday, and she asked a question about her creative work. But everything came up Cups in this Celtic Cross reading, with the 2 of Wands in the Opposition position (card 2). It was the only Wand—and the only creativity card—in the whole reading, which was dominated by Cups—Knight of Cups as Self (card 1), Ace of Cups as Foundation (card 3), 4 of Cups as Higher Power (card 6), Temperance as Near Future (card 5), 5 of Cups as Outcome (card 10). There was no doubt about it—this was about love!

When you first spread out the cards for a reading, note your overall impression. What's this about? It may not be quite so obvious as getting 5 out of 10 cards about emotions. But just

notice how it strikes you. Even as you are turning up cards, notice how you connect them.
You may think, "Oh, this is about that." And
another card comes up, and you think, "And
this card is more about that."

With practice, you'll be able to go deeper
and notice more subtle patterns that underpin
the larger message. By noticing the patterns,
you will gain a sharper definition of the cards.

Charting Your Course

A good way to get in tune with patterns is to
do a Three-Card spread for yourself every day
for a week—the exercise you did back in
Chapter 1. It is interesting to see which cards
fade away and which rise in importance. Look
back over your Three-Card readings for a
week, and you will no doubt see the seeds of
the present moment were in those earlier cards.

Here, let's get some practice. Here is a series
of Three-Card readings for a week.

First notice similar cards and how they move
through Past, Present, and Future. Then notice
the numbers that come up. What is the dominant suit? Which Major Arcana dominates the
week? Which Royal Court card? Any card that
is repeated means a sustained lesson (or ampli-
fied by its mate Royal Court card, as the
Queen of Wands is four days later by the King
of Wands).

What progressions do you see? A progression is moving from Knight of Cups to the 2 of
Cups to the 3 of Cups—from the invitation to
love, to forming a partnership, to happiness.

Another progression is when a card, or card
of the same suit, first shows up in Past, moves
to Present, then Future. It can sometimes show
up in Past and skip to Future. The progression
may be shown in another card in another suit
or in a Major Arcana that references the Past
card through its imagery.

Date	Card 1 Past	Card 2 Present	Card 3 Future
Nov 21	QUEEN of WANDS	KNIGHT of CUPS	
Nov 22	ACE of WANDS	THE CHARIOT	
Nov 23			JUSTICE
Nov 24			
Nov 25	WHEEL of FORTUNE	THE HIEROPHANT	KING of WANDS
Nov 26		THE HERMIT	
Nov 27			

An example: on the first day, you get the Page of Cups in Past; then two days later, you get Temperance in Present. If at the end of the week, you have Page of Cups in Future, it means you did learn the lesson and are ready for the next one.

Fond and Familiar

If you find that you go in streaks where you get similar cards for a while, you're not alone. You might be on a Tower streak or a Knight of Cups streak. (We much prefer the romantic dreamer, the Knight of Cups, to the Tower, we might add.)

It's good to note each time you get a card in your Tarot Journal. You'll be surprised how many times it shows up as you are working through something. You'll get the Page of Cups a lot if you are working through some love lessons, the 8 of Pentacles a lot when you're working to achieve mastery and productivity, the Death card when you're doing some major letting go, and so on.

If you are getting a certain card for a while, notice its placement. The frequency will signal to you that you are working through some big lessons, but the placement will give you insight as to how you're doing.

Suit Your Style

If you're like most people, certain suits will be your constant companions all your life. Other suits may come to the fore as you are working on certain issues; but over the course of your lifetime, you'll have certain ones that are just "you." Some people are just Wands and Swords people; others are just Pentacles and Cups people.

More often, your dominant suits will match the dominant Elements in your astrological birth chart. If you'll remember from Chapter 4, the Power Point signs in your astrological chart are your Sun sign, Moon sign, and Rising sign. For instance, Arlene's are Sun in Aquarius: Air; Moon in Gemini: Air; and Rising in Pisces: Water; Carolyn's are Sun in Sagittarius: Fire; Moon in Aquarius: Air; and Rising in Virgo: Earth.

Of course, you won't know about patterns in previous readings for a new Querent, but you can find out about his or her astrological chart. The Power Points in the chart can give you quick insight into the role the Elements play in the reading. If your Querent has a lot of Air in his chart, as Arlene does, you can be sure that if you see a lot of Swords that these are familiar choices for your Querent.

Temperance _____

American philosopher and psychologist William James once said, "The greatest discovery of any generation is that you can alter your life by altering your attitude." Tarot reminds us constantly that we can alter future events in our lives by altering our attitude. The Tarot capitalizes on your desire to know. It takes that and runs with it—reflecting back your attitudes and the choices you can make about them.

Lantern of Truth _____

Heaven above
Heaven below
Stars above
Stars below
All that is above
Also is below.

Grasp this
And rejoice!

—Alchemical text

Repeating Images

The same holds true for images that repeat a lot in a reading, such as angels or horses. Carolyn went through a phase with a lot of Knights—of all suits. There were a lot of new lessons riding into Carolyn's life during that phase. If you see a lot of Knights in a spread, look for horses on other cards (such as Death). Or look for other symbols of movement. What feels like something is coming, as in the Knight cards? What feels like leaving, as in the 6 of Swords card? You can be sure if you get this combination of a Knight card, Death, and the 6 of Swords that you must leave something behind for something new to come to you.

Within a spread, look for similar images in the cards—the rippling water in the robe of the High Priestess, between the cups of the archangel Michael in Temperance, on the sea behind the 2 of Pentacles, on the near side of the canoe in the 6 of Swords.

Notice other patterns, too, such as the light. For instance, the sun lights the journey of the Fool as he sets out, it adds light to the Moon card, and of course, it's on the Sun card. Notice that in the first five cards the figures are each holding something. The Fool is holding a flower, the Magician a wand, the High Priestess the Torah, the Empress a scepter, the Emperor a sword, and the Hierophant a cross.

Going Interactive

No card is an island. In a spread, the cards are always talking to each other. They play off of each other. Remember our analogy of a group of friends telling stories around the campfire? Well, that holds true when you are looking for patterns. One card picks up the story where another card left off. The next card answers the follow-up question. A card comes up as opposing, and you wonder who it's about. A card comes up in a Celtic Cross spread as an Ally (card 8) or Higher Power (card 6), and you want to know who it is who will help you or who is influencing the situation.

Side by Side

Let's get some practice learning how cards interact with each other by doing some side-by-side pairings. Let's try a few groupings and see what patterns you notice, first using just the Major Arcana. Make notes about the associations revealed in each pair.

Next, let's suppose that the card pairs represent You and your Higher Power. Let's add to each grouping three cards from the Minor Arcana, each one representing Past, Present, and Future, to create a Five-Card spread. How would you analyze these spreads to get at the bigger picture?

What each figure holds in these cards signals the energy the card itself holds.
What pattern emerges across this Major Arcana combination?

DEATH.   THE DEVIL.

THE STAR.   JUDGEMENT.

THE EMPEROR.   THE HANGED MAN.

Notes

What associations do these card pairs reveal?

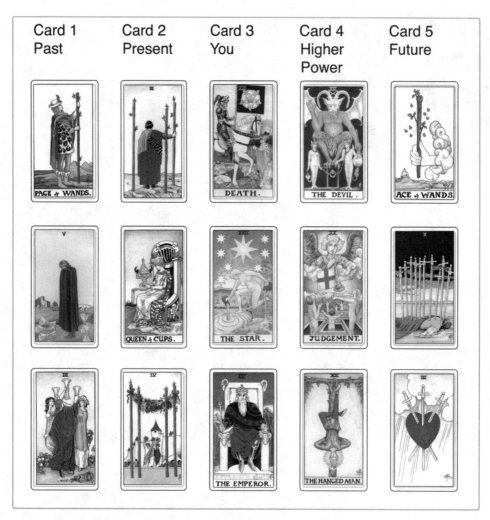

Analyze these Five-Card spreads for associations among the various cards.

What similarities do you notice? Did you notice that the Death/Devil pairing yielded three Wands cards? And that the Star/Judgement pairing yielded three cards about emotions—two Cups cards and the 10 of Swords, which signifies fear of emotional ruin?

In the first spread, the question at hand is clearly about growth and creativity, with the presence of the Wands. Notice, too, the progression: the Page of Wands, which is about learning, shows up in the Past. The Death card indicates you will let go of something, and the Ace of Wands in Future indicates you will start anew.

In the second spread, the Star and Judgement together add up for some significant insights and awakenings. The cards around them indicate this will be about matters of the heart. Put the wisdom of the Queen of Cups into the mix, and you will definitely gain a deeper understanding of love and compassion. The 5 of Cups card indicates the question may have come after a lost love or broken heart, but the 10 of Swords in Future indicates that the questions will finally be resolved and there will be closure.

In the Emperor/Hanged Man pairing, the combination of the discipline of the Emperor and the sacrifice of the Hanged Man indicates that some sacrifice will need to be made. The 3 of Cups and 4 of Wands both point to family. One is about celebrating together; the other is about coming home to celebrate. This indicates the sacrifice in question will be about family. It will be necessary, but there will be some sorrow around it, and you will need to take time to grieve.

The image of light is common to these three cards.

Synchronicities

A *synchronicity* is when two events occur at the same time, unrelated by cause and effect. Let's take a look at these three cards: the Hanged Man, the Hermit, and 2 of Wands. Light always represents illumination. There is a connection between the light of the lantern the Hermit uses to illumine his spiritual quest and the halo on the Hanged Man who is making a sacrifice to break an old pattern. Notice that the Hermit holds a staff that looks like the wands in the 2 of Wands, a card that represents command of one's domain. If these cards came up in a reading, the link would be the illumination received from going within and making a sacrifice. The result would be confidence gained to rule over one's domain.

Setting Off Sparks

A Soul Mate spread is a good one on which to practice looking for synchronicities and sparks. A synchronicity is when two unrelated events occur at the same time—such as when you and your soul mate have the same idea and say, "Great minds think alike." So synchronicities define the compatibility in your relationship.

Sparks are what fly when we put the two of you together. It's not about fighting with each other—but it can be friendly banter. Yes, as in flirting. It's where your differences make the relationship lively. It's where the two of you learn more about yourselves by the way you interact together.

Use the following sample Soul Mate spread to look for synchronicities and sparks. How are these two people alike? How are they teaching each other? Where do they disagree?

> **Tarot Reader**
>
> A **synchronicity** is a meaningful coincidence. Two events may occur by different causes at the same moment in time, but they are linked. Often when you become aware of a synchronicity, you come to see a transcendent truth.

> **Foolproof**
>
> Certain positions in a spread always modify one another, such as the Higher Power (card 6) and Outcome (card 10) cards. They are called modifiers to one another, which works the same as an adjective that modifies a noun. If that's way too much grammar for you, then understand that it's the difference between "spicy soup" and "sweet soup." Spicy or sweet tells us what kind of soup it is.

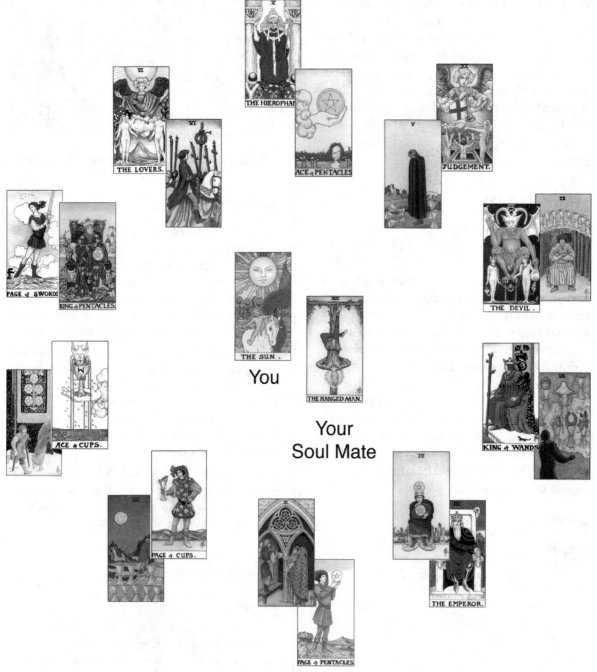

You

Your
Soul Mate

Examine this Soul Mate spread for synchronicities and sparks.

Looking for Themes

Throughout the deck, you will find certain cards naturally go together, united by themes. We have discussed some of those themes in

Chapters 4 through 7, in the creativity, wise heart, decision maker, and prosperity cards. But other cards naturally go together, united by the theme of truth or intuition or change. Here's a quick look at them.

Truth cards. These six cards define different brands of the truth. Some are the truth of the mind, such as Justice, who is holding a sword. Others are the truth of the heart, such as the Star, who is pouring water into a pond.

Intuition cards. These six cards represent looking beneath the surface to what is not immediately apparent.

Agents of change. These five cards show you change is ahead. Each card represents a particular kind of change.

Truth Cards

Here are Tarot's truth cards.

- The High Priestess — The truth within
- The Hermit — A personal truth quest
- Justice — Win-win solutions
- The Star — Inner clarity
- Judgement — An awakening to a new day; the highest truth
- Ace of Swords — Cutting to the honest truth; let's get real

Ask the Cards

Choose one of the six truth cards. Before you give or receive a reading, use that card to focus your thoughts on opening yourself to receive the truth. You may want to focus on a symbol from that card, such as the lantern of the Hermit or the trumpet of the angel Gabriel on the Judgement card.

Tarot's Intuition Cards

Here are Tarot's intuition cards.

- The High Priestess — Trusting your intuition
- The Empress — Tuning in to the earth, loved ones
- The Hermit — Honing your intuition through self-knowledge
- The Moon — Paying attention to the undercurrents
- Queen of Wands — Balance intuition and logic
- Queen of Cups — Mastery of emotional authenticity

Agents of Change

Here are Tarot's cards of change.

- Death — Letting go of what no longer serves you; allowing for new growth
- The Hanged Man — Making a sacrifice to break an old pattern
- The Tower — Dealing with the unexpected
- Judgement — An awakening to change; the dawn of a new day
- Wheel of Fortune — Taking your chances

Fluctuations and Trends

It's all in the details. It's worth it to spend some time studying the little synchronicities in your readings and see how they add up. It will help you chart a path with clear vision when you do a reading.

The Least You Need to Know

◆ Chart your Three-Day readings for a week to get a gauge on the way cards change over a period of time.

◆ Look through a reading for familiar faces (Major Arcana and Royal Court cards) as well as a predominance of certain suits.

◆ Gain familiarity with how certain cards interact with each other by practicing looking at them in pairs. Many cards supplement or amplify the meaning of other cards.

◆ The Soul Mate spread is a good spread on which to practice looking for synchronicities and sparks between cards.

◆ Certain themes run through the Tarot, such as truth, intuition, and change, linking certain cards together in patterns.

In This Chapter

- ◆ How long? Tarot's suits have the answer
- ◆ Past, Present, or Future positions
- ◆ Fast lane or slow lane? Tuning in
- ◆ Mapping out a year with the Horoscope spread

Chapter 14

It's All in the Timing

When it comes to reading a spread, timing is everything. Has this already happened? Is it happening now? Is it yet to come?

The Tarot not only can tell you what's in the past, but it can tell you what's important about the past. It provides a full picture of the present moment. And for the future, it not only reveals the future, it can also show you how events are converging to make that future what it is.

Tarot's Inner Clock

Believe it or not, the Tarot is very explicit about the timing of things. It's not quite as obvious as a digital clock, but Tarot is pretty clear on what's past, present, and future. It's also pretty clear on about how long it will take for the events to pass or unfold.

What ticks the clock for Tarot? The numbers of the suits, the suits themselves, the position of the cards in a spread, and the astrological associations of the card. All of these factors can help you identify:

- What's in the past
- What's happening now
- What's on the horizon
- When it's going to happen
- How long you have to wait
- How long you're going to be working on it
- How long ago the event happened

Temperance

Always remember that the Tarot is a snapshot of the present moment, so when it shows you the past it's in the context of how that past event is influencing the present moment. In other words, the Tarot only highlights the aspects of the past that are influencing your choices right now.

Remember from Chapter 3 that each Tarot Minor Arcana suit has its own particular brand of timing:

Wands	Days to weeks
Cups	Weeks to months
Swords	Hours to days
Pentacles	Months to years

The numbers on the cards, both in the Major and Minor Arcana, tell you how many days, weeks, or months. The Ace through 10 are just what you think they would be—1 through 10. Pages are 11, and Knights are 12. And who's to say about the Queen and King? Their timing has its own royal grace.

Right Time, Right Place

This Magic 7 reading is for a woman named Ava. Let's use it to get a better gauge of how to interpret a spread for timing. Ava wanted to know when she would start to feel better about a relationship that had ended abruptly. It was a relationship that had been wrong from the start, and so she wanted to know when she would learn from it, breaking old patterns and starting anew.

In this spread, the position dictates whether the card falls in Past, Present, or Future. The 2 of Cups and 4 of Swords are about past events that have shaped Ava's desire for new patterns in her relationships. The 2 of Cups indicates that in her past, she has begun her relationships in a spirit of good faith and trust, with optimism about the relationship being mutually satisfying. The 4 of Swords, though, indicates that she has been hurt and may have needed some time to retreat and contemplate her recent choices.

Ava's question for this Magic 7 spread was about how long it would take her to feel better about a relationship that had ended.

The suits give the first indication of the time frame in which this question will be played out—Cups and Swords are dominant with three Cups and three Swords, in just seven cards. Cups are weeks to months, whereas Swords are hours to days; so in general, we are talking about a fairly fast change. The head may come before the heart, but changes are only days to weeks away for Ava.

Now let's consider the numbers:

◆ **Past.** The 2 of Cups in the Past position tells us that in the past two weeks to two months, she has attempted to start new relationships. But the 4 of Swords in the Past position tempers that, indicating that in the past four hours or days (we think days) she has recognized the need to step back, take care of herself, and really reach down into herself to contemplate what she values in a relationship.

◆ **Present.** In the Present position, we have the King of Cups, Ace of Cups, and Knight of Swords. We can figure out the time frame of the King of Cups—who could very well be the wise, loving person who teaches her new lessons—by examining the other cards. The Ace of Cups indicates this could happen within one week or one month, whereas the Knight of Swords tells her to stay alert for the next 12 days.

◆ **Future.** In the Future position, we have the Ace of Swords and the Knight of Wands. The Ace of Swords, which represents a new direction, is right on the horizon—within one hour or one day. The Knight of Wands adds some dimension to what this new direction will be— a focused, inspired vision of something new—and tells us that it will unfold over the next 12 days or weeks.

So it's all coming soon.

Foolproof

What if some of the cards in Ava's reading were reversed? Any time reversed cards come up, expect the timing to be slowed down. The number and the suit of the card indicate how long it will take for the energy to become unblocked and move forward. For instance, if the Ace of Cups had come up reversed, it would mean that Ava's chance to open her heart would be delayed by one week to one month. The delays reflect the ups and downs of our energy—either to slow things down because of our fears or speed things up because of our enthusiasm.

Other Spreads, Other Positions

In the Celtic Cross spread, we look to the fifth and tenth positions for clues about timing. The fifth position is Near Future. The card that falls here is about events that are just now taking shape. It's what's just over the horizon. So if you have a choice between days or weeks, choose days; if you have a choice between weeks or months, choose weeks. The tenth position is long-term Outcome. This is something that has been in the works for some time.

Other spreads don't designate timing for positions. As a general rule, however, the timing in a spread flows from the first cards to the ultimate card, and often the last card is the ultimate outcome of the question. This is true of the Soul Mate spread, for instance, in which the final two cards sum up the relationship.

Good Things Come to Those Who Wait

Remember the spread we did in Chapter 11 about when Martha would get married? Arlene told her it would take about three years—and that's what happened. How did Arlene know?

The predominance of 3s in this reading are just one of the many indicators that Martha's desire to get married will be fulfilled in three years.

Just for review, here's Martha's reading:

Lots of 3s show up here: the 3 of Swords, the 3 of Wands, the Empress. But it's the reversed cards—and the positions they show up in—that indicate it will be a while before Martha gets married. The 6 of Wands R showed that it would be six weeks before Martha would meet somebody. The reversed card slows down the fast energy of Swords.

It's in the Stars

You can add another layer of interpretation by considering the astrological associations with the cards. Every card is hooked to an astrological sign, even the Minor Arcana. What this means is that aspects of that card are intensified during certain times of the year—when the sun is in that astrological sign, for instance. Let's use the Ace of Wands to show what we mean.

Often the Ace stands for the time of year. Because Wands are a Fire element, they are also associated with the three Fire signs: Aries, Leo, and Sagittarius. Those times of the year (Aries, March 21 through April 19; Leo, July 21 through August 19; and Sagittarius, November 21 through December 19) will be more intense for the lessons and choices of this card. The same is true for the other Tarot suits and the astrological signs to which they are linked.

Beneath the Surface

Timing is about more than past, present, or future. It's more than charting out the days, weeks, months, or years on the calendar. Interpreting timing in the Tarot is about knowing when the *energy* will flow smoothly—or things are going to be tough going. Of course, reversed cards are a good indication of when there will be delays. But some cards are about moving swiftly; others are about treading lightly.

Tarot Reader

What do we mean by **energy** of the cards? Energy in the scientific sense is a force of nature harnessed for use, such as coal, petroleum, or natural gas. Energy such as electromagnetic fields or calories sustains the human body. So energy is a vitalizing force that brings life to all people and things. The energy of the cards in Tarot is the life behind their story.

The yin/yang balance of time and no time is as timeless as Tarot.

Dorothy's Ruby Slippers used energy to leap across time and space and find the way home.

Tuning In

Much of interpreting the cards is about intuition. Pay attention to your first thoughts as the cards are turned over. Try not to analyze the spread just yet or focus on any one card. Instead, just tune in to the energy of the cards. Which ones feel new? Which ones feel like "been there, done that"?

A good exercise to get you used to the way the energy of the cards flows from day to day is to once again do Three-Card spreads every day for a week. Chart them in your Tarot Journal. Make notes about what energy is blocked and when it's freed. Notice how many days it takes for that energy to change. Notice what cards appeared when the energy moved. Look back over the cards from the earlier part of the week. Is it clear to you what energy they were signaling ahead?

Lantern of Truth

A good hitter has timing. A good pitcher upsets timing.
—Warren Spahn, American baseball pitcher

In a daily Three-Card spread, the first card is usually about recent events that are fading, or it can be about the early part of your day. The second card is the heart of your day and is the one that is most about what's right here, right now. The third card sifts out from your day what might be important in shaping the days and weeks ahead—so it has a more forward spin.

Now let's analyze this week of daily spreads. First, notice any repeated cards. Repeating cards indicate themes in our lives, showing us patterns we are attracting. Notice, too, whether they have moved in the sequence, as the Hierophant did from December 20 to December 21. When a card repeats, it means it's an important lesson. When that card is a Major Arcana, you can be sure, it's a *big* important lesson. When the card is the Hierophant, the teacher, there is no doubt you're learning something. The Queen of Cups came up twice, indicating there is certainly a nurturing, emotionally wise woman influencing events.

Second, notice the predominance of one suit or another. For instance, this sequence starts off heavy on Swords, with the 2 of Swords and 10 of Swords appearing on the first day, then the 9 of Swords on the second. But on the second day, well, there's lots of emotion to go around, with the 7 of Cups, the Star, and the Moon. After that, it shifts, and we see don't see the Swords suit. December 19 appears to be a day for going within, being introspective and contemplating with the wisdom of the heart the thoughts and decisions of the previous two days.

Certain suits will appear then disappear. This reflects that the energy around you for the week fluctuates. Cups are more emotional days, whereas Swords are more strife or just serious thinking. Wands bring you good energy directed toward your goals, whereas Pentacles are days of gain. These chart the ebb and flow of life.

Third, notice the numbers. Two 9s on December 18 indicate the Querent is completing some lessons about money, and this is supported by the plentiful presence of Pentacles, in particular two Royal Court cards, the King and the Queen. Two 8s indicate mastery—about work, in the case of the Pentacles, and about clear thinking, in the case of the Swords. The 4s suggest a foundation is being laid for these lessons, so they will stick in a solid, can't-forget-it kind of way. The 2s point to collaboration—the Querent will continue the work of learning these lessons in partnership with others.

Which of these cards is about the past? Certainly, the 9s and 10s are, and notice that they appear early in the week, indicating something has been completed.

The cards that point to lessons and choices in the present are the Royal Court cards, which show up as guides to help the Querent gain more self-knowledge about the present situation.

Which cards point to the future? The 2s show the choice to take steps in a new endeavor, and the Wheel of Fortune shows the Querent that the future is what she (or he) makes of it.

Ask the Cards

Did you know you can ask the cards about the past, too? You can use Horoscope, Three-Card, or Seven-Card spreads to look back. The cards can give you insight into past events and help you get some closure. Try it! You will leave the reading saying, "Oh, that's what that meant!" And you may have a better idea of what you want to choose in the coming weeks, months, or years.

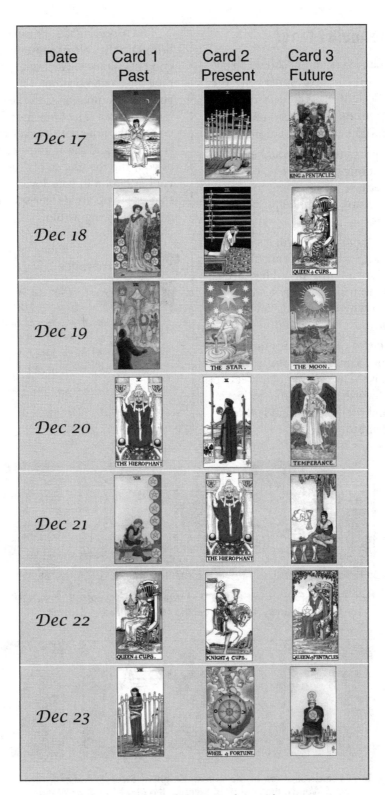

Seven days of Three-Card spreads.

Should I Yin or Should I Yang?

We can find the Tarot version of "should I stay or should I go?" in the Decision spread and the Yin/Yang spread. Both of these spreads can be used to know when to make a decision or when to wait for more insight and information.

The Yin/Yang spread tells you whether to wait, because conditions may improve, or whether to bolt, because it isn't going to get any better. The Decision spread helps you collect all the data sets.

Before you try a Yin/Yang spread, it's good to get acquainted with which cards are about waiting and which are about acting. Here are a few. Take a minute to make some notes in your Tarot Journal about why these cards fall in one column or the other.

When the Fool card comes up, it's time to just go. The Ace of Swords is the initiator, and the Ace of Wands is the beginning of a creative project. The 6 of Swords says it's time to leave the past behind, and the Magician says all factors are full speed ahead.

The Moon signals it's time to go within, which brings up the role of contemplation in making good decisions. Several other cards suggest it's time for contemplation. The 7 of Pentacles tells you that it's time to assess the effort you have put into a project. The Queen of Pentacles nudges you to take time out to acknowledge your gifts and talents and the abundance they have brought to you, and the Queen of Cups bids you to turn your attention to your loved ones. The Hermit suggests there are deeper spiritual truths to be gained by going within.

Temperance

Only you know for sure whether you're ready. Even if the cards are telling you to go forward, if you feel shaky about it, listen to that. It may be that more time needs to elapse or you need more support around you. Take the time to listen to that still, small voice.

Tarot's cards of waiting or delay: 2 of Wands, 3 of Wands, 2 of Swords, Page of Wands, 4 of Swords, the Moon, Queen of Swords.

Tarot's cards of action or movement: Knight of Swords, Ace of Swords, Ace of Wands, the Fool, 6 of Swords, the Magician, 8 of Wands.

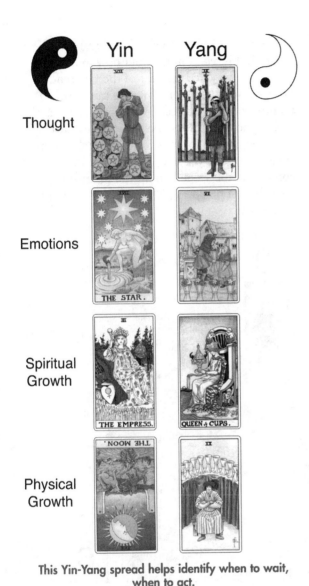

	Yin	Yang
Thought		
Emotions		
Spiritual Growth		
Physical Growth		

This Yin-Yang spread helps identify when to wait, when to act.

Past Decisions that Created the Situation

Conditions of the Present Moment

Future Outcomes of Your Choices

Bob wanted to know if he should stay with his current employer.

Nancy asked whether she should wait a year to buy a house. The Moon R said for her to definitely wait. Together, the 9 of Cups and the Moon (18) indicated she was better off waiting 9 to 18 months. Nancy ultimately ended up delaying, and it was the best decision for her. A year later, a better deal came along.

Swords and Wands are in the Present Decision position of the reading, so Bob is doing a lot of thinking about the employer. Some negative events had happened in the past there, but things have been turning around, so his mind-set is both releasing fears and allowing for a sense of victory. In the Future Decision position, the prognosis is mixed (5 of Pentacles) but with a good possibility of a prosperous future (the Empress) given time and patience (which may yield the clarity of the Star).

Specifically, the timing in the Future position indicates that he would make a decision in late winter (5 of Pentacles) or from February to April. The Star is associated with Aquarius, the Sun sign that falls in February; the Empress is associated with Taurus, which falls in late April.

The Granddaddy of Timing

The Horoscope spread is the granddaddy when it comes to timing in a spread. Each card maps out your year, month by month. The energy of that card defines the events that influence your life for that month. It shows you which events will come to the fore.

The card itself will let you know whether it will unfold slowly or happen pretty darn quick. The number and suit of the card will tell you about how long the card will influence events.

Here is a sample spread for you to interpret.

From this, you can map out how long these cards will influence the year of the Querent. For instance, the 10 of Pentacles can mean 10 months (or even 10 years, which in this case, it's such a good card, we hope so!). So this card will be in the picture for most of the year. Its influence will be strengthened by the 9 of Pentacles coming on the scene also in March, casting a nice glow of prosperity on the last nine months of the year.

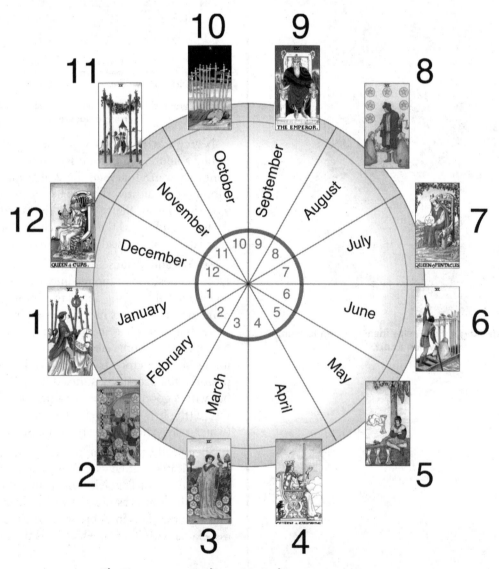

The Horoscope spread uses 12 cards to map out your year.

When It Clicks, It Clicks

So take a picture of the moment with the Tarot. The Tarot will show you what's clicking now and what's not. The Tarot will show you what's coming up right away and what is being held up.

The Least You Need to Know

- To determine timing of events in a spread, look to the numbers of the suits, the suits themselves, the position of the cards, and astrological associations of the cards.
- Suits such as Swords indicate swiftly occurring events, whereas Pentacles indicate that the events are grinding out slowly.
- Spreads such as the daily Three-Card reading and the Magic 7 often are arranged in Past, Present, and Future.
- The Near Future (card 5) and Outcome (card 10) positions of the Celtic Cross indicate future events. The Foundation (card 3) and Recent Past (card 4) positions indicate events from the past that are influencing the present.
- By tuning in to the energy of the cards, you can gain an intuitive sense of the speed of unfolding events.
- The Horoscope spread ties events to the calendar year.

In This Part

Part 5

Doing Readings

It's time to put it to the test. Getting a Tarot reading just right is easy—you just need to practice a few key steps with each reading, and pretty soon you'll have it down. This section is all about how to prepare your deck. We give you a checklist that will guide you through a reading, and we provide a visual glossary of all the Tarot cards for handy reference.

In This Chapter

- ◆ Getting yourself ready for a reading
- ◆ Find a deck that's right for you
- ◆ "Seasoning" your deck
- ◆ Shuffling and dealing
- ◆ How and where to store your deck

Chapter **15**

"Wearing In" Your Tarot Deck

Meeting your Tarot deck is a little bit like going out on a first date—it's exciting, yet just a little nerve-wracking. You want to make a good impression, and you certainly hope this deck is right for you.

It can be just as exhilarating as it is unsettling to break in a new deck. And like dating, it's a matchmaking process that often just needs to stand up to the test of time. In this chapter, we show you how to get to know your deck.

Preparing Yourself

The best way to prepare your deck for a reading is to prepare yourself—you want to be a great first-date guy or gal! If you're ready, you can be sure your deck will be ready for you.

Tarot is a reflection of your state of mind. In preparing yourself for a reading, you create the opening to receive the information the Tarot can deliver. The more you prepare, the more open you are, the more information you get.

Welcoming the Energy

It can be helpful to design a ritual that welcomes the energy of the Tarot. As you practice, you'll find that you can personalize this ritual. Come up with a ritual that feels right to you by trying different ideas.

Atmosphere is important to setting the tone, and if you have a place where you regularly do readings for people, great! But we understand that you may not be setting up Tarot readings as a full-time endeavor. Or you may do them out and about, at bookstores, crafts fairs, parties with friends, or festivals. Still, it's good to have a place that's just for you, when you do your own readings. It should be a quiet place free of distractions and interruptions, and it should be clutter-free.

Many people like to carry their cards in a silk purse or wrap them in silk or velvet. There is no right or wrong. We have found that Tarot does prefer natural fibers, but a glass, tin, or wooden box on the coffee table or bookshelf will work, too. Some people like to have a special tablecloth or scarf on which they can spread out the cards. Choose colors, patterns, fabrics, and textures that get you in the right frame of mind. Again, it's all about what works for you.

Many other objects can set the mood for a reading: a candle, chimes, a smooth stone. In the Southwest, where Carolyn lives, people often use Zuni fetishes, carvings of animals in semiprecious stone that represent the energy, strength, and wisdom of that animal. Other people like to do rituals before a reading to cleanse the mind and present a clear and open heart. One ritual involves asking your Querent to take a pinch of sea salt and sprinkle it over a bowl of water. The salt represents what your Querent would like to let go of. Then have your Querent pick a seed from a bowl and place it on a plate. The seed represents what your Querent wants to bring forth. We love to use lavender for peace and healing.

The goal of any ritual is to set an intention for the reading. It allows your Querent to get clear on the question and to focus on the reading.

Then, of course, there's *you.* You have to get in the right frame of mind, clearing away any distractions. Often Arlene uses an affirmation as a way to get herself to focus before giving a reading. Before a reading, Arlene says a prayer of focus, something like, *"Please allow this reading to flow correctly for the Querent. May all information that comes through this reading be helpful and accurate for the Querent."* Arlene lights a candle to help clear her mind of her day's worries and get to a point of inner peace. Sometimes she reads something inspirational, or sometimes she

just watches a stand-up comedian on Comedy Central. Often before a day full of readings she does a reading for herself.

> **Temperance**
>
> Don't get into a rut with your rituals. There's a fine line between ritual and superstition, and it's usually the difference between having a fresh, vibrant mind and being in a rut. Let your pre-reading ritual be a comfort for you, grounding you in a state of peace and openness. But always be open to modifying your routine a bit, just to keep things interesting.

Welcoming the Truth

Let's remember that the truth is inescapable in Tarot. To get the most out of a reading, you must welcome the truth, whatever form it might take. If you're like the rest of us, you have hopes and expectations about what the reading will tell you. It may tell you just that—but more often, it has a different, and clearer, take on the truth. Your reading may present some choices that you'll have to make if you want to realize those hopes and expectations.

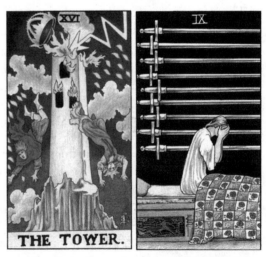

Cards such as the Tower or the 9 of Swords don't exactly tell us what we'd like to hear.

To test this truth, it's good to do a lot of readings for yourself to get acquainted with it. Carolyn tested this with a series of seven readings, asking the Tarot with the persistence of a White House reporter who has sniffed out a scandal. The Tarot was remarkably and insistently consistent with its answers. The answer, of course, was "not now, focus on the work at hand."

So how do you open yourself to the truth? First, try the direct approach. Just ask, and open yourself to the truth. Understand that the truth isn't necessarily what you want to hear. We call this purifying your intent. But a simpler way of saying it is to really get the question right. If you do that, you'll get the truth.

Then again, another way to do it is to ask the *wrong* question. That will do it, too. Because the Tarot will always point you to the right question. We define purifying your intent as purging out any preconceived notions about the answer. Most of the time, you are looking for a certain outcome. And if you don't get it, you won't see the outcome that is meant for you. But the Tarot cards don't let you slide. If the answer is really, really, really that you must wait a little longer, you'll get that answer in a hundred different ways. If the answer is that you really, really, really have to complete one more assignment before you can reap the benefit, then the Tarot cards will present that to you again and again.

Choosing a Deck

For this book, we have used the Universal Waite deck from U.S. Games Systems, Inc. because this deck has generally been used to teach beginners about the Tarot. It's also a classic that forms a great foundation for any reading. Some people find they are comfortable just using this one. The Waite deck is used in many countries and cultures because its images, colors, and numeric symbols convey messages that cross cultural lines.

But there are countless other decks out there, and we'd be remiss if we didn't clue you in on them. As you get more familiar with this deck, you will find different shades of meaning for the cards in other decks.

U.S. Games publishes the Universal Waite deck, along with hundreds of other decks, available by calling 1-800-544-2637 or by going online to http://usgamesinc.com. You'll find decks there for every culture—African, Native American, Egyptian, Celtic. You'll find decks illustrated in various art styles, from art nouveau to Renaissance.

You'll also find decks that have guides such as animals or angels. Some have a celestial theme (weaving in a lot of astrology) or a goddess theme or medicine wheel theme. In other decks, the page may be a princess, and the knight may be a prince. Some flatten out the hierarchy of the Royal Court cards, and some are less patriarchal.

How do you choose a deck when there are so many out there? We suggest you get to know the Universal Waite deck first, getting a firm grounding in the symbols and meanings of the cards. Then go shopping! If you start your search at a metaphysical or New Age bookstore, you may get good advice from the people there. You may also find some used decks—which is fun, because you can get a feel for the previous owner's energy. Also you may get to view each card, so you can see the imagery of the full deck before plunking down some cash.

When you choose a deck, zoom in on certain cards. You may have certain cards that are important to you, such as your Life Path card. Or if you are like Arlene and Carolyn, who are still trying to make peace with their Life Path cards (the Hierophant and the Emperor, respectively), you may want to identify four to five of your personal favorites. Then pull out those cards from various decks and compare the imagery. Chances are, if these cards feel right, the whole deck is just right for you.

'Tis the Seasoning

Once you have selected a deck that's right for you, it's important to wear it in. We call the process of getting to know your deck "seasoning." Here's a ritual Arlene uses. Do this with the cards face up:

1. Divide the Major Arcana from the Minor Arcana.

2. Take the suits out of the deck, and separate them. Now you have 4 stacks of 14 (Wands, Cups, Swords, and Pentacles) and another stack of Major Arcana.

3. Work first with the Major Arcana stack. Place each Major Arcana card one at a time on the table, making four stacks.

4. Now pick up the Minor Arcana stacks. From each stack of Minor Arcana, deal one card to each Major Arcana stack, first Wands, then Cups, Swords, and Pentacles.

5. Repeat until all suits cards have been placed on the four Major Arcana stacks.

6. Put the whole deck together and shuffle it many times until you feel it's mixed well.

7. Put your deck down and let it sit, or "season."

You may let your deck "season" by placing it in its special purse or case. Or, if you plan to use it right away, you may let it sit on the table where you perform your pre-reading ritual.

Many people like to perform a dedication before a deck's first reading, setting up with a new tablecloth, fresh candles, and chimes. Find a quotation that has meaning for you, something that signifies your intention. Say a dedication out loud, such as *"May all that flows from this deck be wise, true, and life-affirming."*

After you season your deck the first time, take the time to get to know it. We suggest starting off with a week of Three-Card readings. Gradually add the Celtic Cross and other spreads.

Season your deck often and well—a little like seasoning your cast iron skillet. You can do a seasoning ritual before doing a day of readings (or a week—it depends on how frequently you do readings). One of the benefits of making it a ritual is that you have seen each card at the top of the day, making contact with each form of energy in the deck.

Before a Reading

Believe or not, it's quite important *how* you shuffle a Tarot deck. When you or your Querent are shuffling the deck, you are making the first connection with the energy of the cards. Allow your Querent to shuffle the cards. It serves the purpose of getting the Querent to focus more deeply on the question.

Some people prefer to shuffle the deck by dropping cards from one hand to the other; others shuffle by blending two halves together, snapping the cards together. Either way is fine. The essential goal is to get the Querent, the question, and the cards connected.

Foolproof

If you're one of those people who don't like to get the deck "messy" with reversed cards, keep your deck pure as you shuffle by keeping the two halves pointing the same direction as you blend them. That way, when a reversed card does show up, you know that the energy of that card is definitely reversed. And regardless of how the cards fall on the table from the shuffle, that is the answer. Upright or reversed—the cards will speak to you!

For some spreads, you will fan out the cards, as you do for the Wish spread, and your Querent will pull a card.

For other spreads, such as the Soul Mate or Yin/Yang spread, you will have your Querent pull 22 or 16 cards, respectively, as they are fanned out on the table. Then you will have your Querent shuffle those cards.

Unless you are using one of these spreads, for most whole-deck spreads you will ask your Querent to cut the deck in three. The three stacks can signify whatever has the most meaning for your Querent, but they should represent a trinity. It can be a trinity in the traditional Christian sense of "Father, Son, and Holy Ghost," or "girl, mother, and grandmother," "sun, star, and moon," "Earth, heart, heaven," "body, mind, and spirit." This dividing of the deck into three is called "blessing the deck," and it is done out on the table.

Each person has his or her own way of shuffling the deck. Some people have a certain number of times they shuffle. Some cut between shuffles. Some prepare their decks by sorting them a certain way—separating Major and Minor Arcana, separating into suits. Then they shuffle!

Guiding Light Card

Sometimes you may want to choose a card for a reading that symbolizes the Querent or the question. The Wish spread is an example of that. The Life Path spread is another. Often Arlene will ask Querents to choose a Royal Court card for a Horoscope spread, someone who represents the Querent.

Ask the Cards

How should you go about choosing a Royal Court card that represents you? First of all, instinct goes a long way to answering the question. You might spread out all 16 Royals and see which one jumps out at you. Or you might go back through a series of readings and see which one comes up most often for you. Take into account where it comes up in a spread. If it shows up in the Self position, that means a lot!

Other times, you may want to choose a card that takes the question further or just helps you or your Querent focus. After a Celtic Cross reading, you may want to do a subsequent reading with the Outcome (card 10) position as the Self (card 1). Or you may want to choose a card that is puzzling to you and do a Magic 7 or Celtic Cross spread to get to the heart of the matter.

Preparing the Question

All of the steps we have described so far in this chapter are about preparing for the question. The clearer you are on the question and why you're asking, the better. The more you are focused on the question, without distractions, without other worries and fears creeping in, the more the cards are going to be on point. And remember, the Foundation (card 3) position in the Celtic Cross spread provides insight into why you asked the question.

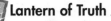

Lantern of Truth _____

Ritual is the way you carry the presence of the sacred. Ritual is the spark that must not go out.

—Christina Baldwin, American author and educator

Between Readings

It matters how you store your deck between readings. Some people like to *cleanse the deck.* That can be a ritual at the end of a session, such as the following:

◆ Ringing a chime

◆ Lighting a candle

◆ Reciting an affirmation, poem, or quotation

Other people cleanse the deck by sorting through it. Some people just go through to set reversed cards upright so that the next day they start anew. Others like to sort through, separating Major and Minor Arcana, or even sorting by suit. Whether you like to do this every time you put your deck away or not, it's a good idea to do this regularly—sort of like an oil change for your car every 3,000 miles.

Tarot Reader _____

Cleansing the deck means getting your deck back to zero. It's like erasing the chalkboard after you fill it up. You cleanse the deck of all energy from the question, the Querent, and the message of the cards. Some people do this with an affirmation, shuffling, or sorting. Visualize your deck returning to the state of the Fool, about to set out on the Journey of Life.

Some people find that it's important how and where they store their decks. They like to wrap their cards in a beautiful fabric, such as velvet, linen, taffeta, or silk. Some people find silk pouches for their decks. Cards should be wrapped loosely.

Some people use an affirmation each time they bring out their deck and unwrap it, greeting the deck. Arlene updates her affirmation from time to time, but here is one she likes to use: *"May this deck help translate the wisdom, awareness, and humor of your life's journey via the Tarot's symbology."*

Your Companion

It doesn't matter which deck ends up being your favorite. It doesn't matter whether you have more than one. Just take the time to get to know each other. Soon you'll build up a great fondness and deep trust.

Honor your Tarot deck with integrity and respect, and you'll have a wonderful partnership.

The Least You Need to Know

◆ Welcome the energy of the Tarot by preparing your deck and your place for a reading.

◆ Choose a deck that's right for you by finding one that has imagery that speaks to you.

◆ Let your Querent shuffle the deck. It's important that the question, the Querent, and the Tarot connect.

◆ The clearer you can be about why you are asking the question, the better prepared the deck will be for the question.

◆ Many people store their decks in fabric such as velvet, silk, or satin.

◆ It's important to cleanse your deck between readings, through a ritual that you design especially for you and your deck.

In This Chapter

- ◆ Assessing the energy
- ◆ Checking in with archetypes
- ◆ Tallying suits, numbers, and images
- ◆ Testing your knowledge

Chapter 16

Tarot Reader's Checklist

You have a lot to remember when examining a spread. You are taking in the meanings of the cards, the placements, the patterns, and the energy of the Querent. You want to make sure you listen to your intuition and don't miss anything.

In this chapter, we give you a checklist that will get you well on your way to developing your own style. With this handy guide, you will be sure to cover all the bases.

Step-by-Step Readings

The first thing to notice as you are doing a reading is the Querent and his or her state of mind. You may already perceive him or her as anxious or confident, angry or happy, sad or generous in spirit. You may already have an inkling what kind of question he or she is going to ask—whether it's about love or career, children or travel, home or money. Take note of this information you are receiving.

Preparation Checklist

Start with the following list of words to notice the kind of energy you are aware of with this person. You can put checks beside the ones that fit. This only takes a few seconds, and the act of committing it to paper can be just the thing that makes you more aware of your intuition about your Querent's energy.

Impression of your Querent's energy.
How does it feel? Put check marks by those
that apply. Feel free to add to this list.

Giving	Receiving
Expanding	Contracting
Open	Closed
Active	Passive
Rapid	Slow
Forward	Backward

As time goes on, you'll come up with a few of
your own to add to your Tarot checklist. And further down the road, you won't even be directly
conscious of taking this in. Somehow you'll just
know. That's the basis of intuition. But what you
are doing here is bringing your intuition to *consciousness*, the state of cognitive awareness.

> **Tarot Reader**
>
> **Consciousness** is the state of being
> aware of your feelings. You allow your-
> self to examine your instincts and intuitions in
> a deep and conscious way. By bringing a
> vague sensation or awareness to your top
> level of thought, you can clarify and solidify
> your understanding of the Tarot cards.

Impression of the question itself. Next
take note of the question at hand. Write it
down. As you do, notice your impression of
this question. How does it add to your impression of the Querent?

_____

_____

_____

Impression of the cards. As you lay out the
cards, pay attention to your initial reactions to
them. It's helpful to have a blank spread sheet
where you can jot down keywords for each
card, or keep your Tarot Journal at hand.

Remember that some cards can have many lay-
ers of meaning. But generally your first
impression of what a card means is something
to heed.

Reading Checklist

When you have a spread laid out before you,
analyze it for these factors:

Destiny vs. Free Will. Take note of the
number of Major Arcana and Minor Arcana. If
Major Arcana cards dominate, Destiny is a
strong force at work on the situation. If they
are in the majority, that's certainly true; but
even when 4 out of 10 cards in a Celtic Cross
show up as Major Arcana, that can be powerful
Destiny. On the other hand, if you have fewer
than four, you have lots of choices. Notice that
in the following spread, five Major Arcana
cards are present, indicating the Querent is
working on some major life lessons.

Life Path card. Before a reading, it's a good
idea to determine your Querent's Life Path
card. If it shows up in a reading, you can bet
some big lessons are happening. Find out your
Querent's Life Path card by finding out his or
her birthday. (Refer to Chapter 2 for how to
calculate the numerology of your birth date.)

> **Foolproof**
>
> Sometimes it's just as important to note
> what's absent from a reading as what is
> present. It's not essential to have every
> Element present in a reading for it to be
> clear. But if your question is pointedly about
> love and there are no Cups, or if your ques-
> tion is pointedly about money and there are
> no Pentacles—that's information, too. It may
> mean you have other work to do in the
> background before you will get the answer
> to the question.

This Celtic Cross spread has five Major Arcana, indicating that Destiny is a strong force acting on the question at hand.

Dominant suit. Which suit dominates? How dominant is it?

____ Wands (creativity, growth, vision)

____ Cups (emotions, love)

____ Swords (thought, power, action, decisions)

____ Pentacles (resources, talents, health, money)

Notice in the Celtic Cross spread illustrated above that four of the five Minor Arcana are Pentacles. Now that's dominant!

Archetypes. Which archetypes are present? Look for the ones that pertain to the question itself, as well as the intent behind the question. By that we mean, if the question is about love, look for the wise heart archetypes. But if the question is about acceptance, look for the truth archetypes, or if the question is about trusting, look for the intuition archetypes.

◆ **Creativity archetypes.** The Magician, the Lovers, the Chariot, Strength, the Moon, King of Wands, Queen of Wands, Knight of Wands

◆ **Wise heart archetypes.** The High Priestess, the Empress, the Lovers,

Strength, Temperance, the Star, King of Cups, Queen of Cups, Knight of Cups

♦ **Decision-maker archetypes.** The High Priestess, the Emperor, the Hierophant, Justice, Temperance, King of Swords, Queen of Swords, Knight of Swords

♦ **Truth archetypes.** Justice, Temperance, the Tower, Judgement, King of Swords, Queen of Swords

♦ **Intuition archetypes.** The High Priestess, the Empress, the Hermit, the Moon, Queen of Wands, Queen of Cups

♦ **Prosperity archetypes.** The Magician, the Empress, Strength, the Sun, 9 of Pentacles, 10 of Pentacles

Royal Court cards. Take note of how many Royal Court cards are present. Note which Royal Court cards are present and where they are. If two appear in the same suit, as with the previous spread, where the Knight of Pentacles and Page of Pentacles are present, you can be sure that influence is strong.

Emotions. Which emotional archetypes are present? What images of emotions are present? Are any of the wise heart archetypes here?

Numbers. What numbers are dominant? Include the numbers from the Major and Minor Arcana. Tally them up. Which ones recur?

Images. What images repeat?

Absent suits. What suits are absent?

Timing. What is about the past? The present? The future? What events are diminishing in importance? What events can still be influenced?

Placement. If your spread has a specific placement for Past, Present, or Future, take that into account.

Suits. Notice what the suits tell you about whether what's happening is occurring in the next days, weeks, months, or years.

Numbers. Look at the numbers to see how many days, weeks, months, or years.

Major Arcana. Again note the number of Major Arcana, especially those near the card for which you are determining the timing. A Major Arcana card could mean that the lesson being learned is part of a larger lesson that is unfolding during this cycle of life.

Movement. Which cards show forward movement? If you have a lot of Swords, some Knights or cards with images of transportation (such as the boat in the 6 of Swords or the 2 of Pentacles), there is a lot of movement.

Astrological symbols and connections. Look for astrological symbols (such as the Venus symbol on the High Priestess). Also take note of which cards are connected with astrological signs. (Chapter 17 includes a list of astrological signs related to the Major Arcana.)

Temperance

What if you forget to check each item on this list when you give a reading? Relax! Your reading doesn't have to be done in microscopic detail. The essence of the reading will come through.

Putting It to the Test

In this section, we use our checklist to analyze several types of spreads so that you can get the hang of it.

About Creativity

When you analyze a spread for creative aspects, take special note of the presence of the suit of Wands and look for any of the creativity archetypes we identified in Chapter 4.

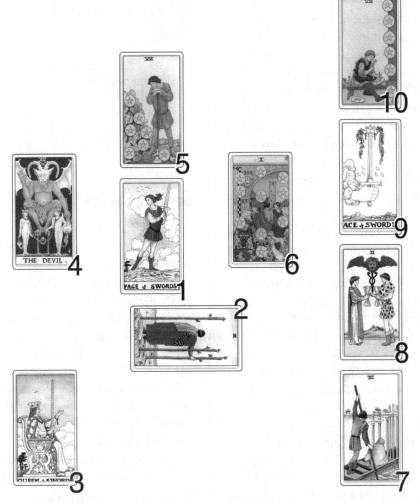

What creativity archetypes are present in this reading?

1. **Self:** Page of Swords
2. **Opposing Force:** 3 of Wands
3. **Background/Foundation:** Queen of Swords
4. **Recent Past:** The Devil
5. **Near Future:** 7 of Pentacles
6. **Higher Power:** 10 of Pentacles
7. **Issues/Fears:** 6 of Swords
8. **Allies/Others:** 2 of Cups
9. **Advice:** Ace of Swords
10. **Outcome:** 8 of Pentacles

In your Tarot Journal, jot down your initial impression of each card. Write down keywords for each card, referring to Chapter 17 if you need to do so.

Creativity cards. Notice any creativity cards that came up. Note any we have named or any others that, in context of position and of the question of the Querent, point to creativity. What about the Devil? This indicates that sensuality is a source of creative energy for this woman, but because it's in the Recent Past (card 4) position, that may be fading in importance. Now the focus turns to completing a project: 7 of Pentacles in Near Future (card 5).

Dominant suit. The suit of Swords, which is about thoughts and ideas, is dominant in this reading. What does that tell you about the Querent's creative style? Also strong is the suit of Pentacles (resources, abundance, results of hard work). What might this indicate?

Challenges and strengths. From this sample reading, what do you think the Querent's struggles will be? Look to Opposing Force (card 2) and Issues/Fears (card 7) positions, the 3 of Wands and 6 of Swords, respectively. The 3 of Wands suggests that the Querent needs to wait patiently for other resources, allies, and supporters to help with her endeavors. Look to the Higher Power (card 6) and Allies and Supporters (card 8) positions to find her strengths. The 10 of Pentacles in Higher Power (card 6) suggests that she has a strong familylike base of support and she is surrounded with abundance. Very good! The 2 of Cups is nudging her to create rewarding partnerships based on a healthy give-and-take.

Advice and lessons. What advice would you give her, based on the Ace of Swords, which symbolizes new ideas and new directions? The Sword also suggests that she cut away at the old ways of thinking and doing (something that is supported by the presence of many swords in the reading, overall). Should she form a partnership? Which two cards point to partnership? What do these cards tell her about hard work?

This Celtic Cross spread shows us how all the components of interpretation must come together to achieve the optimum state of creativity. The women in the Celtic Cross creativity spread was clearly going to need to call on the strength of Swords (swift, clear thinking), the grounding of Pentacles (wise investment of creative resources), and the heart of the Cups (collaboration and rewarding alliances) to achieve her goal.

Ask the Cards

Try a creativity reading about yourself. Take a few minutes to do a spread for yourself and make notes in your Tarot Journal. Notice any creativity archetypes. Notice cards from other suits that support creativity. Notice cards that create tension by posing difficult choices. What feels right and easy about your reading? What feels challenging?

Seeking the Truth

Much of Tarot is about seeking the truth. The Tarot is always truthful—whether it's what you want to hear or not.

Sometimes Querents have questions that really get to the heart of the matter. The plain truth shows up in the Issues/Fear (card 7) position of the Celtic Cross or the Truth card in the Path to Peace. In the case of the latter spread, you are directly asking for the truth. It's a truth you already have learned but not necessarily confronted. The Truth card in this spread validates it for you so you can examine the Path to Peace.

The truth is a dominant factor in the Wish spread, which gives a complete picture of all factors around your wish.

About Love, Prosperity, and the Future

On the following pages, practice your talents as a true Tarot Reader.

- **Love.** Use the Tarot checklist at the beginning of this chapter to analyze this Wish spread.
- **Prosperity.** Analyze this spread for prosperity. The Querent, Paula, a doctor, asked, "*Will my prosperity increase in the coming year?*"
- **The Future.** The Horoscope spread maps out a whole year.

Truth   Conflict

Acceptance   Ultimate
Peace

Path to the Past   Path to the Future

   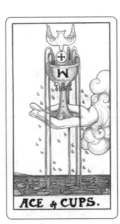   

Anger   Sorrow   Lessons

Present

Analyze this Path to Peace spread for Truth.

About the Wish

  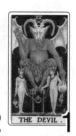    

Conditions
Surrounding the Wish

Opposition
to the Wish

Outcome

What You
Will Learn

Analyze this Wish spread for signs of new love.

Past

Future

Present

Analyze this Seven-Card spread for prosperity.

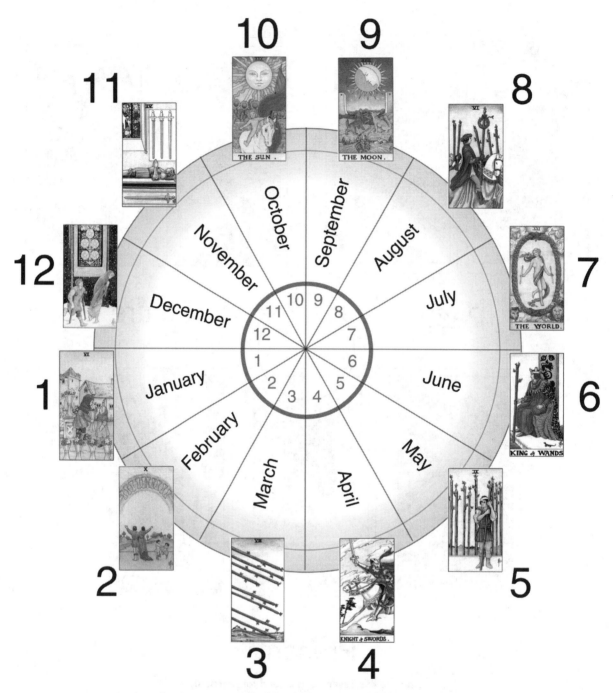

Analyze this Horoscope spread for the year to get a full picture of the future.

Lantern of Truth _____

Trust your instinct to the end, though you can render no reason.

—Ralph Waldo Emerson, American poet

Upward and Onward

In closing, we thought we'd let you take a look at a reading Arlene and Carolyn did together to show the collective energy surrounding the launch of this new Tarot book in the coming year. This Three-Card reading was done in the first week of a new year.

Past   Present   Future

Arlene and Carolyn's reading on the collective energy surrounding this Tarot book.

The King of Pentacles is the essence of Earth behaving as Air—like a diamond. He's a true resource, with a gift for identifying opportunities and taking advantage of them, a pillar of practicality and dependability, an expert with experience built on hard work whose word is as good as gold.

The 6 of Pentacles hints at a time of prosperity and profit, success, and generosity. The World predicts the attainment of ideals, the culmination of work, resulting in prosperity, security, and joy. Well, we certainly hope so—for ourselves, and for *you*, our readers, as you continue on your Life Journey with the Tarot!

Now you see how much fun this can all be. During the time we were writing this book, we, too, learned a lot through the cards that came up for us. Realize that Tarot can be a terrific tool for gaining insight into knowledge you may already have within—or just help you accept unexpected or challenging events as they come up. It can help you know yourself better and identify allies and supporters who will guide you along the Journey of Life.

The Least You Need to Know

- Start a reading by analyzing the overall energy you feel coming from the cards.
- Always take note of the distribution of Major and Minor Arcana in a reading.
- Knowing your Querent's Life Path card will help you provide insight on your Querent's unique talents, abilities, and challenges.
- Look through a reading for dominant suits, recurring themes, and repeating patterns.
- Remember to heed the lessons and roles the Royal Court cards present in a reading.
- Examine a reading for themes such as creativity, love, and prosperity.

In This Chapter

◆ Key concepts of the Major and Minor Arcana

◆ Astrological and numerological associations

◆ Spotlight on the Royal Court

◆ A journey through all of the suit cards:
Wands, Cups, Swords, Pentacles

Chapter 17

What All the Cards Mean

From the Fool to the World, from the Royal Court cards to the day-to-day suit cards of the Minor Arcana, every Tarot card has a meaning. The meaning comes from several sources, chief among them whether the card is part of the Major Arcana or Minor Arcana, what suit it is, or the number on the card.

Meanings also come from the color, imagery, and symbolism on the card and the presence of the Elements of Fire, Water, Air, and Earth. Many cards tie into astrological signs of the zodiac, and others make reference to Christianity, Judaism, and mythology. This chapter provides a handy guide to all the cards in the Tarot deck.

The Major Arcana

The 22 cards of the Major Arcana represent the Journey of Life, progressing from the Fool to the World. Each card represents an archetype, and each is numbered, starting with 0 for the Fool and ending with 22 for the World.

0 The Fool: New Adventures

Archetype: The pioneer.

Astrology: Aries (the big push!).

Numerology: 0, a soul waiting to be born.

Meaning: The Fool is the energetic adventurer, setting off on a new journey with fresh hope. The Fool is free of worries and has an air of immortality about him. He has no preconceived notions, so his ideas are fresh and original, free of the limitations of fear or bitterness. He's willing to take the leap of faith. Anything is possible! He doesn't buy into established notions, so sometimes he plays the trickster. He is in such close contact with his instinctive side that he doesn't need to look down. The little dog at his feet represents his animal instincts. He acts by insight, not logic; by intuition, not conventional wisdom.

Upright: Fresh hope, taking chances.

Reversed: Thoughtless, unprepared.

I The Magician: Make It Happen

Archetype: The alchemist.

Astrology: Aries (invention).

Numerology: 1, the number of initiative, new beginnings.

Meaning: The Magician has vision and focus. He unleashes creative power. His wand, raised aloft toward heaven, connects him with divine revelation. His other hand, pointed toward the earth, symbolizes his role as a conduit of creation energy, manifesting visions into reality. He initiates the curriculum of self-realization that is part of the Journey of Life. He demonstrates the power of transcending the ego—and the empowerment we feel as a result of unifying all of our energies, symbolized by emblems of all four Tarot suits on his table: Wands, Cups, Swords, and Pentacles. Where the Fool dreams of it and sets out for a new horizon to seek it, the Magician visualizes and manifests.

Upright: Focused, empowered creativity.

Reversed: Squandering your talent, wasted brilliance, scattered energy or resources.

II The High Priestess: The Truth Within

Archetypes: The wise woman, sage, goddess.

Astrology: Pisces (intuition), Virgo (sacred service).

Numerology: 2, the number of balance; she balances logic and emotion with intuition.

Meaning: Intuition is what it's all about with the High Priestess. Because she expresses confidence in the truths that are not immediately seen, she is a vessel for transformation. She is the female expression of the Magician—she is the one who gives birth to insight. She harkens us to lift the veil to the subconscious, to examine and understand hidden truths within. She represents a quiet, rooted power—persistent, constant, guided by love and patience. She is an annunciation of the mysteries of our deep subconscious.

Upright: Intuition, the subconscious, inner truths.

Reversed: Blunted intuition, blocked insight.

III The Empress: The Nurturer

Archetypes: Earth mother, Demeter, Madonna (Mary).

Astrology: Taurus (home), Libra (beauty).

Numerology: 3, the number of creativity, abundance, and self-expression.

Meaning: The Empress is about spirit being born as flesh. She unites heaven and Earth. She brings the liberation and transformation, the lightness of spirit, into reality, into our human realm. She is fertile—she goes about this task with grace and abundance. She gives life, and she cultivates all that perpetuates life. She is the queen of the garden, the ruler of the home. She presides over beauty as well as the liberation that gives rise to new beauty. She gives form to our desires and our wishes, and she nourishes them. She is both action and contemplation, and she rules with love.

Upright: Giving birth to desires, wishes, all that sustains.

Reversed: Halted growth; fallow ground.

IV The Emperor: Father of Civilization

Archetypes: Father, architect/master builder.

Astrology: Scorpio (power), Aries (drive).

Numerology: 4, the number of good foundations. This number is about discipline and organization, the foundations of building any creative project.

Meaning: The Emperor brings order and establishes a solid foundation for the wild dreams of the Fool, the visions of the Magician, the insights of the High Priestess, and the abundance of the Empress. It is through his leadership, discipline, and strategic planning that new endeavors come forth. He brings rational, logical thought to these ideas, connecting them to reality in very practical ways. The Emperor is hands-on.

Upright: Solid foundation, strategic planning.

Reversed: Time to make a plan, knuckle down.

V The Hierophant: The Word

 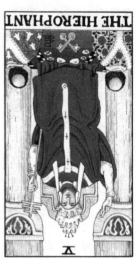

Archetypes: Teacher, the pope.

Astrology: Taurus (structure).

Numerology: 5, the number of action and change (a turning-point number, particularly in the Minor Arcana suits of the Tarot).

Meaning: The Hierophant is the official word. He represents the time-tested wisdom. He is a wise educator who helps us learn from other people's experiences. He upholds traditional values and reminds us of the common good. He reminds us of the reason for the rules, and he's able to speak a common language so that all can understand where he's coming from. He is a preservationist—someone who honors traditions and holds them sacred, even as others test the limits. He's the conventional one in the bunch. He reminds us to consider how we appear to the rest of the world. He represents our need for social approval. He helps us fit in.

Upright: Traditions, conventional wisdom.

Reversed: What rules?

VI The Lovers: Soul Mates

Archetypes: Romeo and Juliet, Psyche and Eros, Isis and Osiris.

Astrology: Gemini (twin energy).

Numerology: 6, the number for home and harmony.

Meaning: At this point in the Journey of Life, you have come to the crossroads. You must make a choice—a choice that unifies and harmonizes two opposites. This card is about the synergy that happens when two vibrant forces come together. It can literally mean the force of love, which makes you choose for reasons that even you don't completely understand, which makes you surrender to a higher power (as in, "swept off your feet"). It may mean that you find a someone—a soul mate—who is so perfectly attuned to you, and you to him/her, that you dare not resist. Or it may mean that you gain some spiritual self-knowledge that creates harmony within. This card is about choosing between dualities—good and evil, for instance—and making peace with them.

Upright: Wise choices, harmony between opposites.

Reversed: Divisiveness, differences.

VII The Chariot: Carry Me Home

Archetype: The hero.

Astrology: Sagittarius (enterprise).

Numerology: 7, the number of spiritual idealism and wisdom.

Meaning: The Chariot is the vehicle that leads you into battle. This card is about pursuing success with vigor and confidence. The charioteer is courageous and well equipped. Having made the choices in the Lovers card, the charioteer has a focused purpose. The charioteer is prepared to meet the challenge.

Upright: Pursuit of spiritual idealism; purposeful action.

Reversed: Giving up the fight, losing direction.

VIII Strength: Love and Courage

Archetype: The healer.

Astrology: Leo (will).

Numerology: 8, mastery. The infinity symbol above her head, which appears also in the Magician, represents the eternal cycle of growth.

Meaning: The Strength card shows us that the key to courage is unconditional acceptance of self. Through love, we gain fortitude. Through compassion, we become stronger. In this card, the woman's strength is not in a magic wand—or any other tool or weapon. It's in her fearlessness. This is how she tames the lion. Love is the key, because it is always stronger than fear or hate.

Upright: Conquering fear through love.

Reversed: Letting fear reign.

IX The Hermit: Spiritual Quest

Archetypes: The hermit, the mystic, the spiritual master.

Astrology: Virgo (the labyrinth).

Numerology: 9, the number of completion. The Hermit completes a cycle in the Journey of Life.

Meaning: The Hermit looks upon the Lantern of Truth as he takes the path of introspection and contemplation. When he comes up in a reading, he signals it's time to go within. What you'll find there is your own inner peace as well as universal truths. The six-pointed star in his lantern represents enlightenment and harmony. The Hermit is all about illumination and inner contentment. He is going on a spiritual quest.

Upright: Time for contemplation.

Reversed: Resistance to your own inner voice.

X Wheel of Fortune: Time for a Change

Archetype: The gambler.

Astrology: Four signs show up here: Aquarius (intellect), Taurus (grounding), Leo (creativity), and Scorpio (desire). All of these zodiac signs are fixed, which means their energy is solid and not mutable. Notice there is one sign for each season—winter, spring, summer, fall—and each Element—Air, Earth, Fire, and Water. The presence of all suggest that anything is still possible.

Numerology: 10, which reduces to 1 (1+0), starting over. It's about initiatives and new beginnings—only now with the wisdom obtained in the Hermit.

Meaning: The Wheel of Fortune brings good luck. All factors are favorable as you start a new cycle. It almost always indicates good fortune ahead—happiness, abundance, a feeling of elevation. That's because at this point on the Journey of Life, you have learned your lessons. You are wiser, and so you are ready to take your chances with Fate and Free Will.

Upright: Let's roll! You cash in on your good karma.

Reversed: Hold the phone! Take time out to examine where you have invested your energies. Is this what you intended? Get centered, like a wheel. Go back to your values.

XI Justice: Do the Right Thing

Archetypes: Lady Justice, the mediator.

Astrology: Libra (balance).

Numerology: 11, a master number in numerology that reduces to 2 (1+1). Eleven represents the balance of the laws of heaven and laws of humans. Like the 2, 11 is about harmony and balance.

Meaning: Justice is about balancing all the interests, looking for the truth and setting things aright. Justice helps us gain perspective—not just looking at the situation through our own self-interest, but considering what's win-win for all involved. If someone has been unfair, Justice restores the situation. Justice neither defends not attacks with her sword. She only seeks the truth. And in the truth, peace is inevitable.

Upright: Seeking higher truth.

Reversed: Get back in balance, rethink the situation.

XII The Hanged Man: The Pattern Breaker

Archetypes: Jesus, redeemer or savior, the messiah.

Astrology: Pisces (metamorphosis).

Numerology: 12, which reduces to 3 (1+2), a trinity. This card vibrates with a high spiritual intensity because of its associations with redemption.

Meaning: The Hanged Man offers himself as a sacrifice to gain knowledge for all. This card is about surrender to a higher purpose. It's about changing all of your old patterns, being willing to let go. The man is hanging upside down, which reminds us that sometimes we have to turn all that we think we know upside down to see the truth. Notice that the man in the card has a look of peace about him, and his head is surrounded by a halo. Through selflessness, we find greater clarity. Through vulnerability, we find illumination.

Upright: Letting go, releasing old patterns.

Reversed: It's over and done with. You can't go back to the way things were. It's time for a change of consciousness.

XIII Death: Transformation

Archetypes: Hindu goddess Kali, the mythic Phoenix.

Astrology: Scorpio (epiphany).

Numerology: 13, which reduces to 4 (1+3), meaning something is transformed and can be reborn to build anew on the foundation of lessons learned. Thirteen is a karmic number in numerology and has to do with learning to grow by overcoming obstacles with maturity and accepting change.

Meaning: The Death card brings about a big change—the end of a cycle, the beginning of a new one. It's not just a passage. You must leave behind ideas and beliefs from your past that are no longer vital and alive to birth new ideas. It parallels the cycle of nature, as in the leaves that fall from the trees in autumn, which decompose, providing nutrients for the soil so that new growth can occur in the spring. Death humbles all, but it also exults; in rebirth, you go to a higher level of understanding.

Upright: Regeneration, rebirth.

Reversed: Stillbirth, stagnation, standstill.

XIV Temperance: Elixir of Harmony

Archetypes: Archangel Michael; peacemaker; the alchemist; the North American goddess Gyhldeptis, who synthesizes divergent energies into a whole.

Astrology: Cancer (home).

Numerology: 14, which reduces to 5 (1+ 4), the number of change and transformation. This card is peaceful, but it's about transforming again and again, with patience. Fourteen is a karmic number in numerology and deals with lessons in responsibility and right action.

Meaning: Temperance is the intermingling of opposites—of yin and yang, of spirit and flesh, of conscious and unconscious; of seen and unseen. Temperance is a good give-and-take, a benevolent synergy. It's also about adapting—you don't resist changes; you go with the flow. It's about the harmonious flow of time—past, present, and future exist in harmony in your psyche. Temperance reminds us there is a happy medium—a place where we can achieve a balance, keeping our emotions on an even keel, exercising self-control and moderation. Temperance just feels good.

Upright: Patience, going with the flow.

Reversed: Out of balance.

XV The Devil: Temptation

 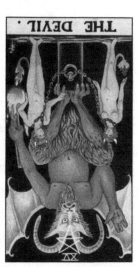

Archetypes: Satan; Hades, the Greek god of the underworld; the Greek god Dionysus; the hedonist.

Astrology: Capricorn (ties that bind).

Numerology: 15, reduced to 6 (1+ 5), which represents bondage—being obligated through others, through fear.

Meaning: This is the "sex, drugs, and rock'n'roll" card. The Devil tempts us—with sensual pleasures, with indulgences. It's about wild behavior and unbridled desires. When it's tuned too high, it can be about obsession or addiction. Giving in to those temptations can result in bondage. But it can also be a reminder that sometimes we need to experience the pleasures of life. There is a mirthfulness to the Devil. At its best, the Devil is about letting loose, being spontaneous. If you explore without fear, shame, or excess, the Devil card is potent indeed, pointing the way to transcend the material and earthly bonds of the flesh. The Devil card reminds us not to let our pleasures become addictions, though.

Upright: Sensuality, indulgence.

Reversed: Freedom from the chains of fear.

XVI The Tower: Unexpected Liberation

Archetype: The liberator.

Astrology: Taurus (stubbornness), Aquarius (innovation).

Numerology: 16, reduced to 7 (1+6), the number of spiritual breakthroughs and shake-ups. In numerology, 16 is a karmic number, and it indicates a lesson in loss and love that needs to be revisited.

Meaning: This is the breakthrough card. Everything you thought you knew before—think again! This card is about upheaval—a dramatic change. It can be good (a new baby) or bad (you get fired). Whatever it is, it will rock your world. It can change your life, or just your perspective. And even if it seems bad (losing your job), ultimately the change is for the best. You have a major shift in perception—a miraculous insight. You come out of it with a new understanding of yourself.

Upright: A life shift, total change in perspective.

Reversed: Earth tremors, listen to the rumblings of change.

XVII The Star: Ray of Hope

Archetypes: Fairy godmother; angel; Aquarius, the water bearer.

Astrology: Aquarius (humanitarianism).

Numerology: 17, reduced to 8 (1+7), hope and spiritual prosperity.

Meaning: Now you have faith that all of your brightest hopes and wishes will come true. All is calm; all is clear. The great eight-pointed star above the woman at the water provides inspiration—the inspiration that comes from mastery (represented in the number eight). The light of the star represents spiritual energy and truth. This card is about believing in miracles.

Upright: Renewed faith, clarity, a wish come true.

Reversed: To restore hope, get in alignment with your higher spiritual purpose.

XVIII The Moon: The Power of the Imagination

Archetypes: Greek goddess Artemis, the goddess of the hunt; Celtic goddess Boudica.

Astrology: Cancer (feeling), Pisces (flow).

Numerology: 18, reduced to 9 (1+8), another cycle of completion. The mastery at this level is higher.

Meaning: The Moon card lifts your awareness to the untamed power of your imagination. You have tapped into the universality of human experience through the collective unconscious. With the Moon, emotions are intensified—in a full moon crazy sort of way. But underneath, there are currents of wisdom. Sometimes the truth comes out during the full moon. Let yourself dream a little!

Upright: Imagination, intuition, dreams.

Reversed: New awareness; good common sense.

XIX The Sun: The Light of the World

Archetype: The child.

Astrology: Leo (heart).

Numerology: 19, reduced to 1 (1+9 = 10; 1+0 = 1). Nineteen represents a starting over with the innocence of a child. It is a karmic number in numerology that coincides with learning the right use of compassion and power.

Meaning: With the Sun, all is well. Your light shines from the center. You have learned many lessons, and with that comes calm contentment. Still, from this safe place, where you have mastered wisdom and peace, you have a childlike wonder about the world. All four Elements—Air, Earth, Fire, and Water—show up here, blossoming as the four sunflowers, which suggest abundance.

Upright: Contentment, attainment of happiness.

Reversed: Diminished growth.

XX Judgement: Coming to Terms

Archetype: Prophet.

Astrology: Scorpio (intensity).

Numerology: 20, reduced to 2 (2+0), cooperation with universal spiritual principles.

Meaning: Judgement is about coming to completion—integrating the mistakes of the past, looking upon the truth, and living it. You can forgive and move on; you have healed and are renewed. You see the greater purpose for your life. Notice the red and white on the cross of the archangel Gabriel: red shows the lifeblood of passion, while white shines the pure light of spirit. Judgement is the final step on the road to realizing self-actualization, the World.

Upright: Cosmic wake-up call, awakening.

Reversed: Denial.

XXI The World: Glimpse of Eternity

Archetypes: Visionary; the Enlightened One.

Astrology: Capricorn (achievement).

Numerology: 21, reduced to 3 (2+1), the culmination of self-expression.

Meaning: The World is about triumph. You have become a whole person, wise in body, mind, and spirit. You have attained the highest wisdom, fulfilling your purpose. It's the culmination of all of your talents and skills. You have come full circle, back to the innocence of the Fool, but with the wisdom of the ages.

Upright: Attainment, self-actualization.

Reversed: Failure to learn the lessons.

The Minor Arcana

Within the four suits of Tarot's Minor Arcana, all numbers represent common themes. Aces always show new beginnings. 5s always show turning points. 10s represent the completion of the cycle. Notice that the numbers correspond with meanings in numerology; we include a handy guide here.

1 Initiative

2 Partnership

3 Expression, communication

4 Solidity, security

5 Change, action, chaos

6 Harmony, peace, resolution

7 Spiritual test, wisdom

8 Mastery, manifesting

9 Completion, responsibility

10 Attainment, conclusion

Remember also from Chapters 9 and 10 that all Royal Court cards represent roles you play or significant people in your life.

Wands

Wands represent the creative force and personal growth, and their Element is Fire, the energy of enterprise. Wands reveal personal drive and power to move on your life goals.

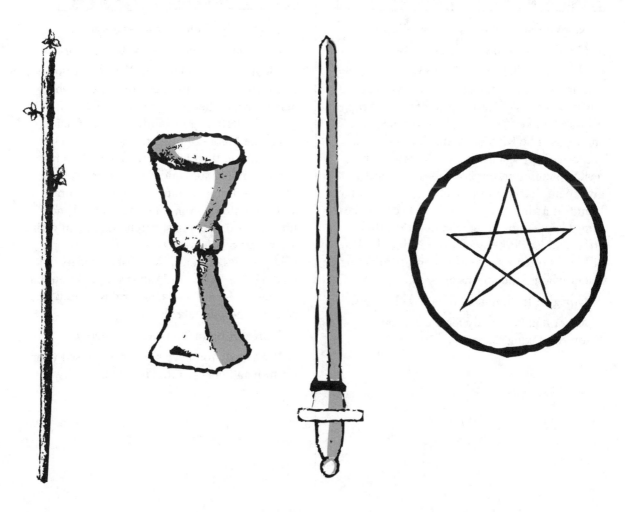

King of Wands

Keywords: Expansive, charismatic vision.

His role: To show you your vision.

Meaning: The King of Wands brings clarity and order to the many manifestations of creativity. Clusters of leaves sprout from the top of his wand, or staff, symbolizing new thoughts and ideas. The King of Wands holds his staff authoritatively against the earth between his feet, grounding those thoughts and ideas to give them shape and substance. The King of Wands is a kind, yet firm, ruler. He can make things happen for those who put forth the effort and legwork. In a Tarot reading the King of Wands often represents a mentor, guide, or leader who is ready to inspire you.

Upright: In command of new, bold ideas.

Reversed: Not ready for the challenge, vision still taking shape.

Queen of Wands

Keywords: Radiating self-assurance.

Her role: To encourage you to go for it.

Meaning: The Queen of Wands is calm and confident, with focused creative energy channeled through her intuition. Her right hand holds the staff of possibilities. Her left hand offers the bloom of potential, a lovely flower. The lions on the Queen's throne look to the east (the rising sun) and the west (the setting sun), presenting an aura of strength, courage, and contented power. The Queen of Wands fills her card, looking squarely out at you with a directness that leaves no room for questioning your abilities or goals. When she appears in a reading, the Queen of Wands says, "Dream big … then go for it!" in whatever direction your creative energies take you.

Upright: Boundless creative energy.

Reversed: You have not yet harnessed your warmth and energy into ambition.

Knight of Wands

Keywords: Go for it!

His role: To get your endeavor started, bring movement and action into play.

Meaning: Charging to your aid, the Knight of Wands brings the momentum you need to launch you toward your dreams and goals. His high-spirited steed is chomping at the bit, eager to gallop onward. Visor raised so nothing obstructs his vision, the Knight of Wands looks full-ahead with determination and anticipation. He's ready to give full rein to his horse and to your efforts—and then, look out! Wild horses won't be able to drag you off course as the Knight of Wands leads the charge. The Knight of Wands in a reading says the energy and direction you need are now here for you. Note that the Knight wears a robe of salamanders; the symbol of the force of will, the salamander will also protect you.

Upright: A crusader.

Reversed: Chaotic, misdirected energy.

Page of Wands

Keywords: Enthusiasm, encouraging news.

His role: To inform and equip you for a new endeavor, the messenger of enthusiasm and affirming results.

Meaning: The Page of Wands brings news about your plans and efforts, often in the form of encouragement and support. The Page of Wands looks pleased as he examines the sprouts of growth on his staff. His message is one you'll want to receive, though as the message unfolds in your life it may come to you from unexpected sources. Messages—and their bearers—take many forms. Even when the news seems not-so-good or disappointing, there's often a silver lining such that it turns out to be good news after all. When the Page of Wands appears in a reading, you might anticipate hearing about an important matter in your personal or professional life.

Upright: Message about spiritual growth, creativity.

Reversed: Delay, disappointment.

Ace of Wands

Keywords: The spark.

Meaning: The hand of inspiration emerges from the clouds, sparking a new idea. "Out of thin air," seemingly from nowhere, often come the most amazing, successful ideas. Gift from the Universe or heaven-sent, some might say. In the background of the card the scene is one of fruition and prosperity, supporting growth and abundance. Look at the leaves falling from the staff! Catch one and it may just put your dream right in the palm of your hand. In a reading the Ace of Wands suggests innovative approaches or solutions.

Upright: A new endeavor.

Reversed: False start.

2 of Wands

Keywords: Great expectations.

Meaning: This is the intention card. The man has visualized what he wants, and he focuses on it with great intent. He holds the staff of possibilities in his left hand and the world in his right hand, looking to the sea in anticipation. Are his ships sailing out from port, ready for new endeavors that bring success and profit? Behind him and the firmly anchored staff of present accomplishments are the measures of prosperity already acquired—lush green fields and a grand castle overlooking them. In a Tarot reading the 2 of Wands often signals favorable prospects—perhaps your ship of good fortune has just set sail. You are waiting to see a profit from your enterprise, the new ideas you've set in motion.

Upright: I see it; I believe it; it has already happened.

Reversed: Doubt.

3 of Wands

 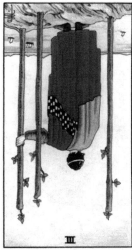

Keywords: Collaboration.

Meaning: Creativity rests on collaboration, on wisely combining your resources with others. Now it is time to anticipate how your venture fares. Like the card's man standing patiently on the shore, you watch as your ships return to you, laden with cargo, the fruits of your efforts. Three is the number of abundance, and the 3 of Wands is the card of potential. In a reading the 3 of Wands suggests you've made the right moves and before long you'll see the fruit of your effort come back to you in some way (and not always the way you expect).

Upright: Put good effort out, and it will come back to you.

Reversed: Get back to the vision; seek collaborators and supporters.

4 of Wands

Keywords: In the flow.

Meaning: This is when it all starts coming together. You are in the continuum. This card depicts a celebration after hard work. You have worked hard and built a good foundation of family, friends, and home. This foundation is itself an achievement, and because it is strong and stable, it can support the design of your dreams. A bountiful arbor welcomes all to share in the joy of the celebration; the high castle walls are solid and safe. When the 4 of Wands appears in a reading, it often points to success and prosperity after you've put forth substantial effort as well as the potential for even greater accomplishments.

Upright: Small victories.

Reversed: Appreciate your accomplishments.

5 of Wands

Keywords: Obstacles and challenges.

Meaning: This card represents a struggle between self-expression and the discipline to sustain a focus. When you are in the middle of a project, you may miss the expansive, creative beginning. Gather discipline and focus to resolve the push-pull between unlimited creativity and stick-to-it-iveness. When you look at the five men on the card, you can see there is no focus in the way they're battling with each other. They are fighting, but without aim or intent. In numerology, 5 is a turning point. When you receive this card in a reading, it's telling you your efforts are intense but potentially futile. Like other 5s in Tarot's Minor Arcana, the 5 of Wands reversed indicates the challenge is past and you can look forward to relief from its pressures. This card, upright or reversed, signals the need to look in a new direction and take your ideas "out of the box" to find a solution with less conflict.

Upright: Time for focus, discipline.

Reversed: Harmony prevails.

6 of Wands

Keywords: Applause.

Meaning: Your discipline pays off. You stuck with it, and you found even more creative solutions. You are even more satisfied with the result. You feel more creative than ever, and your efforts are recognized. You won the battle. And how sweet the taste of success! The 6 of Wands rides triumphantly through an adoring crowd, tall and proud on his white horse. A wreath—the symbol of victory and respect—adorns the staff he holds aloft. When you get the 6 of Wands in a reading, your ideas and efforts are moving toward success and you can be assured that your projects are a forward path.

Upright: Surmounting challenges; finding creative solutions.

Reversed: Opportunities delayed.

7 of Wands

Keywords: Up for the challenge.

Meaning: Your vision is tested by someone from the outside, but now you have the valor to stand your ground. You believe in your project, and you won't compromise or settle for less. The 7 of Wands can't ward off any single blow so he stands at the ready to block all threats. Like him, you may not know who your challenger is, or may face multiple challenges. So you stand firm in your beliefs and confident in your abilities. You are not fighting but rather defending and protecting what you know to be right. When the 7 of Wands appears in a reading, it is telling you to hang in there, you're on the right course and your steadfastness will pay off.

Upright: Stay the course.

Reversed: Surviving a threat.

8 of Wands

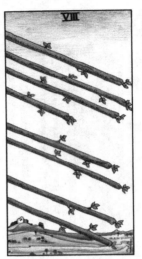 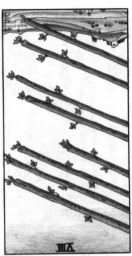

Keywords: In the groove.

Meaning: You are in the home stretch of your project. You feel good luck and enthusiasm are blessing your effort. Results are coming at you from every which way, honed and on target. It's almost too much for you to keep up with but your efforts have generated their own manifestations. You've already done all the work so now all you really have to do is watch the energy of your efforts fly. In numerology 8 is the number of mastery and self-perpetuation. When you receive the 8 of Wands in a Tarot reading, brace yourself! Things are about to start happening for you, and all your efforts will be encouraged.

Upright: Cruisin' right along.

Reversed: A bump in the road.

9 of Wands

Keywords: Spiritual and intuitive strength of vision.

Meaning: You can handle anything. You may have wounds from battle, but you are wiser and stronger. You are on your way. You are well prepared to handle any challenge. But getting what you want isn't easy, and you might be feeling as battered as the poor 9 of Wands appears to be. Worry not, however—appearances are sometimes deceiving. The 9 of Wands has great inner reserves that will carry him through, and so do you. It's time for that final, hard push, and you can do it! When the 9 of Wands appears in a reading, it's a reminder to look within yourself for the strength, determination, tenacity, and courage to bring your ideas and dreams to fruition, and to protect all the good things you have built and accomplished.

Upright: Summon your final reserves.
Reversed: Seek reinforcements.

10 of Wands

Keywords: Too many burdens.

Meaning: This card warns not to take it on all by yourself. It's time to examine your responsibilities. You may be helping others, but at a great cost to yourself. Whether the pinnacle you've reached is lonely or crowded, you're bearing too much of the load. Can you put down one task or responsibility without dropping all of the others? You may have worked yourself into a situation where you cannot. No one is stepping up to give you a hand—maybe they're busy with their own loads or they don't recognize that after helping them you now need help yourself. The 10 of Wands in a Tarot reading is telling you that you're carrying too much yourself. It's time to reprioritize, delegate, and unburden yourself.

Upright: Delegate.
Reversed: Lighten the load.

Cups

Cups represent the emotions and love, and their Element is Water, the realm of the heart.

King of Cups

Keywords: Mastery of compassion, love.

His role: He represents calm dominion over emotions. He is a man who speaks from the heart. He nurtures endeavors in arts, music, nature (particularly the ocean), and home. The king represents logical, compassionate love, the love that comes from a lifetime of experience. He is a great counselor.

Meaning: The King of Cups sits calm and relaxed on his throne, unfazed by the roiling waters that surround him. His dominion is the ocean of the emotions; do you see his Piscean necklace? Pisces is the astrological sign of emotion and intuition. Through wisdom and empathy, the King of Cups brings structure and focus to all that comes from the heart, helping you channel your emotions. When the King of Cups appears in a reading, he often represents someone in your life who is a calming influence, providing comfort and direction in times of emotional turmoil and upheaval.

Upright: Compassion with wisdom.

Reversed: Emotional turbulence.

Queen of Cups

Keywords: The ultimate nurturer.

Her role: She shows us how to give without giving too much. She nurtures our romantic dreams, and she encourages us to trust our intuition.

Meaning: The Queen of Cups is the quintessential nurturer. Her throne rests on a small splash of sandy beach. Gentle ripples lap at the edges of the land. The Queen of Cups sits casually on her throne, the edge of her gown dangling in the water. Do you need a comforting pat on the back or a warm hug? The Queen of Cups has more than enough love to go around! When she shows up in a Tarot reading, she is often nudging you to open your heart and trust in your dreams. After all, look at how ornate her cup appears! She knows how to manifest art and beauty in all her relationships and projects. Whether you are taking a chance with a romantic relationship or pursuing your passion, it's time for you to make that leap of faith.

Upright: Always tuned in to you emotionally.

Reversed: Smothering love.

Knight of Cups

Keywords: Invitation to love.

His role: He encourages us to open our hearts to love. When forgiveness is necessary, he is the one who extends the cup of peace. He can also represent the calling to creativity and self-expression.

Meaning: Sweet and chivalrous, the Knight of Cups guides his horse with deliberation and purpose. He gazes intently straight ahead, letting nothing distract him from his mission. The wings of Mercury, astrology's planetary messenger, adorn his heels and his helmet. You might expect him to dismount and drop to one knee to recite a romantic poem. How could anyone resist? The Knight of Cups often appears in readings when you are falling in love, whether with another person, with a new job or career, or even a place or special interest. He implores you to follow your heart's passion.

Upright: Falling in love; the passionate, romantic side of love.

Reversed: Besotted with love.

Page of Cups

Keywords: Little love notes.

His role: He sends the word: love is in the air. Like all the pages in the Minor Arcana suits cards, he also represents studying and learning. When he comes up, he tells you that you are ready to learn about love.

Meaning: The Page of Cups brings messages of good cheer and comfort, particularly in areas of your life that are emotionally important to you. Is he talking to the fish in his cup (astrology's Pisces, the sign of compassion and emotion)? He's somewhat a silly fellow; it's hard to tell! But that's the essence of the Page of Cups—sweet, fun-loving, and a bit whimsical. When you receive the Page of Cups in a reading, he's telling you that it's time for you to look beneath the surface of your emotions to discover what truly motivates your feelings and interests.

Upright: Sweet, trusting heart.

Reversed: Moody daydreamer.

Ace of Cups

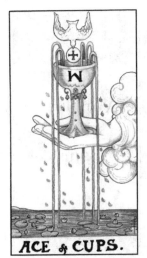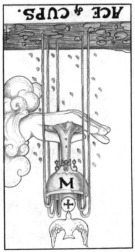

Keywords: Love with wisdom.

Meaning: The heart that is ready to love is a clear, trusting heart. This is the love with integrity card. This is the beginning of a love that is balanced and wise. The white dove in this card is the dove of the spirit, which in many traditions represents the Divine. This is the beginning, the place from which our capacity to love comes. This card represents a spiritual insight that awakens us to new love. Sometimes it means a new baby. When the Ace of Cups appears in a Tarot reading, it reminds you that your capacity to love and be loved is endless.

Upright: Open your heart.

Reversed: Too much, too soon.

2 of Cups

Keywords: Recognizing a soul friend.

Meaning: You meet someone, and you know that person will be your friend, your partner, or your soul mate. A new relationship forms on the basis of equal give and take. This is a relationship that is equally fulfilling for both partners. This card shows a solid partnership being formed. In numerology 2 is the number of balance and harmony. The 2 of Cups shows a man and a woman, the balance of masculine and feminine, yin and yang. As they exchange cups, they remain equal. When you receive the 2 of Cups in a Tarot reading, it suggests a partnership. Though we tend to think in terms of a romantic relationship, the 2 of Cups can represent any kind of equitable partnership in which there are emotional connections, such as between friends, siblings, or business partners. In difficult situations, the 2 of Cups urges empathy and a shared understanding.

Upright: Kindred spirit.

Reversed: Misunderstandings.

3 of Cups

Keywords: Rejoicing in togetherness.

Meaning: There is a lot of love in this room! This card is about acknowledging the gifts of love. Raise your cups to toast your joy and prosperity—both are abundant in the 3 of Cups. When you receive the 3 of Cups in a Tarot reading, it's telling you that you have reason to rejoice. If you are in a new relationship, new job, or new home, this card may represent the "honeymoon" time when exuberance dominates your emotions. Three cheers!

Upright: Joy in uniting with loved ones.

Reversed: Time for apologies.

4 of Cups

Keywords: Restoring yourself.

Meaning: This card can be about taking time out to nurture your individuality within a relationship. It can also signal that you need to be open to receiving love that is being extended to you. The man under the tree is content, yet more satisfaction is being extended to him. This card urges you to make the choice to receive.

When the 4 of Cups appears in a reading, it suggests you are having difficulty accepting what may appear to be gifts or rewards. Maybe you consider yourself undeserving, or you are suspicious of the giver's motivations. The 4 of Cups in a reading encourages you to move past your fears and worries to love yourself and to accept, with joy, love that others offer to you. Sometimes when we feel most alone and aloof from the world is exactly when the inspiration comes and reminds us of the love that waits: three cups (from the 3 of Cups?) sit at the ready, always with you.

Upright: Allegiance to self.

Reversed: Take a new direction.

5 of Cups

Keywords: Despair.

Meaning: Take time out to grieve a loss. Notice that three cups are overturned, but two remain upright and intact. In time, you will heal. Though you cannot recover what has spilled from the three cups (the celebration of the 3 of Cups has passed away from you?), you will be able to fill the cups again. New people and new circumstances will enter your life, and you will again know love and happiness. When the 5 of Cups appears in a reading, you're likely experiencing the end of a relationship. As with other 5s in Tarot's Minor Arcana, the 5 of Cups reversed in a reading signifies that the loss and your pain because of it are now behind you.

Upright: Overcome regret; reach out for love.

Reversed: Hope and happiness return.

6 of Cups

Keywords: Nostalgia.

Meaning: This card can mean that someone from your childhood will come back to you, or it can mean a happy memory will resurface, with some significance to the question at hand. At any rate, it's a perfect moment of balance, pure innocent love. It's the card of good childhood memories that form the basis of present-day happiness. You may feel nostalgic for the past, when life seemed gentler and kinder, and long to bring back these feelings into your current life. The 6 of Cups in a Tarot reading assures you that the innocence and delight of those feelings remains with you, and invites you to reconnect with favorite people, places, and activities.

Upright: Know that you are warm, safe, surrounded by love.

Reversed: Don't live in the past.

7 of Cups

Keywords: Bedazzled, an embarrassment of riches, confusion.

Meaning: This card presents you with too many choices. You are confused, and you must decide what has the most emotional value for you. Take time to step back so you can see the big picture. Maybe you feel you've gotten too much of a good thing in your life, or you got what you thought you wanted but the achievement now feels empty. Perhaps, like the figure on the card, you still want more but can't imagine what more you could possibly want. When you receive the 7 of Cups in a reading, it's telling you that the things that are in abundance are not those that satisfy you at an emotional or spiritual level. Are you lost in the seduction of a dream?

Upright: Shed your illusions.

Reversed: Restored common sense.

8 of Cups

Keywords: Spiritual quest.

Meaning: This card represents getting your emotions in order, which allows you to move ahead with a spiritual or creative quest. The man in this card has done so, taking the steps represented in the first seven cups cards, and is leaving to climb a mountain. You have attained and accepted a great emotional truth. The organization of the cups suggests you've reached a turning point (5 of Cups) and your journey now can lead you toward joy and prosperity (3 of Cups). The Moon, astrology's ruler of emotion and intuition, shines down on the 8 of Cups to lead the way. When the 8 of Cups appears in a reading, it suggests the time has come to follow your true heart.

Upright: Seek the higher path.

Reversed: Come down to Earth.

9 of Cups

Keywords: Wish fulfilled.

Meaning: This card is about contentment. When it comes up in a reading, your relationships will be loving and feel complete, your creativity at a high, your friendships deepening. This is emotional money in the bank. Everyone loves to see the 9 of Cups show up in a reading! This is the card of wishes come true. The man on the card sits like a genie, poised to grant your heart's burning desire. When you receive the 9 of Cups in a Tarot reading, it puts your dreams and goals in the palm of your hand. This card is all about getting, having, or achieving what is most dear to you.

Upright: Contentment.

Reversed: Oh so close … it will come another day.

10 of Cups

Keywords: Happy family, emotional fulfillment.

Meaning: When this card comes up, you are surrounded by loved ones—quite literally your family, or possibly a family of the heart. Contentment and security are yours. Home life, love life, and family life are peaceful. The bonds between all members are solid. The 10 of Cups is the card of emotional completion. All that you've worked for is now securely yours—life partner, family, career, home. The rainbow of love shines brightly in the sky, coloring your life in happiness. When the 10 of Cups appears in a Tarot reading, you are content and fulfilled.

Upright: Permanence of joy, friendship, happiness.

Reversed: Desire for family contentment, but delayed.

Swords

Swords represent the thoughts and ideas, and their Element is Air. Swords show us how we face obstacles and make decisions.

King of Swords

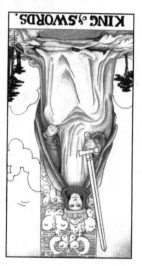

Keywords: Logical adviser, excellent debater.

His role: He tells you to analyze the pros and cons of a situation. He encourages you that you have the power to make good choices.

Meaning: Experienced and analytical, the King of Swords works toward solutions through logic and practicality. He knows there is more than one way to meet every challenge, and he evaluates each option or opportunity to identify its potentials and consequences. He sits forthright on a somewhat austere throne, in full contact with all the Elements. The King of Swords encourages you to empower yourself in the same fashion. You have enough time to explore your options; there is no value in rushing to what appears the obvious solution if it is the wrong answer for your circumstance. When the King of Swords appears in a reading, his message is to examine your situation from all perspectives.

Upright: A brainstormer.

Reversed: Mental exhaustion.

Queen of Swords

Keywords: Clear, logical thought, excellent teacher.

Her role: She represents spirit-penetrating matter, resulting in clarity. She has a sharp mind, like the Greek goddess Athena. She is a keen observer of people. Her role is to encourage you to act on your clear, well-thought-out logic.

Meaning: The Queen of Swords sees beyond the surface. Like the King, she knows things are not always what they appear. But insight and observation, rather than analysis, rule her thoughts and actions. She sits in profile on her throne, looking both inward and outward, with her head above the clouds and feet on the ground. Not much escapes her notice or hides from her scrutiny; secrets and deceptions fall away under her gaze. And don't think she'll let you dally! This Queen is all about action. When the Queen of Swords appears in a Tarot reading, she is telling you, "you know the best thing to do, now do it!"

Upright: Shrewd, discerning, succinct.

Reversed: A muddle, sometimes narrow-minded.

Knight of Swords

Keywords: Cutting to the chase.

His role: He keeps you alert. He just tells the truth. He informs you of something vital. He's a mover and shaker. Notice he is on a racehorse. Movement is fast. He is action that demands results.

Meaning: The Knight of Swords charges fearlessly into the fray. Though he may appear impetuous and even a bit brash, he is skilled and knowledgeable. Beneath his youthful energy lies a vast store of experience and ability that he draws from almost without conscious thought. He wastes no time looking for the path of least resistance but instead cuts through the most direct path. In a reading, his presence usually indicates the need to act quickly—but be careful not to act too quickly!

Upright: Stay on alert.
Reversed: Opposition.

Page of Swords

Keywords: The watchdog.

His role: The Page of Swords keeps you in line with your values. He's a quick thinker, someone with good instincts. He urges you to look deeper into the meaning of the situation at hand. He communicates caution and helpful advice.

Meaning: The Page of Swords brings advice of caution and prudence. Particularly adept at detecting deception and revealing secrets, the Page of Swords watches your back as much as he counsels your actions. With his sword upraised and at the ready, he stands attentively above the landscape. He is prepared to move quickly when circumstances require fast action. When the Page of Swords appears in a reading, he's telling you to be vigilant, especially in your dealings with other people. He may represent someone who has a hidden agenda or who is keeping information from you.

Upright: Skillful vigilance.
Reversed: Hyper-vigilance.

Ace of Swords

Keywords: Sharp, clear direction.

Meaning: This card cuts through the dead wood. This sword is double-edged: it can be constructive by hacking out the old stuff that no longer serves you, or it can cut deep, to the truth that hurts. It can force a situation to come to a head. This card is ultimately about forward-thinking and focused action, so it signals success. It says the new ideas and swift action will win the day. When the Ace of Swords turns up in a Tarot reading, you may be facing a situation that requires fresh thinking and quick response for a favorable outcome.

Upright: Test your mettle.

Reversed: Ease up.

2 of Swords

Keywords: A decision has been made; a decision needs to be made.

Meaning: This card can mean a decision has been made, thus the commanding posture of the woman by the calm sea. Or it can mean that you have been at a stalemate, and it's time to make a decision, because all information has been gathered, and it's time to act. The blindfold suggests justice—as in justice is blind—and that the decision will be fair and honorable, restoring peace. The 2 of Swords in a reading tells you that whatever decision you make, it will resolve the question or challenge in a way that leaves everyone satisfied. The 2 of Swords has confident power and strength. Look at how she's holding those swords! With the intuitive power of the Moon and the help of her blindfold (yes, help!), the 2 of Swords is free to feel with her mind and act decisively on what she intuits as the right decision.

Upright: Time to compromise.

Reversed: A compromise has been made.

3 of Swords

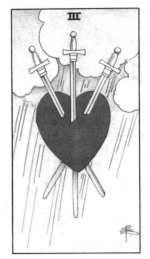 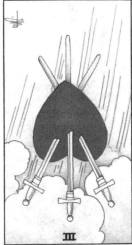

Keywords: Pierced through the heart.

Meaning: This is sorrow experienced at the deepest level. This card may signal a separation, breakup, deep dissatisfaction, or quarrel—about someone or something that really mattered to you. It's a time for pain and sorrow, but the card signals to you to work through your grief, that it's not infinite, and you can get through it. Remember, 3 is the number of creativity. Though your situation may seem as dark and foreboding as the storm clouds on the card, storms are nature's way—sometimes dramatic and even frightening—of clearing the way for new opportunities. But like the darkest storm, this, too, will pass. When you receive the 3 of Swords in a Tarot reading, it both validates your current loss and reminds you that you can heal to become stronger.

Upright: Grieve the loss.

Reversed: You're on the mend from a heart-break.

4 of Swords

 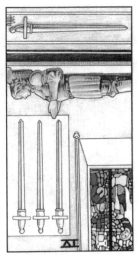

Keywords: Replenish, rejuvenate.

Meaning: This card urges you to take time out. It's time to reflect on what you have accomplished and to replenish yourself for the next step. Often it points to restoring yourself by going back to your roots, exploring your family background or just returning to "home base"—the source of support and love in your life. This card reminds us that introspection, contemplation, and stillness are vital to restoring our well-being and clarity. When the 4 of Swords appears in a reading, it suggests that you set aside your sword, for the moment, and go within yourself. You are safe within the inner sanctum of your being. Think yoga's corpse pose, shavasana.

Upright: Retreat to stillness.

Reversed: You're alive again!

5 of Swords

Keywords: The war zone.

Meaning: This card warns you that you might just be spoiling for a fight—or someone might be bullying you. Examine what you're angry about. Notice any resentments you have building toward others. Notice if you are feeling selfish and insensitive to others' feelings. Have you inadvertently robbed someone of his or her power or energy—or has someone done that to you? This card depicts a conflict that is unequal and unfair, maybe even abusive. Like many of the Minor Arcana, this card presents a choice. You can neutralize it if you heed its advice. When you receive the 5 of Swords in a reading, take a step back to objectively examine a situation. This card represents an opportunity to right things before they become destructive. You are holding on to something that has broken up or broken down, and you may not even realize it as the others walk away. For swordplay to begin again, what is broken must be mended.

Upright: Don't fight it—learn from it!

Reversed: Back on equal footing.

6 of Swords

Keywords: Struggle no more.

Meaning: This card represents more than just a change of scenery. You have decided to leave the strife and seek a higher place. A difficult cycle has come to an end. You are moving out of rough seas to calm waters. You have made the right decision, and the healing has begun. You are bringing with you only what is essential, no heavy baggage. Opportunity awaits on the not-so-distant shore, and the water you must cross is smooth and still. When the 6 of Swords appears in a reading, it indicates completion, acceptance, and hope. Notice the forces of yin and yang, active and receiving, so nicely balanced in this card by the young man who ferries his loved ones through the waters.

Upright: Finding a better way.

Reversed: Stuck—you tried to leave it behind, but something is holding you back.

7 of Swords

Keywords: A deception.

Meaning: This card warns you of conditions around you. It could be you or someone near you, but somewhere near you, someone is being less than honest. You don't know the whole truth. This is sometimes called the "thief" card, but know that someone is deceiving you. You may have to be just as ruthless. The 7 of Swords shows up in a reading to warn you that while you're relaxing and enjoying yourself (see the circus tents in the background?), you are about to lose a good deal of something that is important to you. Don't come out of the tent after the show to find that you've been cut short! But there is also a playfulness to this card—making off with something and being delighted to have gotten away with it. In a reading, this card contains either the lighter or darker energy of sneaky behavior; look carefully at its placement and the surrounding cards.

Upright: Forewarned is forearmed.

Reversed: The truth will out.

8 of Swords

Keywords: Immobilized by fear.

Meaning: This card reveals to you that you are letting your fears imprison you. Notice that there is a castle in the distance—a place of refuge. This woman is blindfolded—blinded by her fear—and can't see the way to safety is near. This card warns you that your fear is rendering you helpless, and it presents the choice that you can let go of those fears. When the 8 of Swords appears in a Tarot reading, it's encouraging you to cut through your fears so you can manifest your dreams and desires (make it to the castle). After all, look at all of the swords waiting to be put into action. In a reading, this card can hold the energy of confused ideas or good energies that you can't figure out how to act upon. What a contrast to the intuitive power of the 2 of Swords!

Upright: Feel the fear, do it anyway.

Reversed: New hope to see beyond the fear.

9 of Swords

Keywords: Despair, nightmares.

Meaning: Some call this the nightmare card. We call this the "being-too-hard-on-yourself card." The woman in the card has lost hope. She is letting anxiety and despair overwhelm her. She is taking on too much. This card reminds you to make a different choice. Previous grief, loss, or depression can all bring out the 9 of Swords. But in the light of day, the oppressive nature of a nightmare fades away. You can see it was only a bad dream. The 9 of Swords in a reading is a call to wake up and see the reality of your situation. Contrast this energy with the peaceful energy of the 4 of Swords. Despair can keep you from accessing peace of mind and the restorative power that allows you to draw the sword of action and accomplish your goals. Look at all those swords! Instead of perceiving them as danger or despair, call on your inner calm, assertive energy, and reach up and grab one!

Upright: Sleepless with worry.

Reversed: Time heals, bringing a new day.

10 of Swords

Keywords: It's over.

Meaning: This card tells you that the cycle you have just experienced is dead—really dead. This card signals that what has just ended has karmic significance, too. It reminds us that a major trauma can break down our will, but it presents the hope that all is not lost. The karmic debt has been paid. The 10 of Swords can also represent a pattern put to rest. In numerology, 10 is the number of completion and rebirth. When you receive the 10 of Swords in a Tarot reading, it tells you the past no longer holds you. You are free to move ahead in a new direction.

Upright: What is done, is done.

Reversed: Dawn of a new day.

Pentacles

Pentacles represent our resources in this world—health, wealth, and talents. Their Element is Earth, and they represent really getting down to business.

King of Pentacles

Keywords: Mastery of prosperity.

His role: He is generous, yet wise with his money. He is proud and self-reliant, and he has the work ethic to make strategic decisions that bring prosperity to his family. He is the ultimate financial adviser.

Meaning: The King of Pentacles holds much wealth and abundance within his control. Wise and experienced, he knows how to manage his resources for perpetual growth. Seeds are as important to him as harvest. The King of Pentacles has worked hard for his riches and so values them for the effort and achievement they represent, yet he is generous in sharing his wealth with others. When the King of Pentacles appears in a Tarot reading, he suggests a solid investment. This may be investment in a person, a project, or situation. The King of Pentacles often represents someone who is solid and secure.

Upright: A wise and benevolent resource.

Reversed: Materialistic dreamer, but can't make it happen.

Queen of Pentacles

Keywords: Down-to-Earth prosperity.

Her role: She reminds you that you are meant to prosper. She is a fertile, creative, and wise woman who knows how to attract the abundance to provide for her loved ones. She is tasteful and generous. She tends a lovely garden. She creates beauty around her. She is scrupulous with money.

Meaning: Natural opulence and beauty surround the Queen of Pentacles. She seems to grow right out of the landscape, being herself the fruit of the gardens she so diligently tends. The arbor above her head is always in bloom, sheltering her in prosperity. The Queen of Pentacles uses her resources to support and nurture prosperity in others. When the Queen of Pentacles turns up in a reading, she suggests abundance and wealth, both in relationships and in circumstances. She may represent a generous benefactor who supports and encourages your efforts and endeavors.

Upright: Abundant love.

Reversed: Hard financial times, financial dependence.

Knight of Pentacles

Keywords: Trustworthy, hardworking.

His role: He is the cultivator, developing new prospects, and his realm is work and creativity, where he works hard, with a thorough, steady hand. He reminds you that you have the skills to get ahead. He symbolizes solidity and stability.

Meaning: The Knight of Pentacles is strong and steady. His steed is a sturdy work horse, capable of carrying him long distances and pulling heavy loads. The Knight of Pentacles knows it is persistent effort that pays off in the end, and he is both capable and willing to put in that effort. When you receive the Knight of Pentacles in a reading, he's telling you to buckle down and stay the course. Determination and persistence carve the road to prosperity, and your efforts will soon produce results. This knight carries the energy of the facilitator; when he appears you will know that you have faithful earth energy to assist and nurture you.

Upright: Nose to the grindstone.

Reversed: Giving in to futility.

Page of Pentacles

Keywords: Stick-to-it-iveness, practicality.

His role: The Page of Pentacles reminds you to study and learn practical things—and just stick with it. He signals that you will learn the skills you need for your endeavor. He models the art of giving careful study before you act.

Meaning: The Page of Pentacles investigates how things work. Ever practical, he is on a constant quest for more effective and efficient ways to work. Though he believes in steady effort, he also believes in not wasting thoughts or actions. The Page of Pentacles examines both his resources and his achievements. He is not about to squander either one. When the Page of Pentacles appears in a Tarot reading, he's telling you to study your situation before committing to a course of action. Maybe the actions you're about to take are the most effective but maybe there are other approaches that can make your efforts more productive. His message is always grounded in earthy practicality.

Upright: Industriousness.

Reversed: No follow through.

Ace of Pentacles

Keywords: Seeds of success.

Meaning: With just this one coin, extended out of the clouds by a benevolent hand, you can make great things. This card heralds the beginning of prosperity. If it comes up when you start a new career or business, your effort will certainly be blessed. This is the seed money. When you receive the Ace of Pentacles in a reading, it suggests you have a great opportunity to turn an idea into an accomplishment. Someone or something is there to give you the resources you need. The earth has given you a wonderful opening in the garden's arbor; are you ready to pass through and make the journey?

Upright: Taking raw passion or vision, turning it into something grounded.

Reversed: Get prepared; get everything in order.

2 of Pentacles

Keywords: Multiplying.

Meaning: Your efforts are multiplying, and you are able to juggle your many resources. You have the capability to balance growth, even with change. You are flexible with your money and weigh the pros and cons well. Though you may question your ability to keep everything moving smoothly, notice the band around the coins to help keep them in place—and notice that the band forms the infinity symbol. When the 2 of Pentacles shows up in a reading, you might be in a situation of determining how to use your resources for optimal productivity. Perhaps you have two competing job offers or an opportunity to move to another city. The 2 of Pentacles tells you that you will find the right, infinitely divine balance.

Upright: Learning about investing your energies.

Reversed: Struggling to stay afloat.

3 of Pentacles

Keywords: Making your luck.

Meaning: Now your efforts and talents are acknowledged. This card tells you that you are on the right track. You have won recognition for your work, and you are creating a reputation for top-quality work—which will bring you more customers. You've worked hard to get to where you are and your talents and abilities are in demand. Like on the card, people are lining up for your services. When you get the 3 of Pentacles in a reading, it suggests that you've finally arrived as a success in your field of endeavor.

Upright: Building a name for yourself.

Reversed: Strive for excellence.

4 of Pentacles

Keywords: Investing in yourself.

Meaning: You have achieved a level of security. You have good judgment, and you are in command of your talents and resources. You are security conscious. Like the man on the card, you are not about to let go of anything you've worked so hard to achieve. This guy has his resources firmly under-foot. The city behind him symbolizes continued demand for his talents. The 4 of Pentacles shows up in a reading to show you that your groundwork has paid off. You are now the master of your resources, and you can use them to build the future of your desires. You are the skyscraper on the skyline! You are the Trump Tower, the Safeco Field, the Eiffel Tower.

Upright: Trust that you have a secure foundation.

Reversed: Don't hold on too tight; don't be a miser.

5 of Pentacles

Keywords: See it, believe it!

Meaning: This card comes up when you need to recognize just how many resources you have. This card depicts two homeless people out in the snow, passing by the warmth of a church. You may need to reach out; but just like the figures in this card, the help is already there. This card reminds you that you don't need to be self-sufficient. It can signal that earlier in life, you experienced abandonment or betrayal. So it presents the choice of trust—trusting that good things are within your reach. You might receive the 5 of Pentacles in a reading when things don't look to be going so well for you. Its message, however, is one of hope—others are there to give you a helping hand. Sometimes it is as powerful to accept help as it is to offer it. Have the courage to accept help, and allow the warmth of friendship and community to reach you.

Upright: Learn interdependence and trust.

Reversed: Triumph over trying times.

6 of Pentacles

Keywords: Generosity.

Meaning: This card signals that you will receive help or money or both—just when you need it. It signals generosity from others and extra benefits. It also may signal you to be generous. The 6 of Pentacles represents balance between resources (your abilities to generate prosperity) and abundance (the fruits of your efforts). In the circle of life, what goes around comes around. Though often you cannot repay those who have been generous to you, you can continue the circle by giving to others who are in need. The 6 of Pentacles appears in a reading as a reminder to share your resources so others may also prosper.

Upright: Generosity begets more prosperity.

Reversed: A bonus, with strings attached.

7 of Pentacles

Keywords: Considering the harvest.

Meaning: This card is the "sow and you will reap" card, because it depicts a farmer who is assessing his crops, preparing them for harvest. It signals that you have put your time and effort into your ambition, and it will pay off. The 7 of Pentacles has worked hard to cultivate and nurture his resources. Even as he pauses to admire the fruits of his labor, he knows he must continue to till the soil and plant the new seeds that will grow into tomorrow's abundance. When you get the 7 of Pentacles in a reading, it suggests you may soon harvest the bounty of your own hard work. Don't stand back too long though—there's another pentacle to plant!

Upright: Patience, hard work.

Reversed: Be cautious where you invest your energy.

8 of Pentacles

Keywords: Mastering your craft.

Meaning: This card shows that you have really gotten it down. You have sharpened your skills. You have paid your dues and put in your time, and you are at the point where your work is at its best. Your hard work has paid off. Like the artisan on the card, you've mastered your processes and manage your resources well. You maintain consistent quality and there is a steady market for your talents or products. The 8 of Pentacles turns up in a reading to tell you your efforts have been worthwhile. You have become a master at your craft and everybody knows it. Yet there is always more to do and to learn, and the 8 of Pentacles is intent on continuing to grow earth energy skyward.

Upright: Keep doing what you do best.

Reversed: Bolster your productivity by nurturing skills, developing tools.

9 of Pentacles

Keywords: It's paid off.

Meaning: This card tells you that you are right on target. This woman is calm and peaceful in the surroundings of her garden—and it's abundant. She is secure, and she not only has achieved much, she is surrounded by loved ones. She is content. This card represents self-sufficiency, independence, and self-mastery. In numerology, 9 is the number of completion. When you receive the 9 of Pentacles in a Tarot reading, it suggests that you have achieved all that you set out to accomplish and then some. You've earned the right to enjoy your abundance! The garden you have planted is yielding its bounty and you are free to enjoy and explore effortlessly its natural splendor. Think of the poet Stanley Kunitz and his marvelous New England garden, tended for a lifetime, and written about in *The Wild Braid*.

Upright: Enjoy the rewards of your hard work.

Reversed: Tend to your security.

10 of Pentacles

Keywords: A lifetime legacy of prosperity.

Meaning: Not only have your hard work and talent paid off, they will leave a legacy for others. You will be able to share this prosperity—financial and emotional—with your loved ones. This card represents the riches you have dreamed of—and being able to share them with those you love. You can fully enjoy your accomplishments. Your abundance now provides security and opportunity for others in your life. When the 10 of Pentacles comes to you in a reading, it tells you that your life—present and future—is secure. You have built a lasting foundation, your project or relationship will endure for the ages and through the generations.

Upright: Pinnacle of prosperity.

Reversed: Family conflicts jeopardize wealth.

The Road Ahead

Now you are ready to try your hand at interpreting the Journey of Life for others. It can be an exciting way to connect with yourself and others. With just a little bit of insight, and a lot of intuition, you can get a good glimpse of wisdom for shaping your past, present, and future. Reading Tarot spreads is an art form that only gets better as you go deeper into the experience. And what a rich experience it is, this story of your life.

The Least You Need to Know

- ◆ Each of the Major Arcana is associated with an archetype.
- ◆ All cards are associated with astrology and the signs of the zodiac.
- ◆ All cards have numbers and draw on the meanings of numerology.
- ◆ The suit cards—Wands, Cups, Swords, and Pentacles—depict the cycles of life, from Ace to 10.
- ◆ Each card holds key energies revealed in upright and reversed meanings.
- ◆ When interpreting the symbols and imagery of a Tarot card in a Tarot reading, it's okay to trust your instinct.

Appendix **A**

Glossary

Tarot Basics

Cups The suit of Cups is about the heart. It's about emotions and creativity. Cups are associated with the Element Water.

Destiny Destiny is what you are given to work with in life. Destiny is about your life's purpose, your life tasks, and your talents and skills. Think of it this way: you are born either a boy or a girl, and you are born to certain parents living in a certain city. That's what you start out with—your destiny—and the rest is up to you.

Free Will Free Will means that you still have a choice about how you will work with what you're given. You can struggle against it—and sometimes that's a good idea. Or you can accept it. You can use it for harm or for good. But the choice is up to you.

Journey of Life Within the Journey of Life are cycles. The first 10 cards of the Major Arcana are the Cycle of Self, in which you learn the basic lessons of life. The next cycle, which begins with the Wheel of Fortune, is the Cycle of Tests. In this cycle, you are presented with challenges that test your values and your strengths. The final cycle is the Cycle of Attainment. It starts with the Star, the card of faith and hope. In this cycle, you begin to see the rewards of the journey.

Major Arcana The 22 cards of the Major Arcana represent the Journey of Life. Each card in the Major Arcana is like a key character acting out a scene from the journey. The Major Arcana are archetypes—personalities that are common to human experience. We all know someone we can think of when we think of the Emperor or the Devil—right? The Major Arcana reveal what we are destined to learn in life.

Minor Arcana The 56 cards of the Minor Arcana represent our everyday choices. They are the plotline, if you will, in the story. They depict life's ups and downs.

Pentacles The suit of Pentacles is about your resources. It can be about material worth and money, but it can also be about your talents and your ability to use them wisely. Pentacles are associated with the Element Earth.

Querent The person who is asking the question of the Tarot. It can be the person for whom you are doing a reading, or it can be yourself. The Querent's energy always influences a reading.

Reversed cards When a card comes up reversed in a spread, it usually means that the energy of that card is blocked or delayed, or the opposite will happen.

Suits Within the Minor Arcana, there are four suits—Wands, Cups, Swords, and Pentacles. (See individual entries for *Wands*, *Cups*, *Swords*, and *Pentacles*.) Each suit has a King, Queen, Knight, Page, and Ace through 10.

Swords The suit of Swords is about thinking and deciding. The cards in this suit show you how you are going about finding the truth and reasoning out your choices. Swords are associated with the Element Air.

Wands The suit of Wands is about passion. It's about having a vision for success and achieving your goals. It's also the Suit of personal growth. Wands are associated with the Element Fire.

Tarot Tools

Astrological Power Points In astrology, three key signs are your Power Points—Sun, Moon, and Ascendant. These core signs determine a lot about your personality. So when the cards that are linked to your Power Point signs come up, pay lots of attention to them.

Life Path card Everyone has a Life Path card, and many people have two. Your Life Path card is a card in the Major Arcana that's all about the unique lessons you must master in your lifetime. Your Life Path card is based on the numerology of your birth date.

Numerology Each card in the Tarot has a number. In numerology, all numbers are reduced to single digits. Each number has a meaning. For instance, the number 1 is about starting new things; 2 is about building partnerships.

Personal Year Each year, you have a Personal Year, which is sort of a curriculum for that year. Your Personal Year is also based on numerology, using your birth date with the current year. This number also correlates with a Major Arcana card. For instance, if your Personal Year is 14, you are having a Temperance kind of year (sorry!).

Timing Each of the suits has its own timing: Wands are days to weeks, Cups are weeks to months, Swords are hours to days, Pentacles are months to years. Timing also is indicated by the position of a card in a spread.

Appendix B

Resources

Arrien, Angeles. *The Tarot Handbook*, Sonoma, CA: Arcus Publishing Co., 1987.

———. *The Tarot Handbook: Practical Applications of Ancient Visual Symbols*. New York: Jeremy P. Tarcher/Putnam, 1997.

Berkowitz, Rita, and Deborah S. Romaine. *Empowering Your Life with Angels*. Indianapolis: Alpha Books, 2003.

Carlson, Laura. *Tarot Unveiled: The Method to Its Magic*. Stamford, CT: U.S. Games Systems, Inc., 1988.

Celestine, *The Mammoth Book of Fortune Telling*. New York: Carroll & Graf, 1997.

Cheiro. *Cheiro's Book of Numbers*. New York: Arcos Publishing Co., 1977.

Connolly, Eileen. *Tarot: a New Handbook for the Apprentice*. North Hollywood, CA: Newcastle Publishing Co., 1979.

Dyer, Wayne W. *The Power of Intention: Learning to Co-Create Your World Your Way*. Santa Monica, CA: Hay House, 2004.

Fairfield, Gail. *Choice Centered Tarot*. Smithville, IN: Ramp Creek Publishing, 1984.

Flynn, Carolyn, and Arlene Tognetti. *The Intuitive Arts on Health: Using Astrology, Tarot, and Psychic Intuition to See Your Future*. Indianapolis: Alpha Books, 2003.

Flynn, Carolyn, and Erica Tismer. *Empowering Your Life with Massage.* Indianapolis: Alpha Books, 2004.

Flynn, Carolyn, and Gary R. McClain, *The Complete Idiot's Guide to Oracles.* Indianapolis: Alpha Books, 2006.

Flynn, Carolyn, and Shari Just, Ph.D. *The Complete Idiot's Guide to Creative Visualization.* Indianapolis: Alpha Books, 2005.

Fox, Matthew. *Creativity: Where the Divine and Human Meet.* New York: Jeremy P. Tarcher, 2002.

Garen, Nancy. *Tarot Made Easy.* New York: Fireside (Simon & Schuster), 1989.

Gerwick-Brodeur, Madeline, and Lisa Lenard. *The Complete Idiot's Guide to Astrology, Third Edition.* Indianapolis: Alpha Books, 2003.

Gleason, Katherine A., and Arlene Tognetti. *The Intuitive Arts on Money: Using Astrology, Tarot, and Psychic Intuition to See Your Future.* Indianapolis: Alpha Books, 2003.

Gray, Eden. *The Complete Guide to the Tarot.* New York: Bantam, 1972.

———. *Mastering the Tarot.* New York: Penguin, 1988.

Greer, Mary. *Tarot for Your Self.* North Hollywood, CA: Newcastle Publishing, 1984.

Jewell, Cathy, and Arlene Tognetti. *The Intuitive Arts on Family: Using Astrology, Tarot, and Psychic Intuition to See Your Future.* Indianapolis: Alpha Books, 2003.

Lenard, Lisa, and Arlene Tognetti. *The Intuitive Arts on Love: Using Astrology, Tarot, and Psychic Intuition to See Your Future.* Indianapolis: Alpha Books, 2003.

Louis, Anthony. *Tarot, Plain and Simple.* St. Paul, MN: Llewellyn, 1997.

Martello, Leo Louis. *Reading the Tarot.* Garden City Park, NY: Avery Publishing Group, 1990.

Myss, Caroline. *Sacred Contracts: Awakening Your Divine Potential.* New York: Harmony Books, 2001.

Pond, David, and Lucy Pond. *The Metaphysical Handbook.* Port Angeles, WA: Reflecting Pond Publications, 1984.

Romaine, Deborah S., and Arlene Tognetti. *The Intuitive Arts on Work: Using Astrology, Tarot, and Psychic Intuition to See Your Future.* Indianapolis: Alpha Books, 2003.

Thibodeau, Lauren, Ph.D. *Natural-Born Intuition: How to Awaken and Develop Your Inner Wisdom.* Franklin Lakes, NJ: New Page Books, 2005.

Tognetti, Arlene, and Lisa Lenard. *The Complete Idiot's Guide to Tarot, Second Edition.* Indianapolis: Alpha Books, 2003.

Wanless, James, and Angeles Arrien, eds. *Wheel of Tarot* (anthology). Carmel, CA: Merrill-West Publishing, 1992.

Wilson, Joyce. *The Complete Book of Palmistry.* New York: Bantam Books, 1980.

Tarot's Classic Spreads (and a Few More!)

Here is a quick guide to the Tarot spreads we teach you how to use in this book. Have fun reading the Tarot, and always hold positive intent.

Celtic Cross This classic 10-card spread is the ultimate storyteller. Many people swear by this spread, and only this one. The Celtic Cross gives you an in-depth look at the situation. It can do a whole-person scan of your life at that moment in time. It derives from the Druid storytelling tradition.

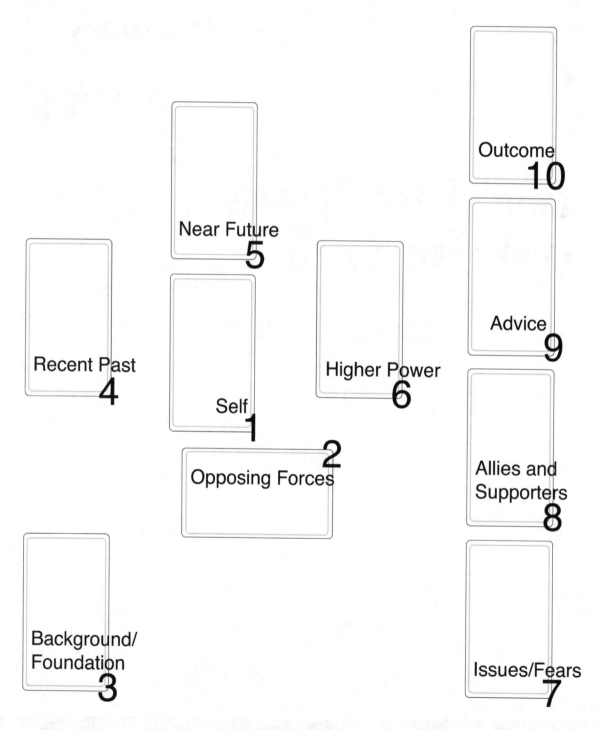

Celtic Cross Cover   This spread doubles the strength of the Celtic Cross by adding a card on top of each of the 10 cards in a Celtic Cross spread. Each card adds a little more to the story of the Celtic Cross.

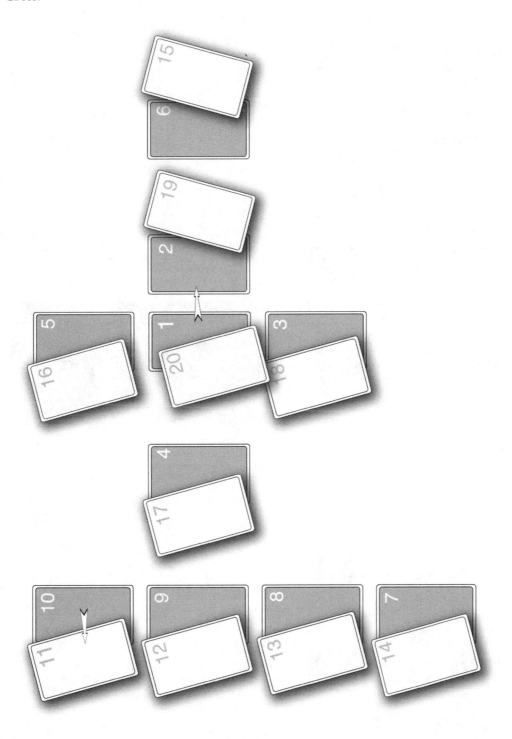

Chakra This seven-card spread is like taking your annual physical checkup. It tells you about seven aspects of your health and well-being, showing how each is in balance.

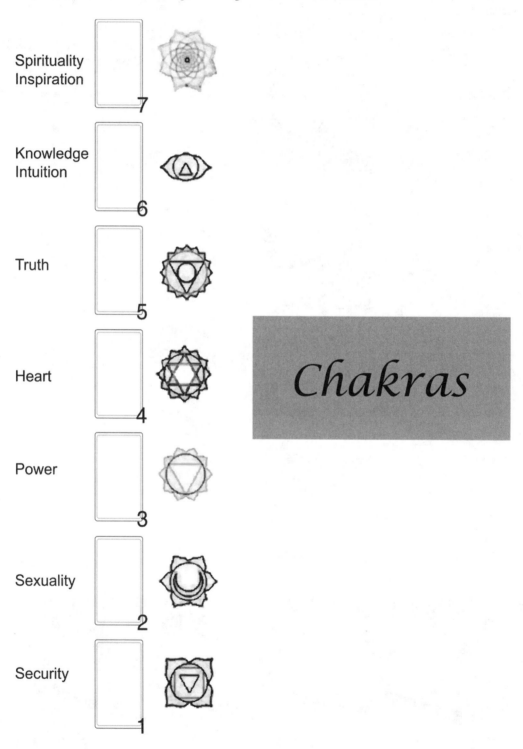

Spirituality
Inspiration

7

Knowledge
Intuition

6

Truth

5

Heart

4

Chakras

Power

3

Sexuality

2

Security

1

Compatibility The nine-card Compatibility spread reveals the foundation of a relationship, as well as the areas for growth.

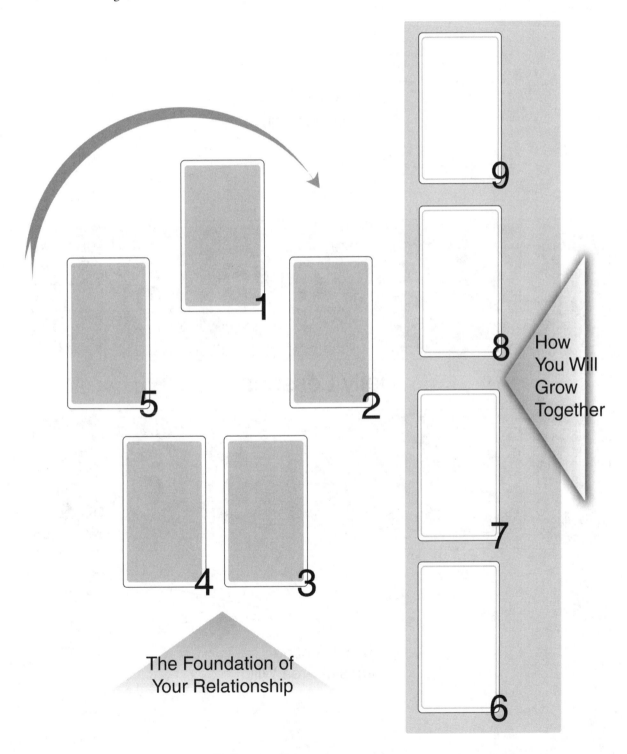

Daily Lessons   This spread uses 14 cards to assess the lessons of the day and explore both karmic forces of Destiny at play, and the application of Free Will to resolve the conditions surrounding the situation.

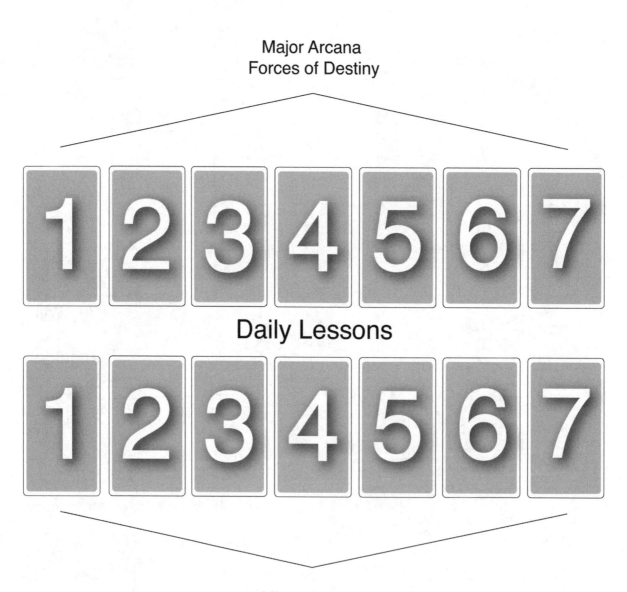

Decision This nine-card spread shows the past decisions that created the situation, the conditions of the present moment, and the future outcome of your choices. This is a good spread for questions of timing, whether or when to do something.

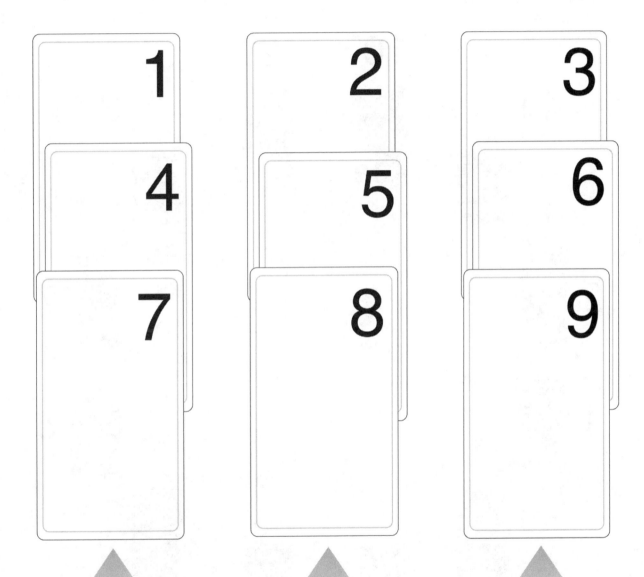

Past Decisions that Created the Situation

Conditions of the Present Moment

Future Outcomes of Your Choices

Destiny   This is the Horoscope spread, using the Major Arcana only, one card for each month in an upcoming year. For added depth, use your astrological birth chart paired with the Major Arcana cards. You may want to enlist the guidance of a professional Tarot/astrology reader to help interpret a Destiny birth chart spread.

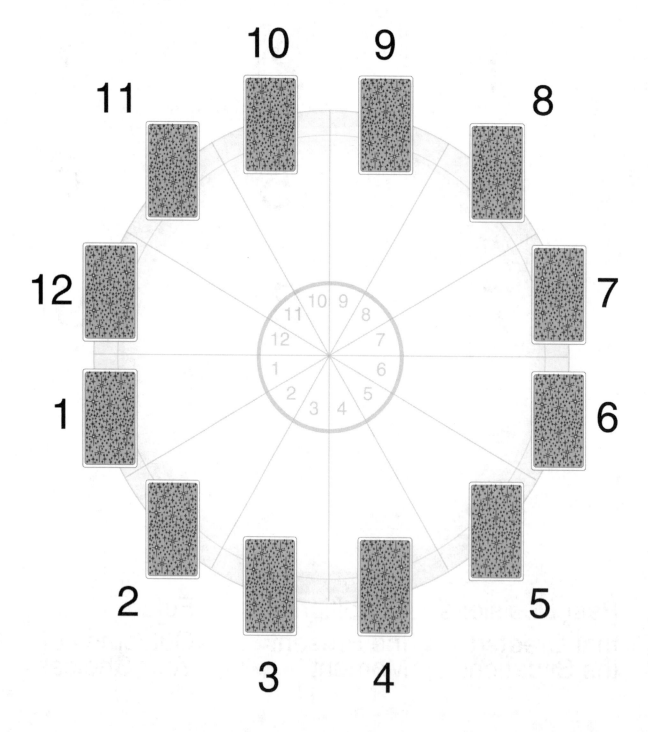

Diamond This four-card spread can be used to look at the influence of the Elements, and is good for exploring balance. See also Karma spread.

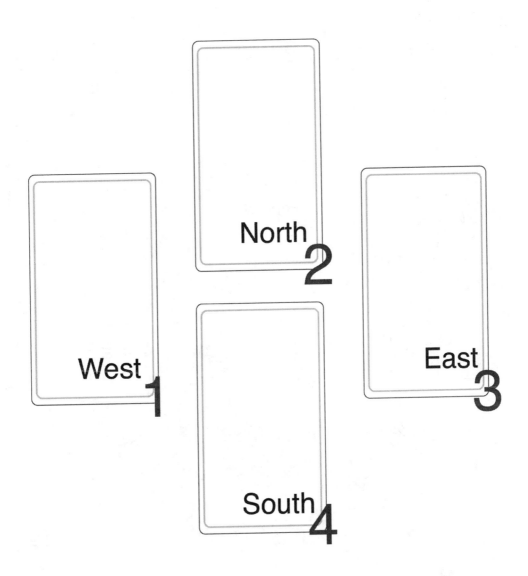

Feng Shui This spread uses the ancient Chinese practice of Feng Shui, a method of arranging spaces to draw in positive energy. Each Tarot card in the spread corresponds to one of the nine areas, called *guas*, of the Feng Shui bagua. The concept of the guas is similar to astrology's zodiac houses.

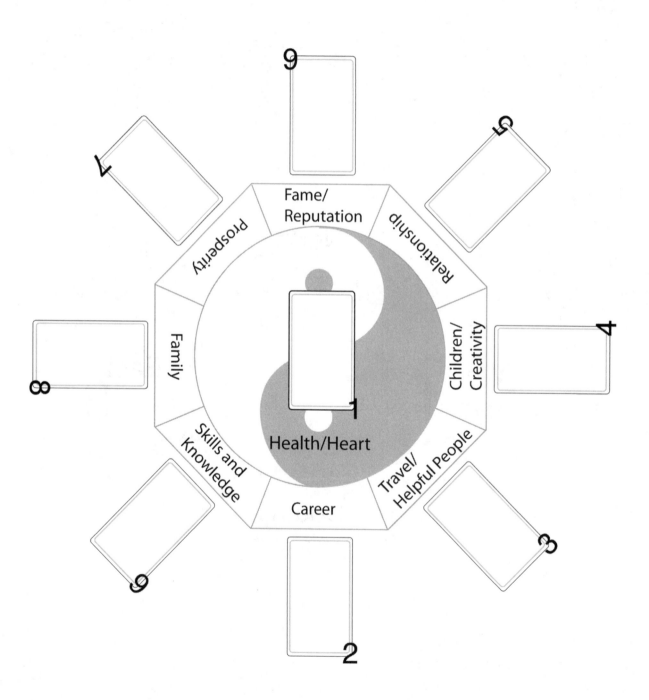

Horoscope This spread uses 12 cards, matching each to a month in the year ahead. Sometimes you match the 12 cards to the houses of the zodiac. This is the Zodiac Horoscope spread.

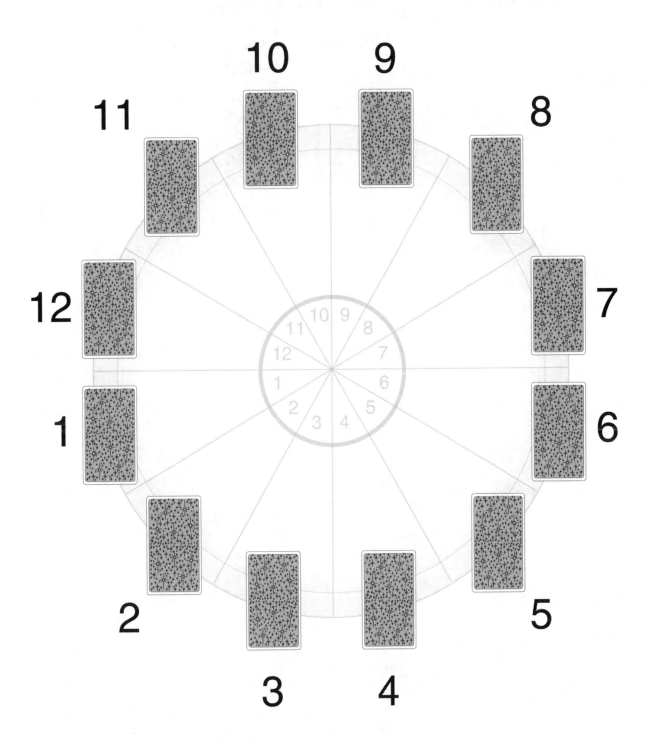

Intuition/Logic This eight-card spread shows you the interplay of intuition and logic in your decision-making style. It can help you trust your decisions more, or it can help you realize that you need to add a little more logic or a little more intuition into your style.

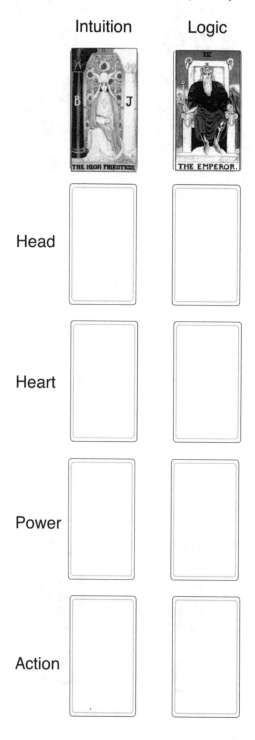

Karma   The Karma spread uses four cards arranged like a diamond. Each card tells about the lessons you must learn to progress to a higher level of awareness.

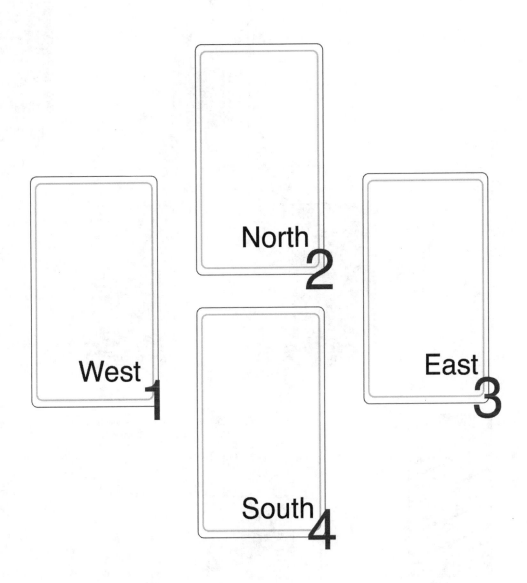

Letting Go   This six-card spread uses two three-card groupings. The first shows what you are hanging on to; the second shows you the ways you are letting go.

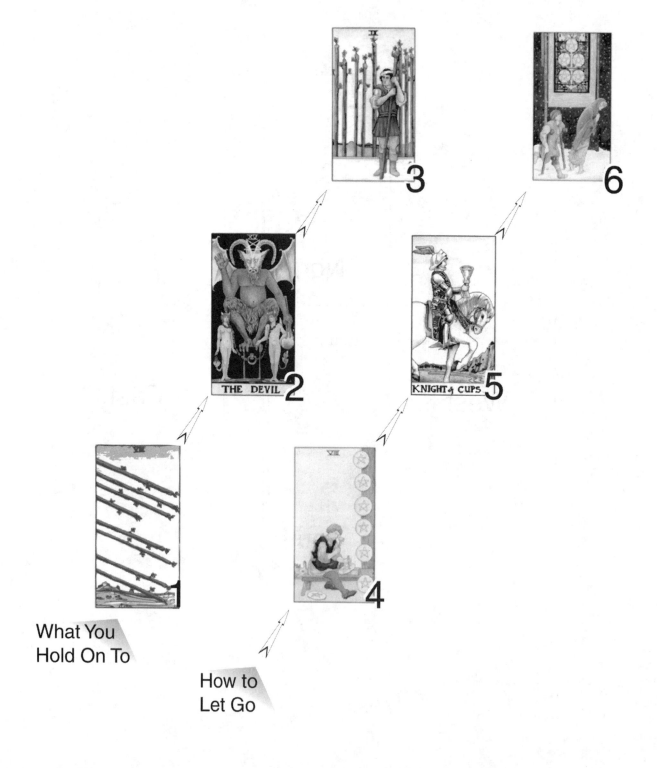

Life Path   This spread uses the Major Arcana only. It's an at-a-glance road map of your life lessons. It consists of five cards arranged around your two (or one) Life Path cards.

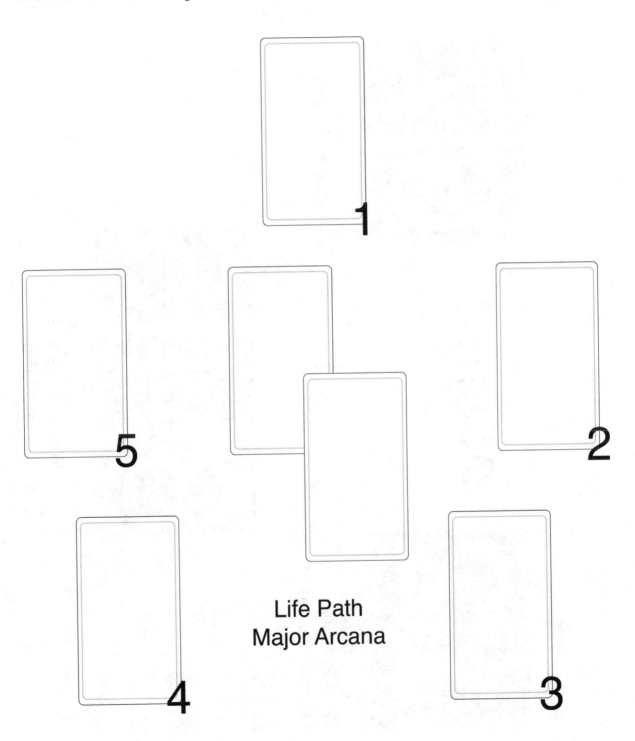

Life Path
Major Arcana

Magic 7 This seven-card spread looks at the spiritual meaning of the number 7. This reading focuses on what has prepared you for your life lessons, where you are spiritually now, and how you will learn.

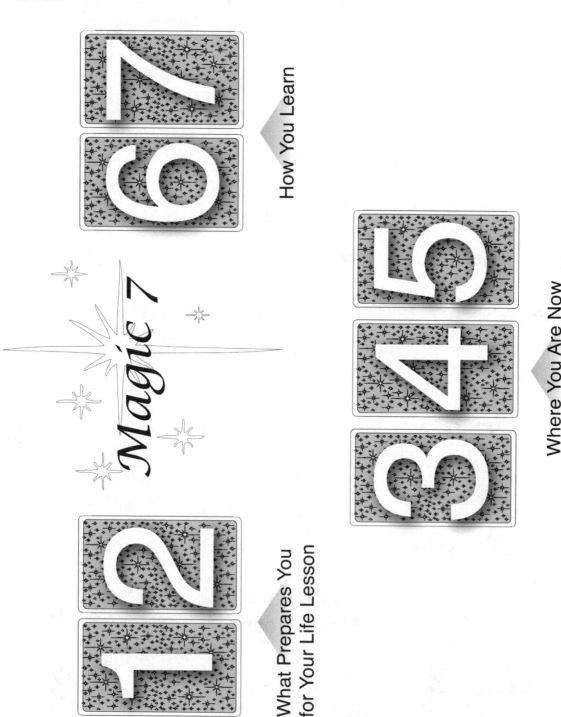

Past, Present, Future   This variation on the Seven-Card spread specifically designates cards as about past, present, or future. It is used well to shed light on questions concerning both short-term and long-term issues. Look to individual cards to add nuances of timing in days, weeks, months, and years.

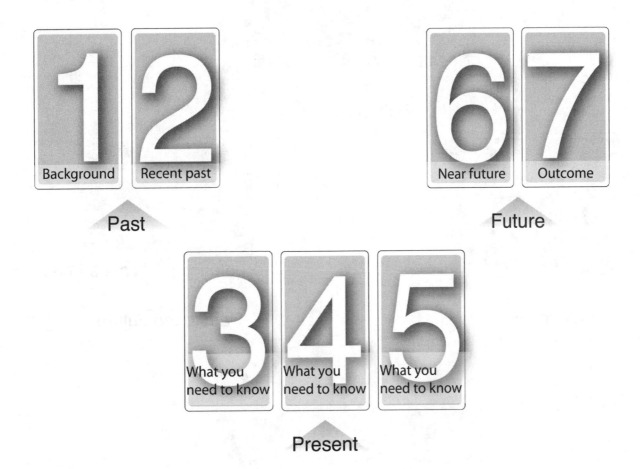

Path to the Heart   This 10-card spread builds upon the Path to Peace spread, but this time adds cards for Needs, Wants, and Desires. It is a great card to examine questions of deep emotional importance.

Path to the Heart

Path to the Past

Path to the Future

Present

Path to Peace   This is a variation on the Seven-Card spread with a specific focus on drawing on higher spiritual knowledge.

Path to the Past

Path to the Future

Present

Seven-Card This workhorse spread gives a great, all-purpose take on any question, and generally casts its answer in the light of past, present, and future resonances in the interpretation of the cards.

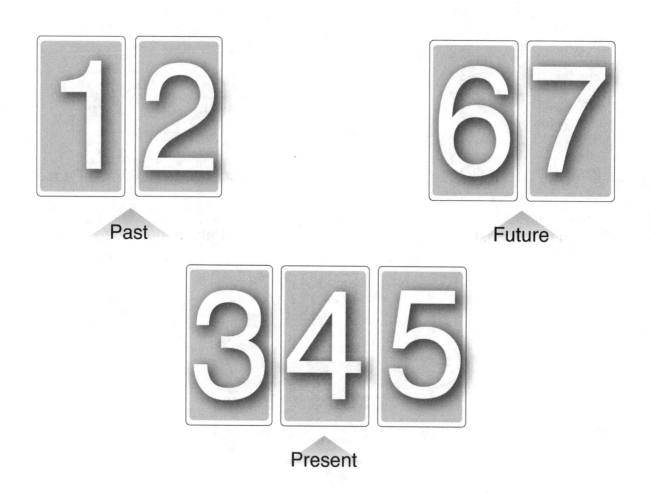

Soul Mate   This 22-card spread uses 11 pairs of cards to show how two soul mates come together. They show where there are sparks and where there is compatibility.

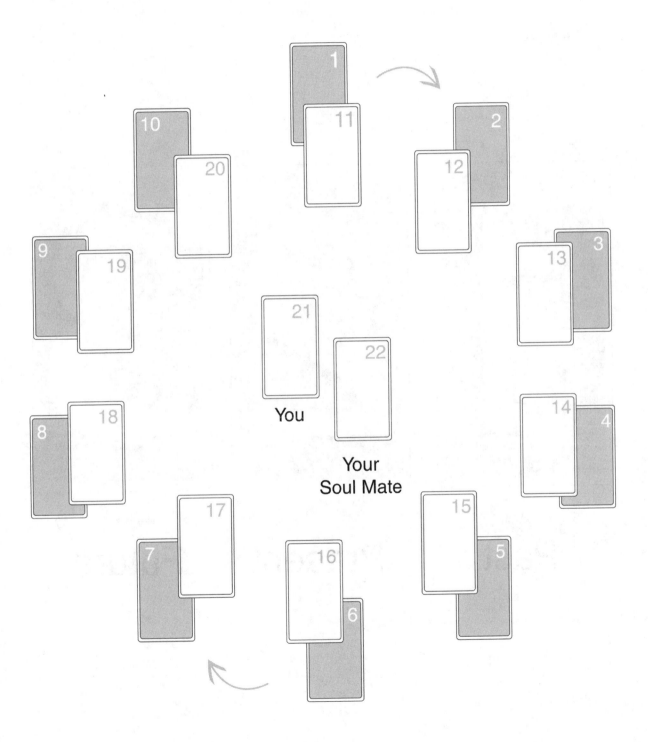

Three-Card The Three-Card spread is good to use for a quick read on what your day might be like.

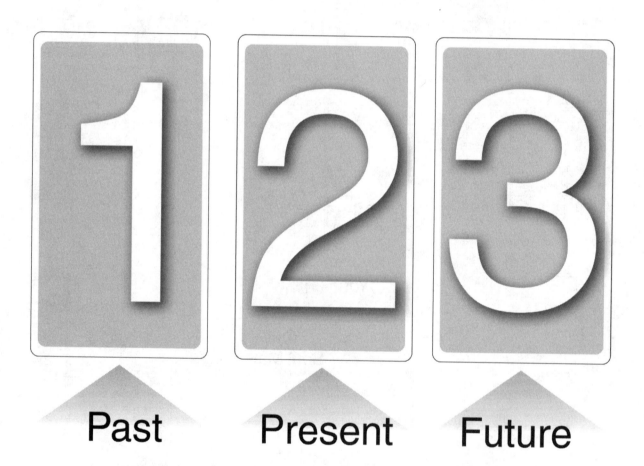

Wish   The 15-card Wish spread gives an in-depth look at the conditions surrounding a wish you may have. It gives insight into why you want the wish and what lessons you may have to learn to get the wish.

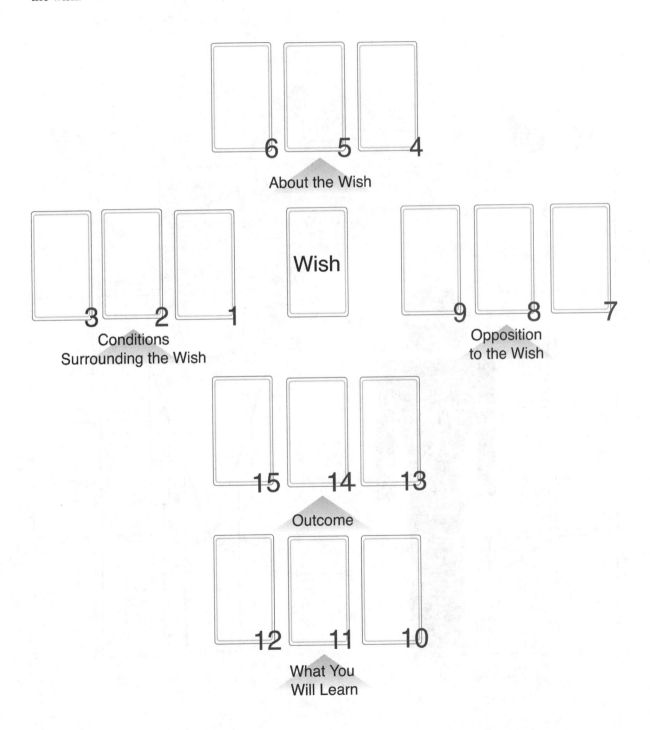

Yin/Yang   The Yin/Yang spread is a good way to compare the personalities of two people. It uses 16 cards, two pairs of four for each person. It is also a great spread to use as an individual, when trying to decide whether or not to do something, or for any question involving the balance of two forces.

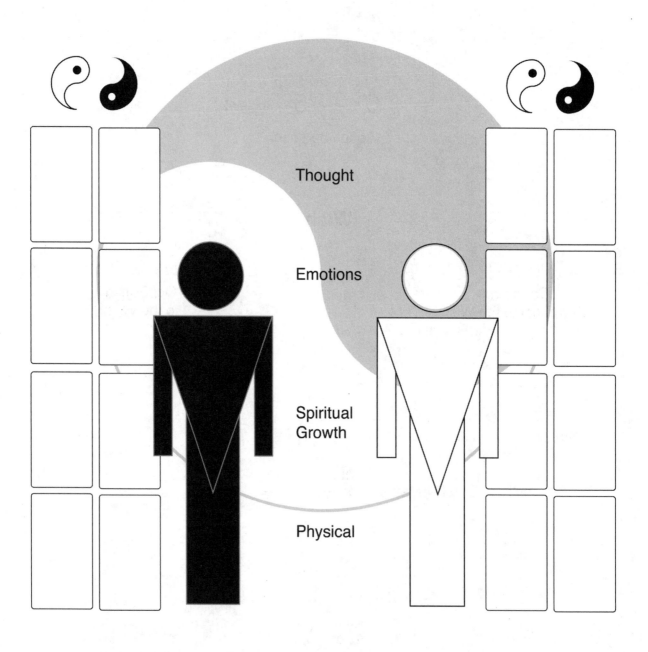

Zodiac Horoscope This 12-card reading pairs your astrological birth chart with Tarot, using the 12 houses of the zodiac. It gives you a full picture of yourself, and it can take a good hour to read.

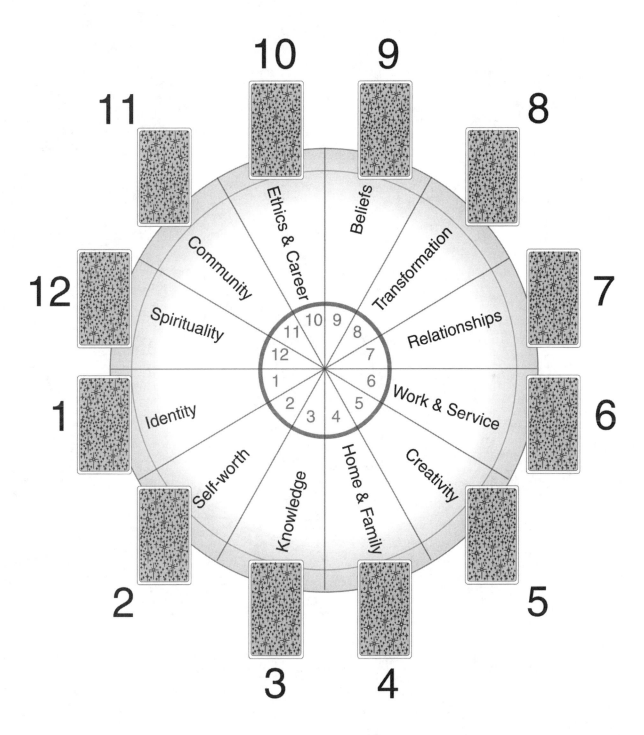

Index

X–Y–Z